Alexander The Great In India

A Reconstruction Of Cleitarchus

by

Andrew Michael Chugg

2009

First Edition

In memory of Bucephalus

Alexander the Great in India

Contents

1.	Introduction	1
2.	A Basis For The Reconstruction of Cleitarchus	3
3.	Book 10: June 327BC – June 326BC	64
	The Invasion Of India, Nysa, Mazaga, Aornus And The Battle Against Porus	
4.	Book 11: July 326BC – May 325BC	93
	Eastwards Through India, The Mutiny On The Hyphasis And The River Voyage To The Siege Of The Oxydracae	
5.	Book 12: June 325BC – June 324BC	121
	Southern India And Its Ocean, The Kedrosian Desert And The Return to Persia	
6.	Alexander's Route Through India	142
7.	Organisation And Sources	144
8.	Bibliography	176
9.	Acknowledgements	181
	Index	182

1. Introduction

This modest publication presents the first fruits of an ongoing project to reconstruct the most influential of all the ancient accounts of the career of Alexander the Great: the history of his reign compiled by Cleitarchus of Alexandria, which has been lost since antiquity. I chose the three Indian books of Cleitarchus to begin the reconstruction mainly because the evidence for Cleitarchus is particularly well preserved in the secondary sources for Alexander's Indian campaigns, but also because the exotic setting is especially well suited to rendering Cleitarchus' equally exotic style. However, it is my intention eventually to produce as complete a reconstruction of Cleitarchus as may prove feasible, so the supporting material in this book already has the scope of the entire work. In particular, the next section provides a detailed technical basis for the reconstruction, incorporating discussions of the evidence and various inferences concerning the nature and organization of Cleitarchus' work.

The reconstructed text is not merely a simple translation of passages from the surviving secondary sources, although virtually every sentence is founded upon evidence from those texts. In particular, it has been necessary to meld overlapping and intersecting accounts together and continually to assess which source should have pre-eminence in the case of (usually slight) disparities. Furthermore, I have thought it fitting to attempt to echo the evidently flowery literary style of Cleitarchus to some extent, especially in the case of speeches and descriptive passages. Yet it would also be true to say that some of that embroidery is already echoed in the surviving Latin and Greek texts of Curtius, Diodorus and even the Metz Epitome. In this sense my own text is not merely a reconstruction, but also an evocation of the original.

Different passages may be attributed to Cleitarchus with widely varying degrees of confidence. Therefore, I have indicated the approximate confidence level using a textual hierarchy running from lowest to highest (attributed fragments of Cleitarchus) as follows: *italic;* plain text; ***italicized bold;* simple bold; <u>**underlined simple bold.**</u> Although grey text has been reserved for connecting passages, where the Cleitarchan version is unfathomable, it has not been necessary to resort to its use for the Indian books. Subject to a few minor exceptions, it is possible to read the reconstruction at a variety of confidence levels by ignoring all text below the desired level of fidelity.

As is explained and argued in detail in the ensuing essay, this reconstruction is particularly founded on the premise that Curtius, Diodorus (Book 17) and the Metz Epitome are all largely abridgements of the History of Alexander by Cleitarchus. We cannot be sure that Curtius did not employ another major source, since it is clear from his work that he knew of the accounts of Alexander by Timagenes, Trogus, Ptolemy etc. Therefore reconstructed text entirely based on material from Curtius is indicated at a lower level of confidence. Higher confidence is assigned to material from the Metz Epitome and Diodorus 17. Still higher confidence is vested in cases where there are detailed matches between these sources and the highest confidence rests with the attributed fragments of Cleitarchus, although they are sadly sparse.

If the premise of a common source for the surviving texts were correct, then it would be expected that a relatively smooth and cogent version of the prototype could be reconstructed by merging them. However, if any of the extant sources had employed a significant secondary source, then it would be anticipated that the attempt to define a prototype that explained all the material in each of them should encounter numerous contradictions. It is a first conclusion of the present research that it has been possible to reconstruct all three of Alexander's years in India without encountering significant contradictions by integrating all the appertaining material in the three main sources (with the exception of a few passages in Curtius where that author is clearly offering his own comments and one instance, where he attacks Cleitarchus by name with reference to Ptolemy's version in a matter that concerned Ptolemy.) This is an important result, because it tends to reinforce the premise that all three extant sources are essentially abridgements of Cleitarchus. Such a (tentative) conclusion is not at all obvious in reading those sources individually.

In the case of Justin, we know from his manuscripts that he epitomised Trogus, although the latter probably used Cleitarchus (or else Timagenes who in turn used Cleitarchus). I have encountered increased difficulties in reconciling his words with the tradition from the other three Vulgate texts, as might be expected for such indirect transmission. The process of reconstruction has also indicated significant amounts of Cleitarchan material in Plutarch, by virtue of some striking parallels between my text (reconstructed from Curtius, the Metz Epitome and Diodorus 17) and some of Plutarch's anecdotes. But it is equally obvious that Plutarch used many early sources (as too did Cleitarchus), so I have used his material sparingly and at low confidence.

Neither do I intend that this should be the final and immutable version of the reconstruction, but rather hope that it may evolve and be revised in the light of new evidence or arguments as they emerge.

Finally, I would also commend the account of Cleitarchus to those readers who have little interest in the technical niceties of source research for Alexander studies. Cleitarchus' account rested on its literary merits for centuries in winning its place as the most popular version of Alexander's campaigns among the Hellenistic Greeks and the Romans. I believe that it retains good measures of readability, atmosphere, coherence and accuracy even in the present metamorphosed and imperfect form, sufficient anyway that it may be read in isolation as an authentic breath of the distant past by readers who are relatively unfamiliar with the particulars of the history of Alexander the Great.

2. A Basis For The Reconstruction Of Cleitarchus

In spite of the objections of Tarn, I regard it as certain that whatever source Diodorus used, it was the same as that employed by Curtius. Schwartz assembled a formidable list of parallels between the two writers, without exhausting the subject. It is adequate to prove the point. To reconstruct this source would be a useful task.

C. Bradford Welles[1]

Introduction

The history of the reign of Alexander the Great written by Cleitarchus of Alexandria ranks as perhaps the most influential of all the many accounts of the King's career, despite the loss of the original text of Cleitarchus' work and the paucity of the attributed fragments collected by Müller and Jacoby. Cleitarchus was evidently the principal source for the authors of the so-called vulgate tradition of Alexander historiography, which survives in the works of Diodorus, Curtius and Justin as well as in the anonymous *Metz Epitome*. Even Plutarch's writings on Alexander incorporate substantial Cleitarchan elements, and there are recognisable, though unattributed, fragments of Cleitarchus in a host of other ancient sources, such as Pliny, Aelian and Polyaenus.

A variety of modern studies have aimed systematically to identify the Cleitarchan passages within the surviving ancient sources. Schwartz and others pioneered the principle that wherever it can be shown that Curtius and Diodorus agree *in detail*, then they employed a common source, who was almost certainly Cleitarchus. More recently, Hammond has produced an entire book with the aim of determining the mix of sources for Diodorus 17, Justin and Curtius. These exercises have resulted in the attribution of large quantities of extant material to the Cleitarchan prototype. Cleitarchan versions of the great majority of the canonical episodes of Alexander's career seem to exist. This fact suggests the tantalizing possibility that the original work may be accessible to substantial reconstruction from the surviving evidence.[2]

Such a reconstruction would necessarily be imperfect, but should nevertheless prove valuable. This is because the reconstruction would itself generate new evidence, since it should reveal patterns and themes from Cleitarchus, which would otherwise be difficult to discern whilst the evidence remained disorganised and amorphous. The whole contains more information and has

---

[1] C. Bradford Welles, *Loeb edition of Diodorus Siculus*, Vol. 8 (Harvard, 1963), Introduction, 12.

[2] For example, A.B. Bosworth, *From Arrian to Alexander* (Oxford, 1988), Introduction, 13 has written, "Cleitarchus, then, is elusive. Is he also irretrievable? My feeling is that it *is* possible to reconstruct something of his work, but the exercise of doing so is particularly arduous."

more structure than the mere agglomeration of its parts, just as the correct interlinkage of its pieces reveals the scene depicted by a jigsaw puzzle. In pursuit of such emergent insights, it is the purpose of this section both to plan and to instigate the reconstruction of Cleitarchus in an English edition.

The order in which this study will proceed may be outlined as follows:

a) Firstly an analysis of the structure of Cleitarchus' book, because this permits an early review of the identified fragments and an understanding of how they fit into the work (surprisingly, some have not previously been placed and the book divisions have not been established.)

b) An analysis of Cleitarchus' sources, since this is a key ingredient in addressing the vexed questions of the date and character of his work.

c) The date of composition of Cleitarchus.

d) The character of Cleitarchus' work: how to recognise Cleitarchan material.

e) A review of the main sources of extant Cleitarchan material.

f) Definition of a *modus operandi* for reconstruction of Cleitarchus' work.

The Organisation of the Work

Relative to his fame and influence, the attributed fragments of Cleitarchus are surprisingly sparse.[3] Nevertheless, we are well-informed on the matter of the title of his history of Alexander, which is his sole attested work. Athenaeus thrice mentions that it was known, albeit blandly, as Περὶ Ἀλεξάνδρου or Περὶ Ἀλεξάνδρου Ἱστορίαι, which I translate as *Concerning Alexander*.[4] Since Athenaeus is corroborated in this matter by the *Florilegium* of Stobaeus[5] and the Scholia on Apollonius Rhodius,[6] there is little doubt that he is correct.

The most important structural issues regarding Cleitarchus' work are the twin questions of the number of books into which it was split and the periods that were covered by each book. Only six of Jacoby's fragments preserve any mention of the book numbers whence they were abstracted. The key evidence for the total number of books is presented by the last and latest of these: fragment 6 describes the disdain for death professed by the Indian gymnosophists and is attributed to Book 12 by Diogenes Laertius.[7]

---

[3] Jacoby, *FGrHist* 137.

[4] Jacoby, *FGrHist* 137 F1, F2, F30 = Athenaeus, *Deipnosophistae* 148D-F, 530A, 586CD.

[5] Jacoby, *FGrHist* 137 F3 = Stobaeus, *Florilegium* 4.20.73.

[6] Jacoby, *FGrHist* 137 F17 = Scholia on Apollonius Rhodius 2.904.

[7] Jacoby, *FGrHist* 137 F6 = Diogenes Laertius 1.6.

A Basis For The Reconstruction Of Cleitarchus

There are only two occasions when this topic is at all likely to have been discussed by Cleitarchus: either in the context of Alexander's meeting with the gymnosophists in India or else at the ceremony for the self-immolation of Calanus (a gymnosophist, who is erroneously called Caranus in Diodorus[8]), which took place in Susianê early in 324BC. The estimate of a total of as many as 15 books for Cleitarchus, which is countenanced in some modern works,[9] might be justified on the assumption that fragment 6 refers to the meeting in India, but actually the suicide of Calanus is intrinsically more likely, because there is a detailed account of Calanus' end in Diodorus, which makes specific reference to the theme of his indifference to his death (note however that this event falls within a large lacuna in Curtius):

True to his own creed, Caranus cheerfully mounted the pyre and perished. Some of those who were present thought him mad, others vainglorious about his ability to bear pain, while others simply marvelled at his fortitude and contempt for death.[10]

In fact the vocabulary of Diodorus (θανάτου καταφρόνησιν) and that of Diogenes Laertius (θανάτου καταφρονεῖν) in fragment 6 are identical.

It is also notable that, were the total 15, the effect of the distribution of the other fragments having book numbers would be to concertina the first half of Alexander's reign into the first third of Cleitarchus' books. For instance, fragment 4 mentions the 50 Spartan hostages surrendered after the defeat of the rebellion of King Agis, which occurred in the sixth year of Alexander's reign and is attributed to Book 5 of Cleitarchus.[11] Conversely, placing the first half of 324BC in book 12 engenders a total of about 13 books up to the point of Alexander's death, which would result in a far more even distribution of Alexander's regnal years across Cleitarchus' books. Furthermore, a 13 book total has the particular attraction of giving virtually exactly one regnal year per book, since the total reign was only months short of 13 years. It will be shown below that the other book-numbered fragments are all broadly consistent with the hypothesis of one book per year to within a matter of a few months.

---

[8] Plutarch, *Alexander* 64.3 explains that Calanus was the nickname of the gymnosophist Sphines, which was derived from his use of the Indian greeting "Kale"; Caranus was the name of one of Alexander's Friends, who was killed by Spitamenes (and also of an apocryphal son of Phillip II in Justin 11.2.3) – Arrian, *Anabasis* 3.5.6 has the inverse error of Calanus for Caranus.

[9] E.g. L. Pearson, *Lost Histories of Alexander the Great* (1960) 213 recognises that Book 12 is the suicide of Calanus, but thinks there were "two or three books more"; A. B. Bosworth, "In Search of Cleitarchus: Review-Discussion of Luisa Prandi: Fortuna è realtà dell'opera di Clitarco, Historia Einzelschriften 104 (Steiner Stuttgart, 1996)" in *Histos* notes that there were "at least 12 books and perhaps as many as 15"; J. C. Yardley & W. Heckel, *Justin: Epitome of the Philippic History of Pompeius Trogus, Vol I, Books 11-12, Alexander the Great* (Oxford 1997) 34 speculate that Cleitarchus' work was published "in 15 books?"

[10] Diodorus 17.107.5 (trans. C. Bradford Welles).

[11] Jacoby, *FGrHist* 137 F4 = Harpocration, s.v. ὁμηρεύοντας.

Cleitarchus may have slightly expanded the duration of some books and contracted others to suit the pattern of events, but it is never necessary to infer that a Cleitarchan book began or ended further than a few months from the corresponding midsummer year boundaries within the reign. This is approximately equivalent to the Attic year boundaries used by Diodorus himself, but is also not too different from divisions at the end of each campaigning season, as seemingly adopted by Thucydides, Xenophon and Hieronymus.[12] It may finally be added that there is evidence from other fragments that Cleitarchus had a fondness for associating things with calendar values: for example, he made the walls of Babylon 365 stades in circumference[13] and also seems to have asserted that Darius' harem comprised 365 women.[14] In this trait he may be emulating his father, Deinon.[15]

Implicit in this discussion is the view that Cleitarchus' work opened with Alexander's accession and closed with his death, which is a relatively orthodox opinion that appears in general to be supported by the evidence. For example, it seems that Diodorus mainly used the universal history of Diyllus as his source for his sixteenth book, which proceeded as far as the assassination of Philip.[16] He only switched to the considerably more detailed account of Cleitarchus at the beginning of Alexander's reign, then he began to use Hieronymus of Cardia from early in Book 18.[17] Furthermore, although his first two books are lost, the indications are that Curtius opened his main account at Alexander's accession. In fact Jacoby's first fragment of Cleitarchus shows that the destruction of Thebes was described in Book 1, so it is unlikely that there was space for a detailed account of Alexander's youth.[18] Nevertheless, Hammond may well be correct in believing that Cleitarchus also treated Philip's last summer.[19] This would be consistent with an overall plan of describing the events of thirteen years across thirteen books, since Alexander died in early June and Attic years ran from mid-summer to mid-summer. Finally, we will find that there are some indications that Cleitarchus introduced his history with a brief account of Alexander's birth and ancestry, because Plutarch was probably utilising

---

[12] Jane Hornblower, *Hieronymus of Cardia*, OUP, 1981, p.101.

[13] Jacoby, *FGrHist* 137 F10 = Diodorus 2.7.3-4.

[14] Curtius 3.3.24, 6.6.8; Diodorus 17.77.6; cf. Justin 12.3.10.

[15] Deinon gave 360: L. Pearson, *Lost Histories*, 221 & 228-229; Plutarch, *Artaxerxes* 27.

[16] E.g. Diodorus 16.76.6, though the Philip mentioned there is probably Cassander's son.

[17] For example, the account of Alexander's catafalque in Diodorus 18.26-27 is a fragment of Hieronymus, because Athenaeus 206E attributes it to him - Jacoby, *FGrHist* 154 F2.

[18] Jacoby, *FGrHist* 137 F1 = Athenaeus, *Deipnosophistae* 148D-F.

[19] Hammond, NGL, *Three Historians of Alexander the Great* (Cambridge, 1983) 92-93; for the chronology of Alexander's accession see Hammond, NGL, "The Regnal Years of Philip and Alexander," *Greek, Roman and Byzantine Studies*, Vol. 33, 1992, 355-373.

Cleitarchus in his introductory account of Alexander's descent from Achilles and Heracles in his *Life of Alexander*.[20]

Location of Jacoby's Fragments and Book Boundaries

The next steps are to assign Jacoby's attributed fragments of Cleitarchus to their correct contexts within each book and to identify the opening and closing events related in each book (see Table 2.1). These issues are interrelated and therefore need to be addressed in parallel. The starting point is the location of the fragments with book numbers (i.e. F1-F6) among the events of Alexander's reign.

Fragment 1 (Athenaeus 148D-F), which is attributed to Book 1, self-evidently relates to the fall of Thebes in October of 335BC and it mentions the wealth of Thebes as having amounted to just 440 talents. The same sum is mentioned by Diodorus 17.14.4, who states that Alexander sold the Theban prisoners and realised a value of 440 silver talents. Bosworth has pointed out that it is not strictly necessary to read Diodorus as stating that the sale of the prisoners raised the entire sum.[21] Rather Diodorus may be abbreviating a longer account, which had listed sales of further resources in realising the total. It is anyway clear that the first book of Cleitarchus extended to the autumn of 335BC.

Fragment 2 (Athenaeus 530A), which mentions the death of Sardanapalus[22] and derives from Book 4, almost certainly belongs to a visit by Alexander to the Assyrian king's tomb at Anchiale near Tarsus in October 333BC, which is attested elsewhere in fragments of Aristobulus and Callisthenes.[23] It fits perfectly into the 13-book annual scheme, since it occurs in the 4th Attic year of Alexander's reign. Cleitarchus is probably echoing his father Deinon's *Persica*, which might in turn have followed Ctesias' *Persica*.[24]

---

[20] Plutarch, *Alexander* 2.1.

[21] A. B. Bosworth, "In Search of Cleitarchus: Review-discussion of Luisa Prandi: Fortuna è realtà dell' opera di Clitarco," *Histos* (University of Durham, electronic journal of historiography), Vol. 1, Aug. 1997.

[22] Cf. Plutarch, *Moralia* 326F & 336C.

[23] Jacoby, *FGrHist* 139 F9a = Athenaeus 530A-B; Jacoby, *FGrHist* 139 F9b = Strabo 14.5.9; Jacoby, *FGrHist* 139 F9c = Arrian, *Anabasis* 2.5.2-4; Jacoby, *FGrHist* 124 F34 = Photius & Suidas s.v. *Sardanapalos* (this mention is attributed to Callisthenes' *Persica*, but it may be a garbled reference to his history of Alexander; see Pearson, *Lost Histories*, 26); Jacoby, *FGrHist* 122 F2 (Amyntas the Bematist) = Athenaeus 529E-530A;

[24] Ctesias, writing in the early 4th century BC, had described the reign of Sardanapalus (see Diodorus 2.23); Cleitarchus seemingly contradicted Ctesias on certain points (see L. Pearson, *Lost Histories*, 230), probably in consequence of his father Deinon having written a *Persica* to rival Ctesias' work on the same theme.

Fragment 3 (Stobaeus, *Florilegium* 4.20.73) from the fifth book tells of Theis Byblios' passionate love for his daughter, Myrra, which is a legend of Byblos, a city on the Lebanese littoral, where Adonis, the son of Theis and Myrra, was worshipped and which Alexander reached in about January of 332BC.[25] This is some five months ahead of the start of book 5 as scheduled by the 13-book scheme. Yet there are strong indications that the epic siege of Tyre, which was so protracted as to extend into the second half of 332BC, was entirely accommodated within the 4th book with book 5 opening after the conclusion of the siege. Logically, the only way to reconcile Fragment 3 with its placing in book 5 is to suppose that it pertains to Alexander's *return* to Syria in the summer of 331BC. Hence we learn that Alexander was probably in Byblos some time in the late Summer of 331BC. The sources are clear that Alexander lingered at Tyre, where he held athletic and musical contests from around mid-June to early July of 331BC, and that he later crossed the Euphrates at Thapsacus (circa early August).[26] Engels has noted, "There were essentially two routes the Macedonians could have followed to the Euphrates: through Coele Syria via Damascus, Homs, Hamah, and Aleppo, a region which was much more agriculturally productive in antiquity than at present; or up the Phoenician coast to Seleucia, the port of Antioch, and inland by the route essentially followed by Cyrus the Younger, Crassus, Trajan, and Julian through the Amuq Plain to the Euphrates. The latter route would, of course, simplify the army's logistic organisation by utilizing sea transport."[27] We now have an independent argument from the third fragment of Cleitarchus to show that Engels was correct to prefer the coastal route, since that was the one that passed through Byblos.

Fragment 4 (Harpocration s.v. ὁμηρεύοντας), which is also attributed to Book 5, mentions the fifty Spartan hostages received by Antipater after he quelled the rebellion of King Agis.[28] This revolt against the Macedonian Hegemony in Greece took place in the summer of 331BC, which is the expected end of Book 5 according to the 13-book scheme. The implication is that Fragment 4 is drawn from a digression on the fighting back in Greece, which closed Book 5.[29]

---

[25] See T. S. Brown, "Clitarchus," *American Journal of Philology*, 71 (1950), 149.

[26] Arrian, *Anabasis* 3.6.1-4; Curtius 4.8.16; Plutarch, *Alexander* 29.

[27] Donald W. Engels, *Alexander the Great and the Logistics of the Macedonian Army*, University of California, 1978, p.65.

[28] The number of 50 is not present in the text of Harpocration (Lexicon of the Attic Orators), but is restored from the epitome of Harpocration used by the author of the Suda, of which only the best manuscript has 50 as the numeral ν′ (in agreement with Diodorus), whilst others have eight as either the numeral η′ or the word ὀκτώ.

[29] The actual departure of the hostages from Greece seems to have been delayed until the next year, since Aeschines 3.133 records that they were preparing to leave in the Summer of 330BC; their arrival with Alexander may be reflected by the comment in Curtius 7.4.32 that Alexander received announcements out of Greece about the Spartan rebellion in about July 329BC.

Conversely, Curtius, Justin and Diodorus all seem to have postponed mention of this rebellion until much later. Curtius and Justin waited until the death of Darius before reviewing events in Europe, whilst even Diodorus delayed mention of the matter until the aftermath of Gaugamela.[30] Cleitarchus' plan for covering the events of each year in a single book may have specially driven him to treat events elsewhere within the year that they actually happened, but his followers in the Roman era evidently cared less about faithfully reflecting the true chronology. Rather they preferred to await a convenient hiatus in Alexander's story to catch up with events elsewhere.

Fragment 5 (Scholia on Aristophanes Av. 487): the greatest conundrum among the fragments with book attributions is presented by the fifth, which assigns a comment about the law that permitted only the Persian monarch to wear the tiara upright to the tenth book of Cleitarchus. According to the 13-book scheme, this cannot have been related earlier than the beginning of 327BC and more probably fits between the summer of 327BC and the middle of 326BC. The most obvious context for such a comment would be an account of a rebellion against Alexander's rule of Persia, for Alexander did not himself wear the tiara.[31] However, this occurs too late in Cleitarchus to be associated with the revolt of Bessus, who had been dead for nearly two years. However, we do know of a more obscure rebellion in Persia led by a certain Baryaxes and Arrian specifically relates that he assumed the title of King of the Persians and Medes and wore the tiara upright. This rebellion evidently occurred whilst Alexander was in India, since Baryaxes was arrested by Atropates, the satrap of Media and presented to Alexander for punishment upon his return in early 324BC.[32] The outbreak of this rebellion is the probable context of Fragment 5. A corollary is that Cleitarchus probably did not write that Bessus wore the tiara upright. Bessus' assumption of the upright tiara was reported by Arrian (from Ptolemy?)[33] But Curtius writes more generally of his adoption of "regal attire" and Diodorus notes that he "had assumed the diadem".[34] Cleitarchus tended to place digressions on events elsewhere at either the start or the end of a book, so these are the two alternative placements for this fragment. The end is preferrable, since Baryaxes probably waited for Alexander to become safely enmeshed in India. This conclusion reveals the history of Cleitarchus in a

---

[30] Curtius 6.1.16-20; Justin 12.1.4-11; Diodorus 17.73.5-6.

[31] Fragment 30 of Eratosthenes in Jacoby (no. 241); Arrian, *Anabasis* 4.7.4 seems to be mistaken on this point, for which see P. A. Brunt, *Arrian*, Appendix XIV, 2, 533 in Vol I; the Vulgate sources refer only to the diadem without mention of the tiara (*kitaris* or *kidaris*): *Metz Epitome* 2; Diodorus 17.77.5; Curtius 6.6.4; Justin 12.3.8; Plutarch, *Alexander* 45.2; Ephippus in Athenaeus 537E.

[32] Arrian, *Anabasis* 6.29.3.

[33] Arrian, *Anabasis* 3.25.3; cf. Xenophon, *Anabasis* 2.5.23.

[34] Curtius 6.6.13; Diodorus 17.83.3.

startling new light, for it provides evidence that his work treated events elsewhere in more detail and in a more chronologically correct order than did Arrian.

Fragment 6 (Diogenes Laertius 1.6): as has already been argued, the sixth and final book-attributed fragment comes from Cleitarchus' account of the self-immolation of Calanus when Alexander was progressing towards Susa in the Spring of 324BC. It was reported in Book 12 of Cleitarchus.

The location of the boundaries between Cleitarchus' books is a topic that is intertwined with the fragment locations. Although the fragments with book numbers are broadly consistent with the scheme of one book per year, they also show that Cleitarchus permitted himself some leeway in his selection of start and finish events, usually for the purpose of avoiding interruption of his accounts of key campaigns. For example, Book 1 seems to have closed a few months late in order to reach the end of campaigning in Greece. Nevertheless, it is clear that the starting point for seeking book boundaries should normally be the summer months of June and July. Since Alexander died near the end of the Attic year, it was particularly convenient for Cleitarchus approximately to follow that prevalent convention. Another important indication of book boundaries is the occurrence of digressions, since Cleitarchus seems to have pursued the tidy policy of placing them preferentially at the beginnings or ends of his books. Due to the secondary authors in some cases having moved the digressions, their Cleitarchan locations can only be reliably identified wherever Diodorus and Curtius relate a particular digression at the same juncture. The book boundaries in Curtius and Justin and the chapter ends in Diodorus 17 do not, of course, in general follow Cleitarchus' scheme, yet in some instances, particularly where a boundary is found at the same point in all the extant followers of Cleitarchus, there may nevertheless be evidence of a Cleitarchan boundary. Finally, certain curious phrases in the text of Diodorus 17 have characteristics which suggest that they may be residual echoes of Cleitarchan book *termini*, especially because these phrases often incorporate the title of Cleitarchus' work - Περὶ Ἀλεξάνδρου.

Book 1: It is likely that Cleitarchus began with an outline of Alexander's birth and ancestry resembling Plutarch, *Alexander* 2.1 & 3.3-5. Hammond has shown that Plutarch's date of 6th Hecatombaeon for Alexander's birth comes from Timaeus, a rough contemporary of Cleitarchus, because Cicero gives many of the same details and names Timaeus as his source.[35] However, there is good evidence that Cleitarchus himself used Timaeus, who was the leading authority on chronological issues in the early 3rd century BC. Fragment 7 of Cleitarchus

---

[35] Hammond, NGL, *Sources for Alexander the Great*, Cambridge 1993; Cicero, *N.D.* 2.69 (*FGrHist* 566 F150a of Timaeus) & Div. 1.47.

couples him with Timaeus as its sources and it mentions the Heracleidae, Alexander's putative ancestors.[36] Then Fragment 36 from Suidas (the Suda) seems to make Cleitarchus a follower of Timaeus and Anaximenes.[37] In this context Plutarch also gives Hegesias as the source of a quip about the conflagration of the Temple at Ephesus on the day of Alexander's birth.[38] Hegesias is another near contemporary of Cleitarchus, but precedes him in a list of ancient writers given by Philodemus, who usually arranged his lists in date order.[39] A famous fragment of Hegesias describes the killing of Betis at the siege of Gaza, but very similar details of this event are given by Curtius, who usually followed Cleitarchus for such histrionic anecdotes.[40] Furthermore, Curtius' version of Gaza emphasises Alexander's emulation of Achilles, which is a familiar Cleitarchan theme. The end of Plutarch's passage cites a prophecy that Alexander would be *aniketos* (= Latin *invictus* = invincible), an epithet for the king, which is strongly associated with the Cleitarchan tradition.[41] Finally, Hegesias was renowned for being perhaps the earliest author to employ a curious metrical device known as Asianic rhythms and there are some hints among the fragments of Cleitarchus that he too occasionally practised this type of prose poetry.[42] In summary, there are indications that both Timaeus and Hegesias were sources for Cleitarchus, so when material is found from both, which is also linked to famous Cleitarchan themes such as *aniketos*, descent from Heracles and Achilles and a fascination for chronology and the calendar and when all these things are seen together in a short passage, then there are grounds to suspect that Cleitarchus is Plutarch's immediate source of inspiration. Book 1 evidently extended as far as the end of the campaigning season in 335BC and the sack of Thebes, since fragment 1, dealing with the aftermath of its fall, is from Book 1. The last known event of the season in the vulgate tradition was Alexander's visit to Delphi whilst heading back towards Macedon.[43]

---

[36] Jacoby, *FGrHist* 137 F7 = Clement of Alexandria, *Strom.* 1.139.4.

[37] Jacoby, *FGrHist* 137 F36 = Suidas: ἔχετον.

[38] *FGrHist* 142 F3 of Hegesias.

[39] Jacoby, *FGrHist* 137 T12 = Philodemus, *Rhet.* 4.1 col. 21.

[40] *FGrHist* 142 F5 of Hegesias; Curtius 4.6.12-16.

[41] Plutarch, *Alexander* 3.5 & 14.4-5; Diodorus 17.93.4, 17.51.3-4; Curtius 4.7.27; Livy 9.18; Justin 11.11.10; Cleitarchus' use of this epithet may reflect contemporary practice, since Hypereides I, col.32, 5 referred to a proposal to erect a statue of Alexander as θεὸς ἀνίκητος according to the interpretation of H. Berve, *Gnomon* V, 1929, 376 n.2.

[42] L. Pearson, *Lost Histories*, 213, n.9 & 227, n.59.

[43] Plutarch 14.4-5; Diodorus 17.93.4; SIG³ 251II, col. II, lines 9-10 (436-7) is an inscription from Delphi recording a gift to the shrine at this time of 150 gold coins minted by Philip II – Alexander is the only likely donor of Macedonian coinage on this scale at this juncture.

Book 2: The second book will have opened with various stories telling of Alexander's theatrical preparations during the winter of 335-334BC for the campaign against the Persian Empire. Surviving versions of the stories are found in Justin and Frontinus (transmitted to them via Trogus) and in Plutarch (probably directly from Cleitarchus).[44] Fragment 7, noting that Alexander's invasion came 820 years after that by the Heracleidae, must be derived from the opening of this book.[45] The evidence for the location of the end of this book is relatively scant, but the Battle of the Granicus in late May or early June 334BC must have been its climax and it was the last major event before midsummer, which would be the normal Cleitarchan book boundary under the 13-book scheme.

Book 3: Opened with the start of the campaigning southwards through Ionia. I infer that Cleitarchus mentioned an otherwise unreported visit of Alexander to the tomb of Themistocles at Magnesia, because Fragments 33 and 34 are from a digression on the career of Themistocles.[46] Cleitarchus seems to have inserted a group of digressions on the death of Memnon[47] and the preparations of Darius at Babylon[48] after the episode of the Gordian knot (where the surviving part of the account of Curtius opens). Alexander probably arrived at Gordion in April of 333BC, but lingered during midsummer, departing perhaps as late as the end of July.[49] This is the most likely end point for the third book.

Book 4: Will have begun with the advance across the Taurus mountains into Cilicia. Fragment 2 shows that events in Cilicia were related in this book. Its climactic events must have been firstly the Battle of Issus (Fragment 8)[50] and subsequently the siege of Tyre (Fragment 9).[51] It ended with the story of the appointment of Balonymus as King of Tyre (which may relate to the appointment of Abdalonymus as King of Sidon). The end of Book 4 seems to

---

[44] Justin 11.5.1-9; Plutarch, *Alexander* 15.2-3; Front. *Strat.* 2.11.3 & 1.11.14.

[45] Jacoby, *FGrHist* 137 F7 = Clement of Alexandria, *Strom.* 1.139.4.

[46] Jacoby, *FGrHist* 137 F33 & F34 = Plutarch, *Themistocles* 27.1-2 & Cicero, *Brut.* 42-43. The surrender of Magnesia (Arrian, *Anabasis* 1.18.1) is the most likely occasion for Cleitarchus' digression on Themistocles, since his tomb lay there. Cleitarchus' father Deinon had evidently told the story of Themistocles, since Plutarch cites Deinon for the same story in F33. It is possible that Cleitarchus drew a comparison between Themistocles' submission to Xerxes and Charidemus' allegiance to Darius, since they were both exiled Athenians serving Persian kings. Arrian, *Anabasis* 1.18.2 may implicitly be contradicting Cleitarchus when he makes a point of stating that Alexander stayed at Ephesus when Magnesia surrendered.

[47] Plutarch, *Alexander* 18.3; Curtius 3.2.1.

[48] Curtius 3.2.2-19; Diodorus 17.30.1-31.2.

[49] Donald W. Engels, *Alexander the Great and the Logistics of the Macedonian Army*, University of California, 1978, p.37.

[50] Jacoby, *FGrHist* 137 F8 = Cicero, *Ad f.* 2.10.3.

[51] Jacoby, *FGrHist* 137 F9 = Schol. Plato *Resp.* 337A (Photius: Σαρδόνιος γέλως).

be marked by a phrase incorporating "Concerning Alexander" (the title of Cleitarchus' book) at Diodorus 17.47.6 (similarly the ends of Books 7 and 12).

Book 5: Opened with a series of digressions on events elsewhere beginning with the conquest of Crete by Agis.[52] It continued the narrative of Alexander's campaign from late summer of 332BC with the siege of Gaza, the advance into Egypt, the visit to Siwa and afterwards the foundation of Alexandria. Cleitarchus probably described Alexander's return up the Levantine coast after Egypt, because this would explain why Fragment 3, which seems to relate to a visit of Alexander to Byblos on the Lebanese coast, is located in Book 5 by Stobaeus. Book 5 seems to have ended on schedule in the summer of 331BC with a digression on events in Europe during that campaigning season and specifically the rebellion of Agis, since Fragment 4 attributes mention of the 50 Spartan hostages received by Antipater to Book 5. Conjecturally, other events in Europe were related by Cleitarchus at this point, such as the death of Alexander of Epirus, given in Justin 12.2.1-15. For example, Curtius 8.1.37 mentions a complaint by Alexander of Epirus (whilst he died of a wound according to Livy) that he had encountered men in Italy, whilst his nephew was up against women in Persia.[53] The relevant section of Livy has some Cleitarchan elements, such as referring to the "Invincible Alexander".[54]

Book 6: Opened with the run-up to the Battle of Gaugamela (called the Battle of Arbela in Cleitarchus). It incorporated Fragment 10 (description of Babylon) and Fragment 11 (the razing of Persepolis).[55] It clearly ended on schedule at midsummer 330BC with the death of Darius, which was also the end of Curtius' fifth book and the 11th book of Justin/Trogus. Diodorus 17.73.4 concludes with the phrase, "And that was the situation in Asia", before catching up with events in Europe, which Cleitarchus had treated at the end of his fifth book. This type of formula is used by Diodorus to indicate major changes in the focus of his account, not only in Book 17, but also in parts of his history based on different sources than Cleitarchus.[56] It is likely that Diodorus is in this instance signalling the end of the sixth book of Cleitarchus.

Book 7: The first events must have been persuasion of the troops to continue the war and the advance to Hecatompylus, but Fragments 12-14,[57] Diodorus

---

[52] Diodorus 17.48.1-2; Curtius 4.1.39-40; note that there are additional digressions in Curtius 4.5.11-22 immediately following Curtius' account of Tyre and including the tale of Aristonicus the Pirate.

[53] Aulus Gellius, NA 17.21.33; Livy 9.19.10-11.

[54] See NGL Hammond, THA 112 on Cleitarchus as Livy's probable source.

[55] Jacoby, FGrHist 137 F10 & F11 = Diodorus 2.7.3-4 (Tzetzes, Chil. 9.569) & Athenaeus 13.37 (576DE).

[56] E.g. "This was the state of affairs concerning Philip," at Diodorus 16.89.3.

[57] Jacoby, FGrHist 137 F12 = Pliny, NH 6.36-38; F13 = Strabo 11.1.5; F14 = Demetrius, De eloc. 304 (Tzetzes, Chil. 7.49, 11.832).

17.75 and Curtius 6.4.1-22 show that Cleitarchus provided significant digressions on the geography of the Caspian region and the natural history of Hyrcania at the beginning of this book. Fragments 15 and 16 relate the visit of Thalestria (or Thalestris), Queen of the Amazons, and Fragment 32 on the castration of a transgressing male also best fits the context of a digression on Amazon practices.[58] Following Alexander's first crossing of the Hindu Kush in the summer of 329BC Diodorus 17.83.3 has a curious tail-piece, Καὶ τὰ μὲν περὶ Ἀλέξανδρον ἐν τούτοις ἦν ("These were the concerns of Alexander"), which probably indicates the end of Book 7 of Cleitarchus. As already seen, it was Diodorus' standard practice to use such phrases to indicate changes of focus or subdivisions for his narrative. However, in this instance he appears to be marking the end of Book 7 of Cleitarchus, especially because he incorporates the title of Cleitarchus' history into his stock expression. Exactly the same sentence appears also at the likely close of Cleitarchus' 12th book in 324BC and there is a similar expression at the apparent end of Book 4 (Diodorus 17.47.6).

Book 8: Began with a digression on events in the camp of Bessus,[59] followed by news reaching Alexander from Greece and elsewhere,[60] then the march to the River Oxus.[61] The end of Book 8 falls in the great lacuna in Diodorus 17, but the *Metz Epitome* has opened and continues to provide corroboration of Cleitarchan elements in Curtius down to Alexander's arrival in the Indus Delta. The closing event of this book seems to have been Alexander's capture of the Rock of Ariamazes (i.e. the Sogdian Rock), which Cleitarchus treated as the climax of the campaigning year of 328BC.[62] This also ended the seventh book of Curtius.

Book 9: Probably opened with Scythian peace overtures including the offer of the Scythian king's daughter to Alexander in marriage.[63] It continued with the first campaign against the Massagetae and the Dahae – Alexander's 3-column campaign through Sogdiana. This book seems to have climaxed in a similar way to Book 8 with the capture of the Rock of Chorienes. It therefore closed in the Spring of 327BC with the marriage of Alexander to Roxane, who had fallen into his hands with the surrender of this stronghold.[64]

---

[58] T. S. brown, "Clitarchus," *American Journal of Philology*, Vol. 71, 149, 1950; Jacoby, *FGrHist* 137 F15 = Plutarch, *Alexander* 46; F16 = Strabo 11.5.4; F32 = Pap. Oxyrh. 2.218 col. 2.

[59] Curtius 7.4.1-19; Diodorus 17.83.7.

[60] Curtius 7.4.32-40; Diodorus 17.83.4-6.

[61] Diodorus, List of Contents for Book 17; Curtius 7.5.9-12; Frontinus, *Strat.* 1.7.7.

[62] *Metz Epitome* 15-18; Curtius 7.11.1-25; Polyaenus 4.3.29; Diodorus 17 – Contents; Strabo 11.11.4.

[63] Curtius 8.1.1-10.

[64] *Metz Epitome* 28-31; Curtius 8.4.20-30; Diodorus 17 – Contents.

Book 10: Commenced with Alexander's preparations for the invasion of India and also mentioned his orders for the training of native youths in Macedonian arms to form the *Epigoni*. Several Fragments (20-22) seem to be from an introductory description of Indian royal processions by virtue of parallels in Curtius.[65] A little later Alexander's visit to Nysa and the discovery of the ivy of Dionysus were related by Cleitarchus (Fragment 17).[66] This was the first book of the Indian campaigns. Its climax was the battle against Porus (the Hydaspes) and it closed with the capture of the wounded Porus in the same place as the close of Curtius' eighth book and within the 89th chapter of Diodorus.[67] This was in June of 326BC. Jacoby Fragment 5 of Cleitarchus, which is stated to be derived from Book 10, was probably part of a digression on the revolt of Baryaxes that concluded this book.[68]

Book 11: Opened with a discussion of Alexander's plans to reach the ends of India and to visit the Ocean.[69] There is copious evidence from the Fragments and other vulgate sources for digressions on the geography and natural history of India near the beginning of this book: specifically, sixteen cubit serpents in Fragment 18[70] (Diodorus 17.90.1 and Curtius 9.1.4) and troops of monkeys and their ensnarement in Fragment 19[71] (Diodorus 17.90.2-3). A visit to salt mines in Fragment 28 probably relates to the start of the voyage down the Hydaspes, when the expedition would have passed the famous and ancient salt mines at Khewra.[72] There is also a fragment of Onesicritus at Strabo 15.1.30, which mentions a mountain of salt in the kingdom of Sopeithes. According to Arrian 6.2.2 Hephaistion was ordered to hurry to the capital of King Sopeithes at the start of the river voyage. Fragment 24 suggesting that Ptolemy was present when Alexander was wounded at the Mallian town was part of the climax of this book.[73] The best indications are that Cleitarchus' 11th book closed soon after the successful treatment of Alexander's Mallian chest wound by Critobulus in the Spring of 325BC. The main evidence for this is the insertion of a digression on a revolt of the Greeks settled in Bactria by both Diodorus and Curtius at this point.[74] Conversely, the vulgate narrative is relatively seamless through

---

[65] Curtius 8.9.23-26; Jacoby, *FGrHist* 137 F20 = Strabo 15.1.69l; *FGrHist* 137 F21 = Aelian, *NA* 17.23; *FGrHist* 137 F22 = Aelian, *NA* 17.22.

[66] Jacoby, *FGrHist* 137 F17 = Scholia on Apollonius Rhodius 2.904.

[67] Curtius 8.14.5; Diodorus 17.89.2; Justin 12.8.7; *Metz Epitome* 61.

[68] It is also feasible that it was in a digression at the beginning of Book 10.

[69] *Metz Epitome* 63; Curtius 9.1.1-6; Diodorus 17.89.3-90.6.

[70] Jacoby, *FGrHist* 137 F18 = Aelian, *NA* 17.2.

[71] Jacoby, *FGrHist* 137 F19 = Aelian, *NA* 17.25.

[72] Jacoby, *FGrHist* 137 F28 = Strabo 5.2.6.

[73] Jacoby, *FGrHist* 137 F24 = Curtius 9.5.21.

[74] Diodorus 17.99.5-6; Curtius 9.7.1-11.

Alexander's visit to the Ocean and subsequent march into Gedrosia, despite this seeming perhaps to modern sensibilities to be a more logical point to close the second book of the Indian campaign.

Book 12: Began with the surrender of the Mallians and Oxydracae and a celebratory banquet, after which the contest between Coragus and Dioxippus took place.[75] Fragment 25 relates the killing of 80,000 Indians in the Kingdom of Sambus.[76] Fragment 23 telling of Mandi women bearing children at age 7 and being old at 40 is difficult to place exactly, but most probably comes from a digression during the progress down the Indus.[77] It is co-attributed to Megasthenes and will be further discussed later. Fragment 26 clearly refers to the tidal bore in the Indus Delta described also by Curtius.[78] The location of Fragment 27 among the Oreitae and the Ichthyophagoi in Gedrosia is self-explanatory.[79] Fragment 29 cites stories told to Alexander about the Indian Ocean voyage and may securely be placed at the return of Nearchus and Onesicritus, since there are matching tales related by these men at Curtius 10.1.11.[80] Fragment 6 shows that Book 12 extended at least as far as the suicide of Calanus. Its end is clearly indicated following the arrival of the *Epigoni* in the summer of 324BC at Diodorus 17.108.3 with a recurrence of the terminal sentence, Καὶ τὰ μὲν περὶ Ἀλέξανδρον ἐν τούτοις ἦν, incorporating the title of Cleitarchus' work.

Book 13: Opened with a digression on the extravagance of Harpalus towards his mistresses (Fragment 30) and an account of his flight to Athens.[81] Subsequently, Cleitarchus evidently claimed that a Roman delegation met Alexander at Babylon in April-May of 323BC (Fragment 31).[82] There is significant evidence that Cleitarchus' account extended beyond Alexander's death in June 323BC in an epilogue focussed on the fate of his corpse. A similar version of the suicide of Sisygambis is found in Diodorus 17 and Curtius. Pausanias 1.6.3 speaks of Alexander's body being laid to rest with Macedonian rites at Memphis in about 321BC and he does so shortly after giving a Cleitarchan version of the story that Ptolemy had saved Alexander's life in India. Similarly, Curtius 7.9.21 speaks of the bones of dead Macedonians being

---

[75] Exclusively a Cleitarchan story: Diodorus 17.100.1-101.6; Curtius 9.7.12-26.

[76] Jacoby, *FGrHist* 137 F25 = Curtius 9.8.15, which had 800,000 (DCCC milia) in the manuscripts, which is usually amended to 80,000 (LXXX milia) on the basis of Diodorus 17.102.5-7, which speaks of "more than eight myriad of the barbarians".

[77] Jacoby, *FGrHist* 137 F23 = Pliny, *NH* 7.28-29.

[78] Jacoby, *FGrHist* 137 F26 = Strabo 7.2.1-2; Curtius 9.9.9-21.

[79] Jacoby, *FGrHist* 137 F27 = Pliny, *NH* 7.30.

[80] Jacoby, *FGrHist* 137 F29 = Pliny, *NH* 6.198.

[81] Jacoby, *FGrHist* 137 F30 = Athenaeus 586C-D; Diodorus 17.108.4-8; Curtius 10.2.1-3.

[82] Jacoby, *FGrHist* 137 F31 = Pliny, *NH* 3.57; cf. Arrian, Anabasis 7.15.5-6.

laid to rest in accordance with the rites of their fatherland in a passage likely to be derived from Cleitarchus. Furthermore, Curtius' account closes with a mention of Alexander's entombment at Memphis. This raises the possibility that both Pausanias and Curtius are following a description of how Alexander's body reached Memphis given by Cleitarchus (Curtius 9.8.22 also shares the statement in Pausanias 1.6.2 that Ptolemy was not sired by Lagus, presumably both following Cleitarchus again.) Another significant indicator for Cleitarchus' account having extended beyond Alexander's death is provided by closely matching comments on the suppression of poisoning rumours under Antipater and Cassander in Diodorus 17.118.2 and Curtius 10.10.18-19 with further echoes in Pausanias 9.7.2 (a matter to which we will return). Additionally, Schachermeyr has argued that Curtius was still drawing on Cleitarchus for his account of events at Babylon after Alexander's death.[83] It is also pertinent that Jane Hornblower has concluded in the context of a detailed study of Book 18 of Diodorus[84] that the historian continued to follow his source for Book 17 (i.e. Cleitarchus) in several chapters near the beginning of Book 18 culminating in the review of the Last Plans (*hypomnemata*), but I cannot see that she has succeeded in excluding Hieronymus as the source for much of this material. She also suspected that Cleitarchus might be the source for Diodorus' version of Alexander's entombment in Alexandria at 18.28.3-6, but I consider that Diodorus was drawing on his personal experience of having visited the tomb in Alexandria for this, since Cleitarchus could not have implied that Ptolemy Soter created the Alexandrian tomb as early as 321BC. Nevertheless, Curtius also mentions the transfer from Memphis to Alexandria in his last sentence. In conclusion, it is likely that Cleitarchus' account extended at least as far as the entombment at Memphis in 321BC and a possibility exists that he finished with the transfer of the body to Alexandria in ~280BC.[85]

Other Fragments: As regards Fragments 35 and 36 and also the aphorisms attributed to Cleitarchus by several Christian writers in the doubtful Fragments 37-52, none can be placed with perfect confidence.[86] However Fragment 36 from the Suda is helpful in that it extends the evidence for Cleitarchus having used Timaeus as a source. And I have found apt contexts for a couple of the aphorisms in the course of reconstructing the Indian campaigns.

---

[83] F. Schachermeyr, "Alexander in Babylon und die Reichsordnung nach seiner Tod", Vienna, 1970, pp. 92 ff.

[84] Jane Hornblower, *Hieronymus of Cardia*, OUP, 1981, pp. 92-97.

[85] A. M. Chugg, "The Sarcophagus of Aleander the Great?" *Greece & Rome*, Vol. 49.1, April 2002, pp.14-15.

[86] There are echoes of the philosophy of the Cynics and mentions of the diadem etc. in F37-52, which is enough to make it seem credible that they were indeed extracted from Cleitarchus' work, but a detailed computer search for close linguistic parallels in the Vulgate sources on Alexander might be required to make further progress on their authenticity and locations within *Concerning Alexander.*

Sources of Cleitarchus

Several strands of evidence make it seem unlikely that Cleitarchus actually accompanied Alexander's expedition.

1) Diodorus 2.7.3 speaks of Cleitarchus and separately of those who "went over [to Asia] with Alexander" in the same sentence, which implies that Diodorus did not believe that Cleitarchus had been a member of Alexander's expedition.

2) Cleitarchus makes some mistakes of a nature that would not be expected of a writer who had actually been present as events unfolded. For example, Cleitarchus seems to have written or at least implied that the Indian river voyage set off from the River Acesines, whereas it actually began on the Hydaspes (according at least to Aristobulus and Nearchus).[87] Others have found errors in Cleitarchus' descriptions of Babylon, Hyrcania and the Caspian region, which make it seem improbable that Cleitarchus ever visited these places in person.[88] Perhaps most telling is the error in Diodorus, where he transfers the appointment of Abdalonymus from Sidon to the aftermath of Tyre, which seems to have been sourced from Cleitarchus.[89]

3) There is no evidence of Cleitarchus' participation in any stage of the expedition, whereas most of the primary sources seem to have been only too keen to emphasise their roles in what was generally regarded as a glorious and illustrious campaign. Although this is an argument from silence, the silence seems significant in this instance, since Aristobulus, Ptolemy, Nearchus and Onesicritus are all known to have given prominence to their own activities.[90]

4) There is copious evidence that Cleitarchus incorporated material from a wide range of primary sources on Alexander's expedition (see below) and it seems improbable that he would have relied so extensively on the testimony of others, if he had direct experience himself.

---

[87] Diodorus 17.95.3-5; Curtius 9.3.20-24; *Metz Epitome* 69-70; Justin 12.9.1; corrected by Arrian, *Anabasis* 5.29.5-6.1.1 & *Indica* 18; Strabo 15.1.17 & 15.1.32; Yardley & Heckel, 255.

[88] J. R. Hamilton, "Cleitarchus & Aristobulus", *Historia*, 1961, Vol. 10, 449.

[89] Diodorus 17.47.1-6; Curtius 4.1.16-26 and Justin 11.10.8-9 correctly give Sidon - either Trogus and Curtius took their information from another source on this point or there is some reason for confusion; Plutarch, *Moralia* 340C-E has "Aralynomos" appointed king of Cypriot Paphos.

[90] Aristobulus told of his work to restore the vandalised tomb of Cyrus (Arrian, *Anabasis* 6.29.10, Strabo 15.3.7); Ptolemy related his mission to arrest Bessus (Arrian, *Anabasis* 3.29.6-30.5); Nearchus concentrated on his command of the fleet for the return voyage from India, especially to correct Onesicritus, who had implied that he had himself led the fleet in his writings (Arrian, *Anabasis* 6.2.3 & *Indica* 18; see Brown, *Onesicritus* 7-11).

A Basis For The Reconstruction Of Cleitarchus

On the assumption therefore that Cleitarchus is not himself a true primary source in the sense of being an eyewitness, it is pertinent to examine whence he drew his material. A list of various writers who may have been among Cleitarchus' sources is presented in Table 2.2. In each case, there is either direct evidence from the ancient sources themselves or else some modern scholar has proposed the writer as featuring among Cleitarchus' sources. The overall picture is that Cleitarchus probably drew on at least ten early or primary sources and may well have used material from twenty or more ancient writers. Table 2.2 also proffers a (subjective) judgement of the degree of probability that Cleitarchus used each listed source.

Onesicritus of Astypalaea – It is almost certain that Onesicritus was a major source for Cleitarchus. For example, T. S. Brown has observed, "The evidence for Cleitarchus' having used Onesicritus… is irresistible."[91] There is scarcely any direct overlap in the attributed fragments, although both authors are reported to have told the story of the visit of the Amazon queen.[92] Onesicritus is often supposed to be its originator, since he seems to be the earliest writer to relate this tale.[93] It is certain that Cleitarchus wrote after Onesicritus, because Cleitarchus also uses stories from Nearchus, who wrote partly to refute Onesicritus. Fragment 28 of Cleitarchus and Fragment 21 of Onesicritus both speak of Indian salt mining, but stronger evidence comes from multiple instances where stories (usually digressions) from Onesicritus are echoed by Diodorus and Curtius. For example, the Cathaean custom of *suttee* and admiration for beauty in the kingdom of Sopeithes are mentioned in Fragment 21 of Onesicritus[94] and appear in the same context in Diodorus 17.91.3-7. Curtius 9.10.3 and 10.1.10 mention respectively the departure and return of the fleet and give the names of *both* Nearchus and Onesicritus as its officers. Since both incidents are covered in similar terms by Diodorus 17.104.3 and 17.106.4-7, their common source is likely to be Cleitarchus, despite the failure of Diodorus to mention the names of the officers. However, Cleitarchus' source is very probably Onesicritus, since Nearchus does not seem to have reported Onesicritus' presence by name in his account of these events.[95] Some at least of the wonders of Hyrcania mentioned in Diodorus 17.75 would seem to be sourced from Onesicritus. For example, the honey-dripping tree of Diodorus resembles the *occhus* tree from which honey distils for two hours each morning in Fragment 3 of Onesicritus and both authors highlight the prolific harvests from Hyrcanian fig trees. Diodorus 17.90.5 appears to refer to the banyan tree,

---

[91] Brown, *Onesicritus* 6.

[92] Jacoby T8 & F1 of Onesicritus and F15 & F1 of Cleitarchus.

[93] E.g. Tarn, *Alexander the Great II, Sources & Studies*, 328.

[94] Strabo 15.1.30.

[95] E.g. Arrian, *Indica* 34.6 following Nearchus; see Brown, *Onesicritus* 10-11 for a detailed argument of the point.

saying that its trunk could barely be embraced by four men. Fragment 22 of Onesicritus in Strabo 15.1.21 says it could scarcely be embraced by five men (although Strabo also notes that Aristobulus mentioned this tree and it also appears in Arrian, *Indica* 11.7 in a fragment of Nearchus). There is an account at Diodorus 17.90.2-3 and in Fragment 19 of Cleitarchus describing a curious technique for capturing monkeys, but this occurs also in Strabo 15.1.29 in a context which makes it look like a fragment of Onesicritus (however, Aristobulus and Nearchus cannot be ruled out as Strabo's source).[96] Cleitarchus' story of Alexander's visit to Delphi may have been sourced from Onesicritus, since Plutarch relates it immediately after the meeting with Diogenes, of whom Onesicritus was a student.[97] The stories of Lysimachus and of the death of his brother Philippus in Curtius 8.1.11-19 and 8.2.34-39 might well have originated with Onesicritus, since he later read his book at the court of Lysimachus.[98] Schachermeyr has speculated that Cleitarchus took the story of Abdalonymus from Onesicritus, because he considered the story to have a colouring of cynical philosophy (especially in Curtius).[99] Finally, the interview with the Indian gymnosophists, which probably originated in Onesicritus' account,[100] though missing from Diodorus and Curtius, appears in the *Metz Epitome* 78-84, which is deeply imbued with Cleitarchan material.

Deinon of Colophon – He was the father of Cleitarchus according to Pliny.[101] He was also the author of a *Persica* (History of Persia).[102] These facts predispose us to expect that Deinon would have been a formative influence on Cleitarchus' conception of the Persian Empire. Nor does the evidence contradict this inference. Cleitarchus seems to have incorporated extensive background material on Asia and on the relationships between certain historically prominent Greeks and the Persians. At least some of this material matches the fragments of Deinon's *Persica*. For example, Cleitarchus seems to be the source for the suggestion that Darius had a concubine for every day of the year and he appears to have inherited this notion from his father.[103] Then Fragments 21 & 22 of Cleitarchus compare Indian birds to Sirens, potentially in homage to his father's assertion that the Sirens were to be found in India.[104] It also appears clear from

---

[96] See Pearson, *Lost Histories* 223-4, Hamilton, *C&A* 451 and Brown, *AJP* 71, p144, n9.

[97] Diogenes Laertius 6.75-76, 6.84; Strabo 15.1.65; Plutarch, *Moralia* 331E & *Alexander* 65.

[98] Plutarch, *Alexander* 46: see Hammond, THA 145-7 on the origins of the stories relating to Lysimachus in Onesicritus.

[99] Schachermeyr, *Alexander der Grosse* 214, n234; cf. Pearson, *Lost Histories* 238; Atkinson, *Commentary on Curtius III & IV*, 283.

[100] Strabo 15.1.63-65; Plutarch, *Alexander* 65.

[101] Jacoby, *FGrHist* 137 T2 = Pliny, *Natural History* 10.136 (where he is "Dinon").

[102] Cornelius Nepos, *Conon* 5; T. S. Brown, *Clitarchus* 135.

[103] Diodorus 17.77.6; Curtius 6.6.8; Plutarch, *Artaxerxes* 27.

[104] Pliny, *Natural History* 10.136.

Fragment 33 that Cleitarchus' stories about Themistocles were extracted from his father's writings, since Plutarch cites both as sources for the same version of Themistocles' career. It should also be suspected that the digressions on Persian history in Diodorus 17.5.3-7.3 and Justin 10 were sourced by Cleitarchus from Deinon. So too the story of Sardanapalus in Fragment 2 (although Alexander's actual visit to the monument of Sardanapalus at Anchiale was told by Callisthenes, Fragment 34). Plutarch, *Alexander* 36.2 has a direct quote from Deinon, which may in this context have been transmitted via Cleitarchus. Hammond suggests that an explanation for the name *Euergetae* given by Diodorus 17.81.1-2 may have come from Deinon via Cleitarchus.[105]

Nearchus of Crete – There are two strong matches between the fragments of Cleitarchus and Nearchus. Firstly, Cleitarchus' Fragment 27 in speaking of the Gedrosians making bread from sun-dried fish matches a fragment from Strabo 15.2.2, which may be from Nearchus, since he is named as a source a few lines above. The only difference is that whereas Nearchus spoke specifically of the Ichthyophagoi, Cleitarchus used the more general term Oreitae. Secondly, Cleitarchus' Fragment 18[106] mentions snakes 16 cubits in length and a serpent of the exact same length appears in Fragment 10 of Nearchus.[107] Nearchus and Cleitarchus both gave accounts of the Banyan tree,[108] but it is perhaps more likely that Cleitarchus was following Onesicritus in this instance, because mention of the number of men required to embrace the trunk was common to Onesicritus and Cleitarchus. The account of whales in Cleitarchus[109] matches closely the Fragments of Nearchus,[110] especially in the use of trumpets to frighten them into diving out of the course of the fleet. However, Onesicritus evidently also mentioned the whales, though terming them "sea-serpents". It is also just feasible that Cleitarchus drew his tale of the capture of Indian monkeys (F19) from Nearchus, but again Onesicritus (or even Aristobulus) is a more probable source.

Callisthenes of Olynthus - Callisthenes told a story that the sea gave way to Alexander during his march along the coast of Pamphylia.[111] The same story recurs in Plutarch[112] and Hammond has argued that this whole section of Plutarch dealing with signs of divine favour for Alexander's cause was drawn

---

[105] Hammond, *THA* 60.

[106] Aelian, *NA* 17.2.

[107] Arrian, *Indica* 15.10.

[108] Diodorus 17.90.5 & Curtius 9.1.9-10 vs. Arrian, *Indica* 11.7.

[109] Curtius 10.1.12 and Diodorus 17.106.7.

[110] Strabo 15.2.12 and Arrian, *Indica* 30.4-5.

[111] Jacoby Fragment 31 of Callisthenes.

[112] Plutarch, *Alexander* 17.2-3.

from Cleitarchus.[113] Then Fragment 2 of Cleitarchus suggests that he told the story of Alexander's visit to the monument of Sardanapalus at Anchiale, but Callisthenes had previously related this, as shown by his Fragment 34. Thirdly, Cleitarchus told that a pair of crows guided Alexander on the road to Siwa,[114] which derives from the account by Callisthenes.[115] Furthermore the Cleitarchan version in Diodorus 17.50.6, that the oracular responses were conveyed via nods and signs, seemingly derives from Callisthenes as in his F14a. Pearson has adduced that Callisthenes was a source for Cleitarchus[116] and this must be correct insofar as story elements originally told by Callisthenes appeared in Cleitarchus. What is less certain is whether Cleitarchus used Callisthenes directly or indirectly through Onesicritus or even Aristobulus.

Timaeus - He is twice coupled with Cleitarchus as a co-source in the context of Jacoby's Fragments of Cleitarchus. According to Fragment 7 both of them cited 820 years as the interval between the invasion of Asia by the Heracleidae and that by Alexander, whilst other authorities gave shorter periods. Cleitarchus was almost certainly following Timaeus in this, since the latter was especially renowned for his work on chronology. Then in Fragment 36 Cleitarchus is specified to have followed Timaeus on a linguistic point. Furthermore Hammond has shown that Plutarch's date for Alexander's birth probably comes from Timaeus,[117] because Cicero attributes the associated stories concerning the conflagration of the temple at Ephesus on the same day to Timaeus.[118] However, given that Timaeus was a source for Cleitarchus, who was in turn a major source for Plutarch's Life of Alexander, the suspicion must be that Plutarch found this information in Cleitarchus. If so, then Cleitarchus must have opened his work with a summary of Alexander's birth and ancestry. Finally, Tarn notes that Diodorus 17.75.7 uses a peculiar phrase μεγίστην ἐπιφάνειαν and a rare verb κηροπλαστεῖν in describing a bee-like creature which he calls an *anthredon*.[119] The same combination occurs in one other place: Diodorus 19.2.9 in a passage Tarn attributes to Timaeus. Tarn poses the question of whether Cleitarchus is using Timaeus, since Diodorus took the matter of the *anthredon* from Cleitarchus (for it is described in Fragment 14 of

---

[113] Hammond, *Sources* 46-7.

[114] Diodorus 17.49.5.

[115] Jacoby Fragment 14a/b of Callisthenes = Strabo 17.1.43 & Plutarch, *Alexander* 27; we know from Arrian, *Anabasis* 3.3.6, that Aristobulus also gave this version, so he would be a possible intermediary.

[116] Pearson, *Lost Histories* 231.

[117] Hammond, *Sources* 19-20.

[118] Cicero, *N. D.* 2.69 & *Div.* 1.47.

[119] Tarn, *Alexander the Great II, Sources & Studies* 90, n.3.

Cleitarchus). Tarn's observation coupled with the other evidence does indeed support the view that Timaeus was a major source for Cleitarchus.[120]

Liber de Morte [Holcias(?)] – As Heckel[121] has noted, it is clear from Justin 12.14, Curtius 10.10.14 and Diodorus 17.118.1-2 that Cleitarchus was aware of the rumour that Alexander was poisoned at Antipater's instigation by his sons Cassander and Iollas using toxin transported in an ass's hoof in the tradition of the *Liber de Morte*.[122] However, on balance Cleitarchus seems to have given the poisoning rumour as an alternative possibility, rather than as the literal truth, much as the matter is presented by Diodorus.

Megasthenes - According to Fragment 23 of Cleitarchus, both he and Megasthenes mentioned an Indian tribe called the Mandi and attributed three hundred villages to them, saying that their women could bear children from age seven and became old at forty. Megasthenes is the source for a parallel description in Arrian's *Indica* 9.1-8, which adds the story of Pandaea.[123] Then Polyaenus 1.3.4 gives the Pandaea story in what has been considered a fragment of Megasthenes,[124] but the usage of the figure of 365 for the number of villages in his version is highly characteristic of Cleitarchus (as noted above). Plutarch, *Alexander* 64 and the *Metz Epitome* 78-84 describe Alexander's interview with the Indian gymnosophists. Cleitarchus is their likely common source, yet elements at least of this version derive ultimately from Megasthenes according to Hammond.[125] Conversely, on the width of Ganges, C. Bradford Welles[126] attributes the details in Diodorus 2.37.2, 17.93.2 and 18.6.2 to Megasthenes, but Strabo 15.1.35 and Arrian, *Indica* 4.7 cite Megasthenes in giving a width of 100 stades, whereas the Cleitarchan figure was 30 or 32 stades.[127] In his digression on India Curtius 8.9.8 mentions the River Iomanes (Jumna), which elsewhere (e.g. Arrian, *Indica* 8.5-6) is mentioned by Megasthenes.[128] Hammond observes that Curtius 8.9 includes material that was not known until after Alexander's time, such as Megasthenes' information on the region of the Ganges.[129] Yet it looks as though at least some of it comes from Cleitarchus, because this chapter

---

[120] Also endorsed by Pearson, *Lost Histories* 216.

[121] W. Heckel, *The Last Days & Testament of Alexander the Great*, Historia Einzelschriften, Heft 56 (Stuttgart, 1988), p.2.

[122] E.g. *Metz Epitome* 88-89.

[123] See also Phlegon. *Mirab.* 33: *Of the Pandaian Land*.

[124] Jacoby *FGrHist* 715: Fragment 58 of Megasthenes in J. W. McCrindle, *Ancient India as Described by Megasthenes and Arrian* (1877).

[125] Hammond, *Sources* 121.

[126] C. Bradford Welles, *Loeb edition of Diodorus*, Vol, 8, 389 note 2.

[127] Diodorus 17.93.2; Plutarch, *Alexander* 62.1; *Metz Epitome* 68-9.

[128] Though the mention of the Iomanes relies on a textual correction by Hedicke.

[129] Hammond, *THA* 148.

of Curtius subsequently mentions the processions of the Indian kings with singing birds on branches, which are in Fragments 20-22 of Cleitarchus. It remains possible that Curtius consulted Megasthenes or another later geographer directly, but it is more likely that he found the geographical material on India in Cleitarchus. Posing the question of whether Cleitarchus used Megasthenes as a source for geographical and ethnographical information on India or the reverse, the former seems more probable, since Megasthenes had personally visited India, whereas Cleitarchus almost certainly had not. Megasthenes lived with Sibyrtius, Satrap of Arachosia and (later?) with Seleucus Nicator.[130] He visited the court of Chandragupta as an ambassador, so he was an authority on the region in his own right and is likely to be the originator of his information in most cases.[131]

Hegesias of Magnesia - Part of the description of Alexander's conduct at the siege of Gaza in Curtius 4.6.13-16 closely parallels Fragment 5 of Hegesias,[132] yet some disparities suggest that Curtius was not following Hegesias directly, but via an intermediary, who is likely to be Hegesias' contemporary, Cleitarchus (since he was Curtius' main source). Pearson has noted some tentative evidence that Cleitarchus sometimes used a metrical scheme known as Asianic rhythms,[133] whereas Strabo suggests that Hegesias was virtually the originator of this style.[134] Cleitarchus' style is also compared to that of Hegesias in Jacoby's T9 & T12 of Cleitarchus. Finally, having noted that some of Plutarch's information on Alexander's birth seems to come from Timaeus via Cleitarchus, by association it is likely that the rest of this passage, which actually cites Hegesias, was also sourced from Cleitarchus.[135]

Polycleitus of Larissa – He probably accompanied Alexander's expedition and he wrote a substantial history of Alexander's reign in around eight or nine books (since his Jacoby Fragment 1 from the 8th book reads like a story from circa 324-323BC).[136] There is uncertainty regarding when he published and his exact identity (although two historical figures of the same name are candidates). Tarn thinks Polycleitus wrote after Megasthenes, because he mentioned the size of tortoises in the Ganges, but Onesicritus seems to have written about the size

---

[130] Arrian, *Anabasis* 5.6.2 & *Indica* 5.3; Clement of Alexandria, *Stromateis* 1.72.4.

[131] Strabo 15.1.36.

[132] Jacoby, *FGrHist* 142 F5 = Dion. Hal., *De comp. Verb.* 123-126 R; Hammond, *THA* 127 notices the resemblances to Curtius' account.

[133] Pearson, *Lost Histories*, 213, n9 & 227, n59 notes evidence of Asianic rhythms especially in F19 (Aelian, *NA* 17.25) & Diodorus 17.13.6.

[134] Jacoby, *FGrHist* 142 T1 = Strabo 14.1.41.

[135] Plutarch, *Alexander* 3.3-5.

[136] Jacoby, *FGrHist* 128 F1 = Athenaeus 539A.

of elephants in Ceylon, though he never saw the place.[137] Polycleitus seems to make similar geographical errors in his Fragment 7 as Cleitarchus in his Fragments 12 & 13 (e.g. confusing the Aral Sea with the Sea of Azov).[138] The sweetish water and sea serpents of the Caspian occur in Plutarch, *Alexander* 44 and Diodorus 17.75 respectively, as also in Polycleitus Fragment 7. Plutarch, *Alexander* 46 couples him with Cleitarchus and others in having told the story of the Queen of the Amazons.[139]

Herodotus - Hammond argues that Plutarch, *Alexander* 17.2-18.2 was mimicking Herodotus in his account of Xerxes being swayed by dreams and oracles, in recounting Alexander's uncertainty regarding his future strategy and in how the ensuing oracles and miracles influenced his policy.[140] Hammond also infers that Plutarch found this idea in Cleitarchus, although he may alternatively have added information from other sources. Furthermore, Hammond suggests that Cleitarchus repeated the same formula for the indecision of Darius regarding the conduct of the campaign that culminated in Issus.[141] At the parade of Darius' forces before Babylon, Charidemus of Athens was pessimistic about their chances against the Macedonians and was executed.[142] This passage has features in common with the conference of Xerxes in Herodotus 7 and Curtius 3.2.2-3 actually refers to Xerxes (as described in Herodotus 7.59) for the method of counting the Persian forces by herding them into an enclosure just large enough to accommodate 10,000 troops. According to Plutarch, *Alexander* 20.1-3, Amyntas, son of Antiochus, gave good advice to Darius, which was ignored, as similarly Herodotus 7.235 & 7.237.1 had presented Demaratus, the Spartan king in exile, as giving good advice to Xerxes, who then disregarded it to his cost. Hammond traces this to Aristobulus and/or Ptolemy, since the same details are given in Arrian 2.6.3-7, but it is not impossible that Cleitarchus adopted this story from Aristobulus.[143] Both Curtius 4.1.27-33 and Diodorus 17.48.2-5 later recount Amyntas' raid on Egypt and they agree so closely that their mutual source must be Cleitarchus. According to Curtius 3.8.1-2 the advice of Amyntas that Darius should fight in open territory was given by Greek troops from the former army of Memnon, but it is likely that Amyntas was already their officer, for he led the Greeks on the Persian side at Issus.[144] It has

---

[137] Tarn, *Alexander II Sources* 8; tortoises in the Ganges - Jacoby, *FGrHist* 128 F10 = Paradox. Vat. Rohd. 10; elephants in Ceylon - Jacoby, *FGrHist* 134 F3 = Pliny, *NH* 6.81.

[138] Jacoby, *FGrHist* 128 F7 = Strabo 11.7.4.

[139] T. S. Brown, *Onesicritus*, 166, n. 84 to Ch. 4 confidently asserts that "Cleitarchus certainly used Polycleitus".

[140] Hammond, *Sources* 45-9.

[141] Hammond, *Sources* 45-9 and *THA* 40-1 & 116.

[142] Curtius 3.2.2-19; Diodorus 17.30.1-31.2.

[143] Hammond, *Sources* 49.

[144] Curtius 3.11.18; cf. W. Heckel, *Who's Who in the Age of Alexander the Great*, s.v. Amyntas [2].

sometimes been argued that Callisthenes was influenced by Herodotus, in which case the possibility arises that Callisthenes is the source of Herodotean echoes in Cleitarchus.[145]

Theopompus of Chios – Cleitarchus evidently gave the same account of the mistresses of Harpalus as Theopompus according to Fragment 30 of Cleitarchus. Since Cleitarchus shortly post-dated Theopompus,[146] there is a good chance that Cleitarchus took his account from Theopompus. This is accentuated by the fact that after Alexander's death Theopompus joined the court of Ptolemy in Egypt, where he died shortly after 320BC.[147] His memory and influence would still have been strong in Egypt when Cleitarchus was active in Alexandria perhaps just a few years later.

Aristobulus of Cassandrea - There are undoubtedly significant similarities between the *History of Alexander* by Aristobulus and some aspects of Cleitarchus' work. Tarn tried to use them to prove that Aristobulus was a source for Cleitarchus, thereby pushing the date of Cleitarchus into the 3rd century BC.[148] However, this argument has been vigorously disputed, notably by Hamilton, essentially on the basis that the similarities are more readily explained by Aristobulus and Cleitarchus having had a common source, who was probably Onesicritus.[149] Specifically, Alexander's visit to a monument and statue of Sardanapalus at Anchiale, 12 miles SW of Tarsus, is told by Athenaeus 530A-B as a fragment of Aristobulus.[150] However, Athenaeus coupled this story with Jacoby Fragment 2 of Cleitarchus (Athenaeus 530A), which gives some historical background on Sardanapalus. It therefore appears likely that Cleitarchus also told the story of the visit to Anchiale, though he was probably echoing his father Deinon's *Persica* (which may in turn have followed Ctesias' *Persica*) for the background history. Tarn points to various Indian names having similar forms in Diodorus and in fragments of Aristobulus, but Hamilton has done much to undermine Tarn's arguments, mainly by proposing Onesicritus as the originator of these forms for the names.[151] The issue revolves especially around alternatives such as Hypasis/Hypanis and Sudracae/Oxydracae. In fact, it is hard to discern the Cleitarchan forms in most of these cases, since

---

[145] L. Prandi, *Callistene. Uno storico tra Aristotele e i re macedoni*, Milan 1985, pp. 82-93.

[146] E.g. according to Pliny, *NH* 3.57 = Fragment 31 of Cleitarchus.

[147] Photius, *Life of Theopompus*.

[148] Tarn, *Alexander II Sources*, 31-36.

[149] J. R. Hamilton, *Cleitarchus & Aristobulus*, Historia 10, 448-458, 1961.

[150] Jacoby Fragment 9a of Aristobulus, with 9b (Strabo 14.5.9) and 9c (Arrian, *Anabasis* 2.5.2-4) also being related; cf. Plutarch, *Moralia* 326F & 336C.

[151] Hamilton, *Cleitarchus & Aristobulus*, 457-8; both Tarn and Hamilton might be criticised for having underplayed the variations in the forms among authors, their various manuscripts and even within manuscripts and they overlook the *Metz Epitome*, which is helpful in supporting Oxydracae as the Cleitarchan form, for example.

Diodorus, Curtius, Justin and the *Metz Epitome* generally give different versions. Sometimes alternative manuscripts of the same author (or even different passages of the same manuscript) have different forms (e.g. variations for the River Hyphasis among manuscripts of Diodorus include: Ὕπανιν, Ὕφασιν, Ὕπανσιν). Consequently, it is difficult to attach much weight to arguments from the name forms. Perhaps the most striking potential parallel between Aristobulus and Cleitarchus is a description of apes appearing to confront Alexander like an army and curious techniques for the capture of monkeys by exploiting their habit of aping humans to persuade them to glue their eyelids shut or to trap themselves in special leggings. A rather garbled and corrupt version of this tale appears in Jacoby Fragment 19 of Cleitarchus, which is from Aelian, *NA* 17.25, and there is a further Cleitarchan rendering in Diodorus 17.90.2-3. A more intelligible version is found in Strabo 15.1.29 and Tarn argues that Strabo got it from Aristobulus, though his case owes much to the supposedly Aristobulan name forms in Strabo's text.[152] However, Pearson and Hamilton agree that Strabo might be following Onesicritus for this tale.[153] Neither can Nearchus be ruled out as Strabo's source. Even if Tarn is correct that Strabo found this material in Aristobulus, then it is still possible as suggested by Brown that both Aristobulus and Cleitarchus took the story from Onesicritus.[154] There remain various instances in which Hammond believes that he detects Aristobulus as the underlying source of passages in the 7th book of Curtius.[155] As Curtius lacks any attributed fragments of Aristobulus and since some of Hammond's attributions to Aristobulus also seem to me to show evidence of derivation from Cleitarchus, these cases potentially indicate the use of Aristobulus by Cleitarchus. For example, Hammond discusses Aristobulus as the source of Curtius 7.6.11-23 & 7.6.25-27 for the advance to the Tanais and the foundation of Alexandria on the Tanais with a circumference of 60 stades in 17 days, mainly due to a general (though not detailed) similarity with events as reported by Arrian 4.1-4.[156] However, the detailed correspondence of Curtius with Justin 12.5.12 and the fact that some aspects are mentioned in the *Metz Epitome* 8-9 are clear indications of Cleitarchus and "Tanais" is a Cleitarchan name for the river. For the rock of Ariamazes, Hammond thinks much of Curtius' account (7.11.1-25) is from Aristobulus,[157] but commonalities with the *Metz Epitome* include a cavern on the ascent path, an altitude of 20 (*Metz Epitome*) or 30 (Curtius) *stadia* and 300 climbers signalling with white cloths and

---

[152] Tarn, *Alexander II Sources*, 30-36.

[153] Pearson, *Lost Histories*, 223-4; Hamilton, *C&A* 451

[154] Brown, *Clitarchus*, AJP 71, 144, note 9.

[155] Hammond, *THA* 151 suggests Aristobulus as the source for Curtius 7.4.22-31, 7.5.1-18, 7.5.27, 7.6.21-3, 7.9.20-1, 7.10.10-14, 7.11.1-26.

[156] Hammond, *THA* 142.

[157] Hammond, *THA* 144.

using iron wedges and ropes. Hence, this would appear to be Cleitarchan material. Hammond also cites similarities between Curtius and Arrian 4.18.4-19.3 and suggests that Alexander's *cupido* in Curtius is a Latin equivalent of *pothos* in Arrian, where such yearning is believed to be a characteristic applied to Alexander particularly by Aristobulus.[158] Nevertheless, it might be countered that Hammond is taking advantage of the lacuna in Diodorus speculatively to attribute some of the more historically cogent passages in Curtius to Aristobulus. Finally, the key role for Aristander's prophecies in Arrian seems to be derived from Aristobulus, but Aristander's influence was also reported by Cleitarchus.[159] In summary, there are enough hints as to justify a suspicion that Cleitarchus was influenced by Aristobulus, but none is sufficiently clear as to establish high confidence in the matter.

Patrocles – Tarn[160] noticed that a geographical observation that the Euxine (Black Sea) is equal to the Caspian (in length) is common to Fragment 12 of Cleitarchus (Pliny, *NH* 6.36-38) and to a fragment of Patrocles.[161] Tarn made this point into the lynchpin of his theory of a late date for Cleitarchus, since he supposed Patrocles, who explored the Caspian in c. 280BC, to have originated the statement. However, Pearson and Brown do not accept this as proof that Patrocles was a source for Cleitarchus.[162] It remains possible that the comments are independent of one another or that Cleitarchus inspired Patrocles.

Ephippus of Olynthus - Hammond suggests that Trogus (Justin 12.12.11-12) may have followed Cleitarchus, who in turn followed Ephippus, for the death and funeral of Hephaistion (since Ephippus wrote a book on the subject).[163] Similarly, Hammond attributes the elaborate description of the funeral of Hephaistion in Diodorus 17.115 to Ephippus, noting that the extravagant funerary dedications from Alexander's Friends in Diodorus 17.115.1 & 17.115.5 are comparable to the gifts made to Alexander himself in Jacoby Fragment 5 of Ephippus (Athenaeus 537E-538B).[164] Strangely, Hammond argues that Diodorus could not have taken the description of Hephaistion's pyre from Cleitarchus on the basis that the description of Alexander's catafalque in Diodorus 18 might have come from the same source, which is Hieronymus of Cardia.[165] However, this is illogical and inconsistent. If Justin is reporting

---

[158] It also seems to have been used of Alexander by Nearchus, e.g. Arrian, *Indica* 20.1.

[159] Diodorus 17.17.6; Curtius 4.2.14, 4.4.12, 4.13.15, 4.15.27, 5.4.2, 7.7.8-29.

[160] Tarn, *Alexander II Sources*, 16-19.

[161] Strabo 11.7.1, probably via Eratosthenes.

[162] Pearson, *Lost Histories*, 227; Brown, *Clitarchus*, AJP 71, 140.

[163] Hammond, *THA* 107-8 & 114; Athenaeus 120D, 146C, 434A & 537D for Ephippus' work.

[164] Hammond, *THA* 75; Droysen, *Hellenismus²* II 126, note 2 has the same suggestion.

[165] Athenaeus 206E.

Hephaistion's funeral from Ephippus via Cleitarchus, then so is Diodorus.[166] Nevertheless, despite the fact that Ephippus is the best-attested primary source on the death and funeral of Hephaistion, he was probably not the only early writer to treat the subject in detail, so it is far from certain that he was the source used by Cleitarchus. However, Ephippus also mentioned that Alexander quaffed from a giant cup before collapsing at his final party, which recurs as the "Cup of Heracles" in the Cleitarchan tradition.[167] There is one other hint that Cleitarchus may have followed Ephippus: the description of the dress adopted by Alexander after the death of Darius given by Ephippus closely matches details given in the Vulgate authors (diadem and purple tunic with the central white stripe etc.)[168]

Berossus - P. Schnabel long ago published a rather intricate argument[169] to the effect that Cleitarchus may have used Berossus, a Chaldean Priest of Bel, as a source on Babylon. In outline, Diodorus within his account of Babylon in his second book states that he sometimes corrects Ctesias from Cleitarchus and others. One such correction in 2.10.1 was to deny that Semiramis constructed the Hanging Gardens in favour of a "later Syrian king". Since Curtius 5.1.35 makes exactly the same statement, including the Cleitarchan "Syrian" instead of the more correct "Assyrian" and the matching detail that the king made them for his wife, there are good grounds to think that both writers took this from Cleitarchus. But whence did Cleitarchus obtain this information? Schnabel pointed out that the *Babyloniaca* of Berossus[170] is the earliest authoritative source for asserting that Nabukodrossoros (Nebuchadnezzar?) was the builder rather than Semiramis and for terming them a present for his queen. However, Berossus dedicated his work to Antiochus I, who came to the throne in 293BC (initially jointly with Seleucus Nicator), so this would push Cleitarchus well into the third century BC. It is possible that an earlier authority made the same statement, but no such source is known.[171]

Demetrius of Phalerum – Richard Billows has argued that Cleitarchus' attention to Alexander's *Tyche* was inspired by a work *Peri Tyches* by Demetrius of Phalerum, which is cited by Polybius as having discussed Alexander's

---

[166] Hammond, *Sources* 137 attributes the parallel account of Hephaistion's death and the funeral arrangements in Plutarch, *Alexander* 72.1-3 to Cleitarchus, but I suspect that Plutarch drew on other sources as well, since his figure for the funeral costs of 10,000 talents agrees with Arrian as opposed to the 12,000 talents in Justin and Diodorus, which should be the Cleitarchan value.

[167] Athenaeus 434A-B; Diodorus 17.117.1-2; Plutarch, *Alexander* 75.3; Justin 12.13.8.

[168] Ephippus in Athenaeus 537E; *Metz Epitome* 2; Diodorus 17.77.5; Curtius 3.3.17-19 & 6.6.4; Justin 12.3.8; Plutarch, *Alexander* 45.2 & *Moralia* 329F-330A (though the latter is attributed to Eratosthenes).

[169] P. Schnabel, *Berossus*, 1923, ch. 3 – this chapter had earlier been published as a separate study.

[170] In the Fragment of Berossus in Josephus, *Contra Apion* 1.141-142.

[171] See also Pearson, *Lost Histories* 230-231.

career.[172] However, the influence of Demetrius could have been indirect or Cleitarchus may have taken up this theme independently.

Chares of Mytilene - Pearson expresses confidence that Chares was a source for Cleitarchus, but he fails to offer any specific evidence and such evidence is hard to detect.[173] Nevertheless, Hammond thinks Curtius 8.11.1-25 supplemented his account of Aornus from Chares especially for the heroic acts of the King, another Alexander and Charus.[174] This is mainly because Curtius mentions the filling of *cavernas* with tree-trunks, whilst Fragment 16 of Chares (Athenaeus 124C) speaks of pits being filled with snow and covered with oak boughs in the context of Aornus (which he calls Petra, since it was known as the Rock in Greek). This would raise the possibility that Cleitarchus took these details from Chares, though it seems more likely that the rather vague similarities between Curtius and Chares are merely coincidental. Fragment 18 of Chares (Aulus Gellius 5.2.1-5) has Bucephalus die of his wounds after carrying Alexander from the midst of the enemy in the Battle of the Hydaspes and also mentions the foundation of the city of Bucephala at the site to honour the King's steed. This is also broadly the story told by Cleitarchus as reflected in the Vulgate sources.[175] It is therefore a possibility that the Cleitarchan version was inspired by the account of Chares. Conversely, Chares' versions of the proskynesis experiment (F14 – Plutarch, *Alexander* 54; Arrian, *Anabasis* 4.12.3-5), the death of Callisthenes (F15 - Plutarch, *Alexander* 55) and the funeral of Calanus (F19 – Athenaeus 437AB; Plutarch, *Alexander* 70) are not noticeably similar to the Cleitarchan versions.

Hieronymus of Cardia - Hammond gives a curious argument that Hieronymus should be seen as the source of the accusation in Diodorus, Curtius, Justin and other Vulgate sources that Antipater, Cassander and Iollas had conspired to poison Alexander.[176] He notes that Curtius 10.10.18-19 and Diodorus 17.118.2 both said that the subsequent power of Antipater and Cassander had caused this rumour to be suppressed. He concludes that it cannot have been published until after Cassander's death in 297BC. He infers that Hieronymus was the likely source, since he wrote his History dealing with events following on from Alexander's death in the early 3rd century BC (but completed it after the death of Pyrrhus in 272BC[177]) and because he was Diodorus' main source in his next

---

[172] Richard Billows, "Polybius and Alexander Historiography" in *Alexander the Great in Fact and Fiction*, ed. A.B. Bosworth and E.J. Baynham, Oxford 2000, 297-299; Polybius 29.21.2.

[173] Pearson, *Lost Histories*, 61 & 131.

[174] Hammond, *THA* 149

[175] See Hammond, *Sources* 111 & 257; Curtius 8.14.34, 9.1.6, 9.3.23; Justin 12.8.4-8; Stephanus Byzantinus, s.v. *boos kephalai*; Diodorus 17.89.6 & 17.95.5; Strabo 15.1.29 and *Metz Epitome* 62.

[176] Hammond, *THA* 78 & *Sources* 146.

[177] Jacoby, *FGrHist* 154 F15.

book.[178] However, the *Liber de Morte* may well be the original written source for the poisoning of Alexander on Antipater's orders. Heckel dates it to ~317BC, before the fall of Eumenes.[179] The close correspondence between Diodorus and Curtius on the matter of the suppression of the story is in fact good evidence that both are still following Cleitarchus, but Cleitarchus is likely to be getting his information from the *Liber de Morte*, rather than from Hieronymus. It is sometimes argued that Curtius 10.6-10.10 is based on Hieronymus,[180] but the similarities between Diodorus 17.118.2 and Curtius 10.10.18-19 and between Diodorus 17.118.3 and Curtius 10.5.19-25 are indications that Curtius may have found at least some of this material in Cleitarchus. If so, then there is a vague possibility that Cleitarchus drew on Hieronymus.

One early history of Alexander's campaigns that Cleitarchus virtually certainly did not use was that compiled by Ptolemy, because Cleitarchus disagrees with Ptolemy's account on too many issues. For example, they specifically differ on whether Ptolemy was present when Alexander received his chest wound in India[181] and on many points regarding Alexander's activities in Egypt.[182] There is also no sign that Cleitarchus had direct access to the *Ephemerides*, although he might have had indirect access if he used Ephippus.[183]

The Date of the *Indica* of Megasthenes

The date at which Cleitarchus wrote and published his history of Alexander is of considerable interest, since it is a key determinant of his relationship with his own sources, the men who were friends and companions of Alexander. However, there seems to be significant evidence that Cleitarchus also sourced material from the *Indica* of Megasthenes, which was based upon its author's experience of India after Alexander's death. The date of composition of the *Indica* is therefore potentially a *terminus post quem* for Cleitarchus' work. But this

---

[178] Hornblower, Jane, *Hieronymus of Cardia*, OUP, 1981.

[179] W. Heckel, *The Last Days & Testament of Alexander the Great*, Historia Einzelschriften, Heft 56 (Stuttgart, 1988), p.71-75.

[180] E.g. R. M. Errington, "From Babylon to Triparadeisos, 323-320BC," *JHS* 90 (1970) 72-75.

[181] Curtius 9.5.21.

[182] E.g. return route from Siwa - Arrian, *Anabasis* 3.4.5 versus Curtius 4.8.1: timing of the foundation of Alexandria - Arrian, *Anabasis* 3.1.5 versus Curtius 4.8.1, Diodorus 17.52: dragons versus crows guiding Alexander in the desert - Arrian, *Anabasis* 3.3.5 versus Diodorus 17.49.5.

[183] A. M. Chugg, "The Journal of Alexander the Great", *Ancient History Bulletin* 19.3-4 (2005) 155-175.

issue is controversial: in particular A. B. Bosworth has recently argued for a revision of Megasthenes' publication date from circa 290BC to circa 310BC.[184]

It is stated by Strabo that Megasthenes visited Palimbothra (Pataliputra) on the Ganges, for the purpose of an embassy to the Indian king, Chandragupta Maurya.[185] It is separately stated by Clement of Alexandria that Megasthenes lived together with Seleucus Nicator, implying he was a member of Seleucus' court.[186] From these attestations and other circumstantial details, it has long been believed that Megasthenes was the ambassador of Seleucus in his negotiations with Chandragupta in 304/3BC. Such is the orthodoxy that Bosworth has disputed. At the core of the issue lies a single sentence from Arrian's *Indica* (5.3): συγγενέσθαι γὰρ Σανδροκόττῳ λέγει, τῷ μεγίστῳ βασιλεῖ Ἰνδῶν, καὶ Πώρου ἔτι τούτου μείζονι. Bosworth offers the translation: [Megasthenes] *says that he met Sandrocottus* [Chandragupta] *the greatest king of the Indians, and also met Porus, who was yet greater than him.* Although the Greek is good, this creates a paradox, since Porus was undoubtedly also an Indian king and was recognized as such by Megasthenes and his contemporaries. For this reason it has become standard practice for modern editors to amend the final phrase to: Πώρου ἔτι τούτῳ μείζονι, giving the translation, [Megasthenes] *says that he met Sandrocottus the greatest king of the Indians, even greater than Porus.* However, Bosworth notices that Arrian, *Anabasis* 5.6.2, states that, *Megasthenes lived with Sibyrtius, satrap of Arachosia, and often speaks of his visiting Sandracottus, the king of the Indians.* He suggests that the paradox may be resolved by supposing that Megasthenes actually acted as the ambassador of Sibyrtius to Chandragupta in the context of the alliance of the eastern satraps against Peithon between 320BC and 318BC. He would have met Porus, who was not murdered by Eudamas until 317BC, *en route.* If he then compiled his *Indica* after Porus' death, but before Chandragupta took over the satrapies of the Indus river system, Megasthenes might have written that Porus had been the greatest ever king of the Indians, but that Chandragupta enjoyed that distinction at the time he wrote. Bosworth supposes that Arrian has then garbled the meaning of his source (by failing to reflect the time distinctions) to generate the received manuscript reading. Bosworth adopts this reasoning to argue that Megasthenes probably wrote before Chandragupta's territories became larger than those of Porus at their greatest extent. Bosworth further observes that Porus had achieved control of virtually the entire Indus river system by the time of Alexander's death, so the critical juncture (at least from a Greek perspective) would be Chandragupta's acquisition of Porus' territories to augment his kingdom on the Ganges. The evidence is scant, but Justin remarks that Chandragupta came into possession of India whilst Seleucus was laying the

---

[184] AB Bosworth, "The Historical Setting of Megasthenes' *Indica*," *CPh* 91 (1996), 113-27.

[185] Strabo 15.1.36.

[186] Clement of Alexandria, *Stromateis* 1.72.4.

foundations of his future power.[187] Bosworth places the extension of Chandragupta's control into the Punjab after 309BC. His acquisitions in the Indus river system were seemingly recent in 305BC, when Seleucus launched an expedition across the Indus and fought with him.[188] We are explicitly told of an alliance negotiated between them in 304/3BC involving an interrelationship by marriage and the gift of 500 elephants to Seleucus,[189] which he deployed to great effect at the Battle of Ipsus in 301BC.

On balance I support Bosworth (and T. S. Brown before him)[190] in rejecting the manuscript emendation of Arrian's *Indica*, even though it is textually minor. As Bosworth points out, it is in general bad practice to impute errors where the Greek of our manuscripts is good and in this case the manuscript reading is contextually superior to the emendation. However, it seems to me that there is a more straightforward way to resolve the apparent paradox, which does not involve the imputation of any kind of error on the part of our ancient sources. I would offer instead a translation of the manuscript reading with a variant nuance: [Megasthenes] *says that he met Sandrocottus the king of the Indians of the greatest stature, and also met Porus, who was of yet greater stature than he.* To appreciate that this is essentially a quip or pun, it is only necessary to know that Porus' most famous attribute was his exceptional tallness. Arrian himself introduces his description of Porus by noting his reported height to have been above 5 cubits.[191] In fact the paradox in the sentence *requires* that "stature" should be interpreted in its sense meaning greatness when it refers to Chandragupta, but in its sense meaning height when it refers to Porus. But in the Greek, μέγας has exactly the same duality in its possible meaning. Indeed, Arrian uses its counterpart noun μέγεθος to describe Porus' height in his *Anabasis*.

This interpretation has the opposite effect to that suggested by Bosworth. It is seen to be necessary for Megathenes to have been aware that the territories of Chandragupta exceeded those that had been controlled by Porus. Probably, that would put the composition of his *Indica* after the negotiations in 304/3BC, because it would have been offensive to his patron Seleucus to imply Chandragupta's acquisition of the Punjab before that time. It also makes it very likely that Megasthenes' embassy to Chandragupta was indeed conducted on behalf of Seleucus. Although I concede that Megasthenes *could* have represented Sibyrtius in India, it seems strange that Sibyrtius should have conducted direct negotiations with a kingdom on the Ganges at a time when his ally Eudamas would have been in a better position to engage in diplomacy with his neighbour

---

[187] Justin 15.4.20.

[188] Appian, *Syriaca* 55; Justin 15.4.12.

[189] Strabo 15.2.9 & 16.2.10; Plutarch, *Alexander* 42.2; Appian, *Syriaca* 55.

[190] T. S. Brown, "The Merits and Weaknesses of Megasthenes," *Phoenix* 11 (1957) 13.

[191] Arrian, *Anabasis* 5.19.1.

Chandragupta on behalf of the eastern satraps and there is of course no actual evidence of such diplomacy anyway. Consequently, I am compelled inexorably to accept the canonical publication date for Megasthenes' *Indica* in the first decade of the third century BC.

The Date of Cleitarchus

Quintillian stated that Timagenes, who flourished in the middle of the 1st century BC and arrived in Rome from Alexandria in 55BC, was born long after Cleitarchus, who tends also to be listed among other writers of the late 4th and early 3rd centuries BC in various of Jacoby's Testimonies (e.g. T12, T14).[192]

We are told by Philippus, quoted by Diogenes Laertius in his *Life of Stilpo of Megara* (2.113), that Stilpo succeeded in poaching Cleitarchus as a pupil from his rival Aristotle the Cyrenaic sophist. It has been argued by Zeller[193] by analysing the list of his known pupils that Stilpo, though born around 380BC, only began actively teaching in around 322BC, yet when he met Demetrius Poliorcetes in 307BC he was said to be living a "life of tranquillity and study".[194] Cleitarchus' studentship therefore probably occurred between these two dates. More recently it has been suggested that the specific occasion of Cleitarchus' recruitment by Stilpo was the visit to Corinth in the summer of 308BC of Ptolemy Soter, when he presided at the Isthmian Games. It is supposed that Aristotle of Cyrene and his pupils, Cleitarchus and Simmias, were among Ptolemy's retinue, since Cyrene was among Ptolemy's possessions and Cleitarchus himself is called an Alexandrian by Philodemus.[195] Diogenes Laertius 2.111 mentions that Stilpo defeated a rival, Diodorus Cronus, in dialectic in the presence of Ptolemy, but he also states a little afterwards that Stilpo refused Ptolemy's invitation to visit Egypt, whereas the Suda observes that Stilpo was entertained by the first Ptolemy.[196] It has been argued that a visit by Ptolemy to Megara at only ~20 miles from Corinth during 308BC is the only

---

[192] See Heckel in the Introduction to *Yardley's translation of Curtius*, 7; Jacoby, *FGrHist* 137 T6 = Quintillian, *Inst.* 10.1.74; Jacoby, *FGrHist* 137 T12 = Philodemus, *Rhet.* 4.1 col. 21; Jacoby, *FGrHist* 137 T14 = Pliny, *NH* 1.6, 1.7, 1.12-13.

[193] Eduard Zeller, *Die Philosophie der Griechen*, 4th ed., Part II, 1 (Leipzig, 1889) 248, n. 2; T. S. brown, "Clitarchus," *American Journal of Philology*, 1950, Vol. 71, 137.

[194] Plutarch, *Life of Demetrius* 9.

[195] *FGrHist* 137 T12 of Cleitarchus; Cleitarchus was probably an immigrant to Alexandria, firstly, because he was probably born before its foundation and, secondly, because his father may have been the Dinon of Colophon mentioned in the list of sources of Varro, *R.R.* 1.1.8 and Pliny, *N.H.*, sources for books 10, 14, 15, 17 & 18, but there are manuscript difficulties, on which see L. Pearson, *Lost Histories*, 226, n.56.

[196] Suidae Lexicon s.v. *Stilpon* – Adler number: sigma 1114.

obvious occasion such that all these references can be correct.[197] Since Diogenes Laertius seems to expect his readers to recognise Stilpo's Cleitarchus and since his era is perfectly consistent with all other evidence on our Cleitarchus, it is likely that Philippus was referring to the famous author of the history of Alexander. The Stilpo connection therefore has the effect of confining Cleitarchus' publication date to between about 320-250BC and is most consistent with a date towards the centre of this period. In fact, the *terminus post quem* may be 310BC if the mention at Diodorus 17.23.2-3 of Agathocles' activities in that year was derived from Cleitarchus, which seems probable.[198] At any rate, few authorities would support a date outside this range, but within it scholars may be sub-divided into two main camps. One party (e.g. F. Jacoby, J. R. Hamilton, W. Heckel…) favour a date in the approximate range 310-300BC, whilst the other (e.g. W. W. Tarn, L. Pearson, N. G. L. Hammond…) would prefer a range of 280-260BC. The evidence for the earlier range may be summarised as follows:

1. Pliny suggests that Cleitarchus wrote before Theophrastus and it is on balance likely that Theophrastus published within a few years either way of 300BC.[199]

2. Cleitarchus appears to have written in ignorance of Ptolemy's mention (penned before his death in 282BC) of his presence elsewhere during the Mallian siege at the time that Alexander received his chest wound; furthermore, it has been suggested that Ptolemy might have been implicitly contradicting Cleitarchus in recording his absence.[200]

---

[197] Luisa Prandi, *Fortuna è realtà dell' opera di Clitarco*, Historia Einzelschriften 104, Steiner, Stuttgart 1996; A. B. Bosworth, "In Search of Cleitarchus: Review-discussion of Luisa Prandi: Fortuna è realtà dell' opera di Clitarco," *Histos* (University of Durham, electronic journal of historiography), Vol. 1, Aug. 1997.

[198] Diodorus might in principle himself have introduced the example of Agathocles out of personal familiarity with the exploits of a fellow Sicilian; however, he is explicit that Agathocles was imitating Alexander's strategy in ridding himself of his fleet, a motivation which probably needed to be sourced from a contemporaneous writer, given the inexactitude of the parallel; yet Diodorus fails to mention the connection with Alexander when recounting Agathocles' boat burning in more detail using a different source (Timaeus?) at 20.7. That Agathocles is called a king at 17.23.2, whereas Diodorus assigns him the title of Dynast or Tyrant elsewhere in books 16, 18, 19 and 20, may be a consequence of sourcing from Cleitarchus.

[199] Pliny, *N. H.* 3.57; see J. R. Hamilton, "Cleitarchus & Aristobulus," *Historia*, 1961, Vol. 10, 452-3 for a detailed analysis of this point.

[200] Curtius 9.5.21; Arrian, *Anabasis* 6.11.8; F. Jacoby, *Real-Encyclopädie* 11, 625 argued that Ptolemy had probably contradicted Cleitarchus, but J. R. Hamilton, "Cleitarchus & Aristobulus" 451-452 considered the evidence inconclusive; Tarn, *Alexander the Great II, Sources & Studies*, 26-28, pointed out that our sources suggest that Ptolemy did not explicitly contradict Cleitarchus and sought to argue that Ptolemy wrote first and Cleitarchus deliberately distorted the truth to glorify Ptolemy's memory: the value of this evidence for the problem of the date of Cleitarchus is further undermined by arguments from Errington, "Bias in Ptolemy's History of Alexander", *Classical*

3. Cleitarchus (F11) made Thais responsible for the burning of Persepolis, whereas Arrian's account, presumably deriving from Ptolemy, effectively denies her any role in the matter.[201] Since Thais was Ptolemy's mistress and the mother of his daughter Eirene and his sons Leontiscus and Lagus, it should have been dangerous for an Alexandrian to contradict Ptolemy regarding her biography. It is therefore argued that this is a further indication that Ptolemy's official version was not known to Cleitarchus when he wrote.[202]

4. It is relatively uncontroversial that Cleitarchus used both Onesicritus and Nearchus, who had probably both published by 310BC, but advocates of an early date for Cleitarchus have also been at pains to point out that it is strangely difficult to *prove* that Cleitarchus used Aristobulus, who wrote between 301BC and about 270BC, despite Aristobulus' history having been second only to Cleitarchus' own in popularity.[203]

Conversely, there are significant reasons to assign a date in the early 3rd century BC to the publication of Cleitarchus' work:

1. The close similarity between Curtius 10.10.18-19 and Diodorus 17.118.2 in speaking of Antipater and Cassander having suppressed the rumour that they had caused Iollas to poison Alexander is a significant indication that these authors found this comment in Cleitarchus.[204] If so, then this is suggestive that Cleitarchus published after the death of Cassander in 297BC, since the perspective of the comment seems to be an overview of the entire reign and it would indeed have been dangerous to promulgate such an accusation whilst Cassander lived.

Quarterly 19, pp233-242, and others that Ptolemy wrote soon after Alexander's death, although the more orthodox view that he wrote in the 280's BC remains preferrable.

[201] Arrian, *Anabasis* 3.18.11-12.

[202] E.g. A. B. Bosworth, "In Search of Cleitarchus: Review-discussion of Luisa Prandi: Fortuna è realtà dell' opera di Clitarco," *Histos* (University of Durham, electronic journal of historiography), Vol. 1, Aug. 1997, paragraph 6.

[203] J. R. Hamilton, "Cleitarchus & Aristobulus"; however this is essentially an argument from silence and should therefore carry little weight.

[204] Diodorus 17.118.2 (Loeb trans.): *"After Alexander's death, Antipater held the supreme authority in Europe and then his son Casander took over the kingdom, so that many historians did not dare write about the drug. Casander, however, is plainly disclosed by his own actions as a bitter enemy to Alexander's policies. He murdered Olympias and threw out her body without burial, and with great enthusiasm restored Thebes, which had been destroyed by Alexander."* Curtius 10.10.18-19 (Yardley trans.): *"Whatever credence such stories gained, they were soon scotched by the power of the people defamed by the gossip. For Antipater usurped the throne of Macedon and of Greece as well, and he was succeeded by his son, after the murder of all who were even distantly related to Alexander."*

Nevertheless, Heckel has recently argued that Diodorus' mentions of Cassander's restoration of Thebes and murder of Olympias at the same juncture suggest that his source, Cleitarchus, wrote before the killings of Roxane, Alexander IV, Barsine and Heracles, since he should otherwise have been expected also to refer to them.[205] However, this is an argument from silence, which should therefore carry little weight. Furthermore, Pausanias 9.7.2 is another author who couples Cassander's rebuilding of Thebes with his role in arranging the execution of Olympias.[206] It is relatively unlikely that these two incidents were coupled in the same way independently by two different writers, so we should suspect that Pausanias is also following Cleitarchus. This is reinforced by our earlier observations that Pausanias 1.6.2-3 probably drew on Cleitarchus for Ptolemy having saved Alexander in the land of the Oxydracae and for Alexander's entombment at Memphis. Yet Pausanias 9.7.2 *does* proceed immediately to note the murders of Alexander's sons and he continues with details of Cassander's death and the fates of Cassander's sons. It appears likely that Cleitarchus gave these details, but that Diodorus abbreviated his source rather arbitrarily.[207] As regards the proposition that Pausanias might be merging other sources with Cleitarchus' account, it should be noted that Curtius 10.10.19 mentions that all Alexander's relations were killed, whilst Pausanias states that all members of Alexander's house were destroyed by Cassander: virtually the same observation in the same context. There is in effect a three-way correspondence between Diodorus, Curtius and Pausanias on these points. Thus it is difficult to evade the conclusion that Cleitarchus was the underlying source for

---

[205] Waldemar Heckel, "The Earliest Evidence for the Plot to Poison Alexander" in *Alexander's Empire: Formulation to Decay*, California 2007, 271; F. Schachermeyr, *Alexander der Grosse: Das Problem seiner Persönlichkeit und seines Wirkens*, (Vienna, 1973) 155, n. 149 also thinks Cleitarchus did not know of the murder of Alexander IV and Roxane, but Curtius 10.10.19 is suggestive of awareness of the murders on the part of Cleitarchus; N.G.L. Hammond, *THA* 78 notices that the implication is that the poisoning story was not reported by Diodorus' source until after the death of Cassander in 297BC and he uses this to argue that Hieronymus was Diodorus' source, yet this contradicts the *Einquellenprinzip* given the similarity of context and language found in Curtius.

[206] Pausanias 9.7.2 (Loeb trans.): "*My own view is that in rebuilding Thebes Cassander was mainly influenced by hatred of Alexander. He destroyed the whole house of Alexander to the bitter end. Olympias he threw to the exasperated Macedonians to be stoned to death; and the sons of Alexander, Heracles by Barsine, and Alexander by Roxane, whom he killed by poison. But he himself was not to come to a good end. He was filled with dropsy, and from the dropsy came worms while he yet lived. Philip, the eldest of his sons, shortly after coming to the throne was seized by a wasting disease, which proved fatal. Antipater, the next son, murdered his mother Thessalonice, the daughter of Philip, son of Amyntas, and of Nicasipolis, charging her with being too fond of Alexander, who was the youngest of Cassander's sons. Getting the support of Demetrius, the son of Antigonus, he deposed with his help and punished his brother Antipater. However, it appeared that in Demetrius he found a murderer and not an ally. So some god was to exact from Cassander a just requital.*"

[207] There is a parallel instance in the misleading arbitrariness with which Diodorus seems to have summarised the matter of the 440 talents raised at Thebes.

every detail in all three accounts. This amounts to a cardinal argument for pushing his date into the early 3rd century BC.

2. It has been argued that Cleitarchus would have been more likely to mention the Romans after Pyrrhus' campaigns against them in around 280BC, which was the first time that they came to prominence on the stage of Greek history.[208] (Badian's suggestion that Cleitarchus actually saw the Roman delegation, because he was present in Babylon, is not persuasive: his argument that Cleitarchus' information had to be based on autopsy, because Pliny *implies* that it was better than hearsay [*fama*] but less good than close study [*diligentius*] is a *non sequitur*.)[209]

3. There is evidence of varying strength that Cleitarchus drew on a range of writers of the early 3rd century BC for aspects of his account of Alexander's reign. These include (as a minimum) Aristobulus, Patrocles, Berossus and Megasthenes.

To show how the multiple, individually inconclusive strands of evidence that Cleitarchus used 3rd century writers can accumulate to make a strong case for a third century date for Cleitarchus, I have assigned conservative probabilities as to whether Cleitarchus used each source as follows (see also Table 2.2): Megasthenes 80%, Aristobulus 40%, Patrocles 35%, Berossus 30%. Thus the probability that Cleitarchus did not use Megasthenes is 1 - 0.8 = 0.2. For Cleitarchus to have a 4th century date, it is necessary that he actually used none of these writers. The probability that he used none of them p_{none} is the product of the probabilities that he did not use each one:[210]

$$p_{none} = (1-p_{Meg}) \text{ x } (1-p_{Aris}) \text{ x } (1-p_{Pat}) \text{ x } (1-p_{Ber}) = 0.2 \text{ x } 0.6 \text{ x } 0.65 \text{ x } 0.7 = 0.05$$

Hence the cumulative evidence suggests high confidence (~95%) that Cleitarchus published in the 3rd century BC, even though none of the individual sourcings can be considered decisive. Clearly, there is room for argument about the exact probabilities that Cleitarchus used each source, but the general point that multiple independent strands of weak evidence combine to provide strong overall evidence will always be valid.

Given that no single fact establishes a definite date for Cleitarchus, it is necessary to be guided by the collective preponderance of the evidence. It

---

[208] E.g. Pearson, *Lost Histories*, 233.

[209] E. Badian, "The Date of Clitarchus," *Proceedings African Classical Associations* 8 (1965) p.10.

[210] On the basis that the evidence for his use of each writer is independent of the evidence that he used any other.

seems to me that it is not unlikely that Pliny was led into assuming that Cleitarchus published soon after Alexander's death by the vividness and detail of his reports and that Ptolemy's history was not widely disseminated until some while after his death.[211] Conversely, the internal evidence that Cleitarchus had some knowledge of contemporaneous authors *and* events down to perhaps 280BC seems to be emerging from a wider range of evidence than has previously been appreciated. I would therefore favour a date shortly after 280BC, whilst conceding that any time in the range 320-250BC remains feasible. I note that in siding with Tarn and his followers on this matter, I do so for rather different reasons: it is the Cleitarchan comments on the poisoning plot, the extirpation of Alexander's family and the restoration of Thebes combined with the likely use of Megasthenes and other early third century sources that weigh particularly strongly in my evaluation. This conclusion also tends to support the suspicion of Jane Hornblower that Cleitarchus ended with the transfer of Alexander's corpse to Alexandria, though again she reached this view by a different route than I.[212] If Cleitarchus wrote in Alexandria under Philadelphus, then the celebration of the transfer of Alexander's remains to his own city by its monarch is by far the most obvious flourish on which to conclude his history of Alexander.

Unattributed Fragments: the *Einquellenprinzip*

A fundamental tool for identifying unattributed fragments of Cleitarchus is the application of the so-called *Einquellenprinzip* (single source principle), which has been pioneered by German scholars, such as Schwartz and Jacoby and more recently reasserted by F. Schachermeyr.[213]

In its original 19th century form the *Einquellen-theorie* asserted that Diodorus slavishly epitomised a succession of earlier historians with little modification of their language or perspectives in compiling his *Bibliotheke*. In so doing, he confined himself to a single source over long sections of his work, often extending to an entire book or more. In the 20th century, Schwartz advocated relaxation of the strict *Einquellenprinzip* to the effect that Diodorus generally

---

[211] It is a normal practice throughout history for prominent individuals to suppress the publication of controversial works, especially autobiographies, until after their deaths: e.g. Procopius, Copernicus, Lord Byron, Charles Darwin, Mark Twain. If Philadelphus eventually published his father's memoirs, might he have sanitised them for public consumption? Is this why Ptolemy's history seems to have been so coldly devoid of characterisation, opinion and anecdotal information? Ptolemy's distortions seem mainly to have been achieved through omission, which is suspiciously characteristic of sanitisation by an editor: for Ptolemy's omissions see Errington, "Bias in Ptolemy's History of Alexander", *Classical Quarterly* 19, pp233-242.

[212] Jane Hornblower, *Hieronymus of Cardia*, OUP, 1981, p.93.

[213] F. Schachermeyr, *Alexander der Grosse: Das Problem seiner Persönlichkeit und seines Wirkens*, (Vienna, 1973), 'Anhang nr. 2: Der Weg zu Kleitarch', 658-662.

based his narrative upon a single main source, but sometimes intermingled material from another source and occasionally offered personal contributions.[214]

In the specific context of Diodorus' account of Alexander in his 17th book the *Einquellenprinzip* concept may be adapted to mean that wherever any pairing among Diodorus 17, Curtius, Justin, the *Metz Epitome* and to a lesser extent Plutarch agree on incidental details (not just on the broad historical outline), then they have a common source, which is Cleitarchus.[215] The reason the common source should be Cleitarchus is that (conservatively) around a third of the attributed fragments of Cleitarchus are found to be closely echoed in Diodorus 17.[216] This is too many for there not to be an intimate connection between Cleitarchus and Diodorus 17. Insofar as it was Diodorus' regular practice to use a single main source for each book/section of his history, then his 17th book is essentially an epitome of Cleitarchus and there is indeed only occasional and questionable evidence that he supplemented Book 17 from alternative writers. Furthermore, it is clear from Jacoby's Testimonies that Cleitarchus was the most widely read account of Alexander's career under the later Roman Republic and the early Empire, which was the era of Diodorus, Trogus and (probably) Curtius. Finally, in this present analysis it has emerged that Diodorus 17 appears to incorporate certain echoes of Cleitarchus' book endings. Consequently, it may reasonably be assumed that Diodorus is mainly following Cleitarchus in his 17th book.

That Cleitarchus was also the principal source for Curtius is suggested by the numerous instances where he is seen to use the same source as Diodorus. A list of such matches was initially formulated by Schwartz and has since been significantly expanded by later scholars.[217] I give such an extended version of this list of matches in Table 2.3. Since Diodorus 17 is a highly summarised version of Cleitarchus' voluminous original, it is likely that many episodes in Curtius, though lacking extensive parallels in Diodorus, were nevertheless sourced from Cleitarchus. An example would be the eulogy of Ptolemy in Curtius 9.8.22-24. However, Curtius exhibits more substantive evidence than Diodorus of having supplemented his account from other early authors: for

---

[214] For a good discussion of the use of sources by Diodorus see Jane Hornblower, *Hieronymus of Cardia*, OUP, 1981, pp 18-32.

[215] For example, J. R. Hamilton, "Cleitarchus & Diodorus 17" in *Greece & the Eastern Mediterranean*, 146 has concluded, "Much of Cleitarchus may be recovered from a comparison of the narratives of Diodorus and Curtius, provided that this is carried out with a proper appreciation of the individual characteristics of the two writers."

[216] See Hamilton, "Cleitarchus & Diodorus 17" in *Greece & the Eastern Mediterranean*, 137-142; E. Badian, "The Date of Clitarchus," *Proceedings African Classical Associations* 8 (1965) 5-11 for minimalism.

[217] E. Schwartz, *Paulys Real-Encyclopädie*, Vol. 4, 1901, s.v. Q. Curtius Rufus, cols. 1871-1891, & Vol 5, 1905, s.v. Diodoros, cols. 682-684; for expansion of Schwartz' list see for example J. R. Hamilton, "Cleitarchus & Diodorus 17" in *Greece & the Eastern Mediterranean*, 127, note 7.

example, he cites Ptolemy's account of Alexander's expedition: in particular he quotes him to contradict Cleitarchus on the question of Ptolemy's presence at the Mallian siege. It should also be noted, that it has been firmly demonstrated that Curtius had read Trogus, whose *Philippic History* was also the source for Justin's *Epitome*.[218] It is clear that Cleitarchus was a major source for Trogus, but he probably also used other sources. Since both Curtius and Justin used Trogus, agreement between them is statistically a less secure indication of Cleitarchus than matches between other pairs of Vulgate authors.

Various scholars have launched assaults on the application of the *Einquellenprinzip* to identify Cleitarchan material. A subtle line of criticism has been to postulate the existence of intermediaries between our surviving ancient sources and Cleitarchus himself. For instance, it has been postulated that Trogus got his Cleitarchan material via Timagenes, a Greek writing in Rome in the second half of the 1st century BC.[219] This has the effect of weakening the *Einquellenprizip* by introducing additional conduits for cross-contamination from other historical traditions (see Figure 2.1 for interrelationships between lost and extant sources). However, the exceptional degree of detail in the agreements between Diodorus 17, Curtius and the attributed fragments of Cleitarchus, the fact that both Diodorus and Curtius cite Cleitarchus by name and the evident popularity and wide dissemination of Cleitarchus' history in their epoch mitigate in favour of them both having known his work from its original text.[220]

A more vigorous mode of assault has been to argue that Diodorus made significant use of a second source for his 17th book. It is instructive in this respect to examine Hammond's attempt to demonstrate that Diodorus continued to resort extensively to the universal history of Diyllus (who had been his principal source for large parts of Book 16) in parallel with Cleitarchus throughout Book 17.[221] Hammond began by expressing a low opinion of Cleitarchus as an historian. He was therefore minded to attribute the more sensible and measured passages in Diodorus 17 to Diyllus and to assign only those episodes that exhibited a degree of sensationalism to Cleitarchus. This *modus operandi* immediately confronted Hammond with the problem that many of the sober passages in Diodorus which he attributes to Diyllus also have close parallels in Curtius. He therefore inferred that Curtius too had resorted extensively to the history of Diyllus in formulating these parts of his narrative. But this was a cardinal error, for, whereas it is just about feasible that both Curtius and Diodorus might have used a combination of Diyllus and Cleitarchus as sources on Alexander's expedition, it is utterly implausible

---

[218] Yardley & Heckel, *Justin – Epitome of the Philippic History*, 7 & 34-36.

[219] E.g. Yardley & Heckel, *Justin – Epitome of the Philippic History*, 30-34.

[220] See Hamilton, "Cleitarchus & Diodorus 17" in *Greece & the Eastern Mediterranean*, 144-146.

[221] Hammond, *THA* 32-35.

(especially on statistical grounds) that both authors independently made the same choice between Cleitarchus and Diyllus as their common source in episode after episode. It may be added that some of the material in Curtius that Hammond felt compelled to assign to Diyllus is simply too detailed to have been found in a universal history.

Similarly Luisa Prandi's attempt to assign Duris as a co-source for Diodorus 17 cannot be sustained in the evidence as has been amply demonstrated by Bosworth in an extensive review published in Histos.[222]

Cleitarchan Style & Themes

Another useful tool in identifying material originating from Cleitarchus is a survey of particular stylistic features and themes that were characteristic of Cleitarchus' work. The identification of such features in pertinent ancient writings (e.g. those relating to Alexander) can then be recognised as indicating potential lost fragments of Cleitarchus. To this end, a proper starting point is a brief review of the testimony on the style and quality of Cleitarchus' writing from a range of his readers in antiquity:

1. Pliny, *NH* 10.136 (Jacoby T2) calls Cleitarchus "a celebrated writer".

2. Quintillian, *Inst.* 10.1.74 (Jacoby T6) writes "Cleitarchus is admired for his talent, but his accuracy has been impugned."

3. Cicero, *Ad f.* 2.10.3 (Jacoby F8) & *Brut.* 42-43 (Jacoby T7/F34) & *De legg.* 1.7 (Jacoby T13) implies that his friend Caelius Rufus was fond of Cleitarchus and mentions Cleitarchus in saying that "It is the privilege of rhetoricians to exceed the truth of history, that they may have an opportunity for embellishment..." and also asserts that Cleitarchus was the only Greek work read by Sisenna, who had sought to imitate him: "and even had he succeeded in this, he would still be considerably below the highest standards."

4. Curtius 9.5.21 (Jacoby T8) criticises Cleitarchus as one of the "framers of ancient histories" who are either negligent or too credulous.

5. Jacoby T9 (anonymous): "And some of the expressions of Callisthenes which are not sublime but high-flown are ridiculed and still more those of Cleitarchus, for the man is frivolous and blows, as Sophocles has it, 'on pigmy hautboys: mouthpiece have they none.' Other examples will be found in Amphicrates and Hegesias and Matris, for often, when these writers seem to themselves to be inspired, they are in no true frenzy, but are simply trifling."

---

[222] Luisa Prandi, *Fortuna è realtà dell' opera di Clitarco*, Historia Einzelschriften 104, Steiner, Stuttgart 1996; A. B. Bosworth, *Histos*, Vol. 1, Aug. 1997; M. Fontana, "Il problema delle fonti per il XVII Libro di Diodoro Siculo," *Kokalos* I (1955), 155-190, also argued for Duris.

6. Demetrius, *De Eloc.* 304 (Jacoby T10) relates, "Often objects which are themselves full of charm lose their attractiveness owing to the choice of words. Cleitarchus, for instance, when describing the wasp... This might have served for a description of some wild ox, or of the Erymanthian boar, rather than a species of bee. The result is that the passage is both repellent and frigid."

7. Philodemus, *Rhet.* 4.1 cols. 7 & 21 (Jacoby T11-12) in a rambling passage, essentially suggests that his own style is not dissimilar to that of Cleitarchus and that this is not a bad thing.

In summary, these commentators considered that Cleitarchus' style was highly rhetorical and sometimes overblown and tasteless. Some were also dubious concerning his accuracy, but the sceptical views are mitigated by Cleitarchus' evident popularity in terms of emulation and citation by others: Philodemus implies that his own style is Cleitarchan and Caelius Rufus quotes him frequently. It is hard not to empathise with the mixed feelings among the ancient writers. Then as today, it was difficult to identify more than a few cases where Cleitarchus could be said to be unambiguously in error. For the most part, we can merely prosecute a charge of sensationalism regarding stories that were nevertheless founded in truth.

Certain characteristics frequently recur in recognisable fragments of Cleitarchus. The following features and themes may provide additional grounds to suspect a direct Cleitarchan influence in cases where there is uncertainty:

1. Alexander's emulation of his putative maternal ancestor Achilles (e.g. visits Achilles' tomb at Troy [Diodorus 17.17.3; Justin 11.5.12; cf. Arrian, *Anabasis* 1.12.1-2; Aelian, *VH* 12.7; Strabo 13.1.32], drags Betis behind his chariot [Curtius 4.6.29, cf. Diodorus 17.48.7, Arrian, *Anabasis* 2.25.4, Homer, *Iliad* 22.395-404], does battle with the River Indus [Diodorus 17.97.1-3, Curtius 9.4.8-14; cf. Homer, *Iliad* 21.228-382]).

2. Alexander's rivalry with his putative paternal ancestor Heracles, especially in the invasion of India (Curtius 8.10.1), in the conquest of Aornus (Curtius 8.11.2, Diodorus 17.85.2, Justin 12.7.12-13, *Metz Epitome* 47, Strabo 15.1.8), in defeating the Sibi or Ibi who were descendants of Heracles (Diodorus 17.96.2, Justin 12.9.2, Curtius 9.4.2), in capturing the land settled by descendants of Heracles' daughter (Polyaenus 1.3.4), in planning to advance to the Pillars of Heracles (Curtius 10.1.17), in quaffing from a Cup of Heracles (Plutarch 75.3, Diodorus 17.117.1-2, Justin 12.13.8, cf. Athenaeus 434A-B).

3. Alexander's emulation of legendary invaders of India: Semiramis (e.g. Curtius 9.6.23), Heracles and Dionysus (Curtius 8.10.1, *Metz Epitome* 34).[223]

4. Alexander's interest in tombs of heroes and kings: Achilles (Diodorus 17.17.3, Justin 11.5.12), Themistocles (F33-34 of Cleitarchus), Sardanapalus at Anchiale (Athenaeus 530A, cf. Plutarch *Moralia* 326F & 336C), Cyrus (Curtius 10.1.30).

5. Alexander's fascination and honour for oracles: Delphi (Diodorus 17.93.4, cf. Plutarch 14.4-5), Didyma (Curtius 7.5.28-35, cf. Strabo 17.1.43), Siwa (Curtius 4.7.25-28, Diodorus 17.49.3-17.51.4, Justin 11.11.2-10, Plutarch 26.6-27.4, Val. Max. 9.5 ext 1).

6. Alexander's exposure to omens: e.g. spring at Xanthus (Plutarch, *Alexander* 17.2-3); Demophon's warnings before the attack on the citadel of the Oxydracae (Curtius 9.4.27-9, Diodorus 17.98.3); return to Babylon (Plutarch, *Alexander* 73.1-4 Diodorus 17.112 Justin 12.13.3-5).

7. Alexander called "World Ruler" (e.g. Plutarch, *Alexander* 18.2 & 27.4, Diodorus 17.51.2, Curtius 4.7.26, Justin 11.11.10).

8. Alexander hailed with the epithet "Aniketos" meaning invincible (Plutarch, *Alexander* 3.5 & 14.4-5, Diodorus 17.93.4, 17.51.3-4, Curtius 4.7.27, Livy 9.18, Justin 11.11.10, cf. Hypereides: Alexander as θεὸς ἀνίκητος).

9. Interest in Persian history based on his father Deinon's book on the subject (e.g. Diodorus 17.5.3-7.3 & 17.81.1-2, Justin 10); seemingly inspired the provision of relatively more information on events at the court of Darius than given by Arrian.

10. Lauding of Greek figures (especially relative to Macedonians): e.g. Charidemus of Athens (Curtius 3.2.10-19, Diodorus 17.30), Thimodes son of Mentor (Curtius 3.3.1, 3.8.1, 3.9.2), Patron (e.g. Curtius 5.11), Dioxippus (Diodorus 17.100.1-101.6, Curtius 9.7.12-26).

11. Supplication of enemies through the display of fronds or branches (e.g. the Branchidae [Curtius 7.5.33], at Massaga [*Metz Epitome* 45], the Indus River tribes [Diodorus 17.96.5] and the Brahmins [Diodorus 17.102.7]).

12. Alexander conceals himself behind curtains (torture of Philotas [Plutarch, *Alexander* 49.6], proskynesis experiment [Curtius 8.5.21]).

13. Fascination with chronology, the calendar and astronomy: making quantities equal to the number of days in the year (Diodorus 2.7.3-4, 17.77.6, Curtius 5.1.26, 6.6.8, Polyaenus 1.3.4); one book per year; lunar

---

[223] Tarn, WW, *Alexander the Great, Vol II, Sources and Studies, Part One, The So-Called 'Vulgate' and its Sources*, Cambridge 1948, 43-51.

eclipse (Curtius 4.10.2); poetic reference to the pole star (Curtius 7.3.7); astronomy and calendar of the Indians (Curtius 8.9.33-6).

14. It has been argued by Pearson that Cleitarchus often modified the figures and units he found in his sources.[224]

15. Emphasis of the role of fortune (*Tyche*) in Alexander's successes (which may have been inspired by a work *Peri Tyches* by Demetrius of Phalerum).[225]

16. Frequent examples of *thaumasia* (wonders) – this is perhaps an inevitable characteristic, since Cleitarchus embraced the writings of Onesicritus, described by Strabo 15.1.28 as the "Chief Pilot of Marvels", as a major source.

17. Use of Asianic rhythms.[226]

18. Sensationalism and prurience (especially in contrast with the censorial attitude of Arrian): e.g. in some instances Cleitarchus seems to have speculated pruriently a little beyond the facts, e.g. Alexander's adoption of Darius' harem (Diodorus 17.77.6, Curtius 6.6.8), amorous liaison with Thalestris (Curtius 6.5.29-32, Diodorus 17.77.3) amorous liaison with Cleophis (Curtius 8.10.35-36, Justin 12.7.9-11).

19. Influence of the Cynical philosophers: pupil of Stilpo (Diogenes Laertius, *Stilpo* 2.113); stalwart veterans versus young shirkers (Diodorus 17.27.1-2) - perhaps this is why Onesicritus, as the pupil of Diogenes, ranked among Cleitarchus' favourite sources; perhaps the aphorisms attributed to Cleitarchus by the Christian Fathers also reflect the cynical bent in his philosophy (F38 F52).[227]

20. Cleitarchus did not seek to demonstrate a deterioration in Alexander's character nor was he hostile in his attitude towards Alexander, for Diodorus 17 shows no significant sign of such antagonism.[228] The negative spin that was superimposed on Cleitarchus' work by Trogus and Curtius represented Roman (Republican) moralising. Cleitarchus' attitude to his subject seems to have been equivocal, for his work was certainly not a eulogy either.

---

[224] See Pearson, *Lost Histories*, 228-9.

[225] Richard Billows, "Polybius and Alexander Historiography" in *Alexander the Great in Fact and Fiction*, ed. A. B. Bosworth and E. J. Baynham, Oxford 2000, 299.

[226] Pearson, *Lost Histories*, 213.

[227] T. S. Brown, "Clitarchus," *American Journal Philology* 71 (1950) 154-155.

[228] E.g. Borza, *PACA* 1968; T. S. Brown, "Clitarchus," 153-5.

21. Some distinctive name forms, such as Syria for Assyria (e.g. Athenaeus 530A).[229]

22. It appears likely that Cleitarchus coloured his History with quotations from various letters addressed to Alexander by key individuals: particularly the sequence of three letters from Darius (First offer: Curtius 4.1.7-14, Justin 11.12.1-2, Diodorus 17.39.1-3; Second Offer: Curtius 4.5.1-8, Justin 11.12.3-4, Arrian 2.25.2, Plutarch 29.4, Val. Max. 6.4 ext 3; Third Offer: Curtius 4.11.1-22, Diodorus 17.54.1-5, Justin 11.12.7-16); also letters from Olympias and Parmenion warning Alexander about Philip the Doctor and Alexander Lyncestes (Diodorus 17.32.1-2, Seneca De Ira 2.23, Val. Max. 3.8 ext 6, Curtius 3.6.4-16); also letters in the *Metz Epitome* 56-58 & 71-74 from Porus to Alexander (cf. Curtius 8.13.2) and from the Indian philosophers to Alexander; letter from Tiridates to Alexander, which is one of the *Einquellenprinzip* commonalities between Diodorus 17.69.1-2 and Curtius 5.5.2-4; also letters from Porus and Taxiles, which reached Alexander after he had returned to Persia (Curtius 10.1.20).

Cleitarchus in Diodorus 17 and Curtius

It is clear that Cleitarchus was a major source for Diodorus 17, because:

1. He had already been a source for Diodorus 2.

2. A high proportion of the fragments of Cleitarchus are closely echoed in Diodorus 17.

3. Cleitarchus' history is known to have been extremely popular in Italy in the late Republican period.

It is also apparent that many episodes in Diodorus have detailed parallels in Curtius.

These facts make it almost inevitable that Cleitarchus was the principal source for both Diodorus 17 and Curtius. As already discussed, Hammond's conjecture that Diyllus was a significant secondary source for Diodorus 17 is untenable, because it requires (on his own admission) that Curtius independently chose Diyllus as a secondary source for exactly the same set of episodes as Diodorus, which is a statistical impossibility. Similarly Luisa Prandi's advocacy of Duris as a secondary source for Diodorus is unconvincing, because her reasons for rejecting Cleitarchus do not stand up to scrutiny (e.g. of Bosworth) and because she cannot escape the same *impasse* as encountered by Hammond. In fact

---

[229] Pearson, *Lost Histories*, 230.

Diodorus 17 appears to be dominated by Cleitarchus, but it is epitomised down to only ~10%-20% of the length of the original.[230]

It is also likely that Diodorus reproduces excerpts from Cleitarchus with a reasonable degree of fidelity. On the basis of a detailed analysis of Diodorus' sources for his entire *Bibliotheke*, Jane Hornblower has concluded: "Diodorus adhered very faithfully to his sources at least over limited sections… He did not copy them word for word… He seems however to be a reliable vehicle for the subject matter of the histories he used, taking over both facts and the inbuilt attitudes and assumptions, and his language frequently echoes, even when it does not repeat, the language of the original."[231]

Cleitarchus is Curtius' main source, but elements may have been taken from other early authors (Ptolemy? Timagenes? Trogus?) Curtius may personally have contributed some rhetorical elements, such as speeches and also sought to evince a progressive deterioration of Alexander's character, which was not present in Cleitarchus, but which may have been partly inspired by Trogus, for it is certain that Curtius had read his *Philippic History*.[232] Curtius almost definitely dates to the early Roman Empire and most probably to the reign of Claudius,[233] whilst Diodorus belongs to the end of the Republican period (not long) before 30BC. Therefore it is not feasible that Diodorus used Curtius. Since Curtius gives much more detail than Diodorus for most of their common episodes, it also follows that Curtius cannot have used Diodorus as his source. The *Einquellenprinzip* provides a sound basis for attributing matching episodes in Curtius and Diodorus 17 to Cleitarchus, wherever they agree on matters of incidental detail. It may safely be extended to other pairings of Vulgate authors in some circumstances: especially, for example, Curtius and the *Metz Epitome*.

Cleitarchus in Trogus

The last datable event mentioned by Trogus is the surrender of Phraates' sons and grandsons as hostages to Augustus in 10BC (Justin 42.5.11-12), but a date of compilation as late as AD9 (as given by the medieval writer Radulfus de Diceto) is possible.[234] Indirect transmission and the curtness of the

---

[230] Diodorus 17 is an exceptionally long book for a Greek work, so it is unlikely that Cleitarchus' 13 books averaged more than 75% of its length – conversely, Cleitarchus' work seems to have been substantial, so it seems improbable that his books averaged less that 40% of the length of Diodorus 17.

[231] Jane Hornblower, *Hieronymus of Cardia*, OUP, 1981, p.32.

[232] J. E. Atkinson, *A Commentary on Quintus Curtius Rufus' Historiae Alexandri Magni, Books 3 & 4*, Amsterdam 1980, 59-61; Yardley & Heckel, *Justin – Epitome of the Philippic History*, 7.

[233] J. E. Atkinson, *A Commentary on Quintus Curtius Rufus' Historiae Alexandri Magni, Books 3 & 4*, Amsterdam 1980, 19-39.

[234] Yardley & Heckel, *Justin – Epitome of the Philippic History* 5-6.

summarisation makes it difficult to prove that Trogus used Cleitarchus: for example, Justin lacks the detail to prove that Trogus echoed any fragments of Cleitarchus (though he mentioned the ivy at Nysa and he used Thalestris, the Cleitarchan name for the Amazon Queen, whilst also giving Minythyia as a variant). However, it is even more difficult to prove that Trogus did not use Cleitarchus either directly or indirectly and Trogus was unambiguously a part of the so-called Vulgate tradition, for it is easy to recognise overlap between Trogus and Cleitarchan material from Curtius and Diodorus. But there are significant circumstantial reasons to suspect that Trogus was inspired and guided by a lost work *On Kings* by Timagenes of Alexandria, who wrote in Rome some time after his arrival there in 55BC.[235] It is therefore possible that Trogus got his Cleitarchan material via Timagenes. Mitigating in favour of direct use of Cleitarchus, however, is the fact that Trogus adopted the death of Darius as the endpoint of his 11th Book, which coincides with the end of Cleitarchus' 6th book and the midpoint of his work. (Conversely, Darius is murdered in the middle of Book 3 of Arrian.) There is concrete evidence in the form of closely matching phraseology that Curtius had read Trogus, although the two books of Trogus that dealt with Alexander's reign were too short to have formed the entire basis for Curtius' *History of Alexander*.[236] Similarly, there were strong parallels with Livy's works in Trogus: the two were contemporaries and may well have been influenced by one another's literary outputs.[237]

Cleitarchus in the *Metz Epitome*

Much of the *Metz Epitome* (specifically sections 1-86) falls clearly within the Cleitarchan tradition, although the *Liber de Morte* (sections 87-123) seems to be derived from a different source: the same as used for the closing sections of Pseudo-Callisthenes (Holcias?).[238] Details are telling: for example, the *Metz Epitome* mentions that Alexander persuaded his companions to wed daughters of the Sogdian aristocracy at the time of his marriage to Roxane. The only other place where this information is to be found is the contents list for Book 17 of

---

[235] J. C. Yardley & W. Heckel, *Justin: Epitome of the Philippic History of Pompeius Trogus, Vol I, Books 11-12, Alexander the Great*, Oxford 1997, 30-34.

[236] J. E. Atkinson, *A Commentary on Quintus Curtius Rufus' Historiae Alexandri Magni, Books 3 & 4*, Amsterdam 1980, 59-61.

[237] Yardley & Heckel, *Justin: Epitome of the Philippic History of Pompeius Trogus, Vol I, Books 11-12, Alexander the Great*, Oxford 1997, 6-8 & 333-336.

[238] P.H. Thomas accepted Pfister's conclusion that the *Liber de Morte* is a separate work from the rest of the *Epitoma Mettensis*, although Otto Wagner treated it as part of the *Epitoma*; see C. L. Howard's review of the Teubner edition in *Classical Philology* 58, 129; Elizabeth Baynham, "An Introduction to the *Metz Epitome*: its traditions and value", *Antichthon* 29 (1995) 60-77, points out that Lellia Ruggini's philological study of the *Metz Epitome* text shows that the two pieces were both the work of the same epitomator, who probably developed them from separate source documents, but intended that they should provide complementary coverage of Alexander's career.

Diodorus (the details being lost in the great lacuna). In general, events in the *Metz Epitome* closely parallel the corresponding episodes in Curtius.[239]

Ostensibly, a particular problem for the view that the *Metz Epitome* is Cleitarchan is the fact that its standard text[240] mentions Chorienes, a figure elsewhere found only in Arrian and believed by some (e.g. Heckel & Brunt)[241] to be an official title of Sisimithres, who fulfils a very similar role in the Vulgate tradition. However, it is instructive that on careful examination of the manuscript evidence this anomaly emerges as an invention of modern textual editors. The manuscript of the *Metz Epitome* read "corianus", which was corrected to Chorienes through comparison with Arrian by Otto Wagner. Conversely, a satrap named "cohortandus" in the manuscripts of Curtius 8.4.21 (or "cohortanus" according to Freinshem's older reading) has conventionally been emended to "Oxyartes" since the Renaissance edition of Aldus. However, it is clear from the context (i.e. hosting of the meeting of Alexander and Roxane) that "corianus" in the *Metz Epitome* is the same individual as "cohortanus" in the manuscripts of Curtius. Therefore these names almost certainly reflect separate Latinisations (and corruptions) of a similar name given in Greek by Cleitarchus, which may well have been Chorienes. The manuscripts, when analysed jointly, therefore seem to vindicate the common (Cleitarchan) derivation of the *Metz Epitome* and Curtius and it would appear that Cleitarchus considered Sisimithres and Corianus to be distinct persons. The correction of "cohortanus" to "Oxyartes" should therefore be rejected; despite the fact that Curtius implies a few sentences later that Roxane is the daughter of "cohortanus". It is easy to see that Curtius (or one of his transcribers) has probably garbled the complex statement found in the *Metz Epitome* that "corianus" invited his own virgin daughters *and* those of his friends to appear before Alexander, who was entranced by the daughter of "oxiatris" among them. This perspective also has the virtue of rescuing us from the need to make Cleitarchus (through Curtius) contradict the clear statements elsewhere (e.g. Arrian 4.20.4) that Oxyartes was not present when Alexander first met Roxane.

In another similar case, it may be argued that the *Metz Epitome* gives the correct Cleitarchan version where Curtius resorts for some reason to a variant. This is the surrender of the rock of Ariamazes. Section 18 of the *Metz Epitome* relates the complex outcome that the occupants of the rock were so much intimidated by the appearance of 300 of Alexander's men at its summit that they slew

---

[239] The parallels are often so close that J. M. Hunt, "An Emendation in the Epitoma Metensis", *Classical Philology* 67, 287-288, uses the phraseology of Curtius to determine the correct reading of a corrupt passage in the *Metz Epitome*.

[240] P. H. Thomas (editor), *Incerti Auctoris Epitoma Rerum Gestarum Alexandri Magni cum Libro de Morte Testamentoque Alexandri*, Teubner, 1966.

[241] W. Heckel, *Who's Who in the Age of Alexander the Great*, Blackwell 2006, s.v. Sisimithres; P. A. Brunt, *Arrian: History of Alexander and Indica*, Loeb, Harvard, Vol. 1, 1976, 407, note 1.

Ariamazes then surrendered to Alexander, who pardoned them all. Yet Curtius 7.11.28 suggests that Ariamazes himself together with his family and nobles surrendered to Alexander who then scourged and crucified them all at the foot of the rock. In cases of discrepancies between the *Metz Epitome* and Curtius it is inherently more likely that the latter is differing from Cleitarchus than the former, since Curtius is by far the more heterogeneous work. It should also be noted that, if Alexander had truly brutally executed the high status occupants of the Rock of Ariamazes after they had surrendered to him, then it would be astonishing that Sisimithres and his family readily surrendered to Alexander in his turn following a siege of his rock a few months later, as is also related by Curtius 8.2.28-33.

Another name in the *Metz Epitome* that might superficially appear to follow Arrian's usage is "oxudrac" or "oxidragas" for the Indian tribe that Arrian himself calls the "Oxydrakai" in his *Anabasis* (6.4.3 and 6.11.3), but the "Oudrakai" in his *Indica* 4.9.[242] However, Arrian uses "Oxydrakai" particularly in the context of refuting unnamed "Vulgate" sources, which stated that Alexander had received his chest wound among them. We know that Cleitarchus was prominent among these sources, so it is feasible that Arrian was actually following Cleitarchus' spelling of the tribe's name in order to make the target of his criticism the more apparent. This is supported by the fact that Pausanias 1.6.2 uses "Oxydrakai" in citing the Cleitarchan version of Alexander's wounding as true history and similarly Plutarch, *Moralia* 343D. Conversely, Curtius (9.4.15 and 9.4.26) uses "Sudracae", but he states that he was influenced by Ptolemy's account for this episode in his history (9.5.21). The manuscript readings for Diodorus 17.98.1 (Συρακοῦσαι) and Justin 12.9.3 ("Sugambri") are so wildly variant that they can scarcely be used to decide the issue. Furthermore, the manuscripts of Strabo arbitrarily used either spelling at 15.1.8 and 15.1.33 and several used both forms in different places e.g. one gave ὀξύδρακας at 15.1.8 and συδράκαι at 15.1.33.[243] A rather mixed range of spellings is found among various other ancient texts.[244] In the light of this impenetrable confusion in the manuscripts, it is altogether unsafe to assume as many have that "Oxydrakai" is from Ptolemy/Aristobulus and "Sudracae" derives from the Cleitarchan Vulgate. In actuality, there is a strong possibility that "Oxydrakai" is the authentic Cleitarchan spelling and that the confusion

---

[242] Yardley & Heckel, *Justin: Epitome of the Philippic History of Pompeius Trogus, Vol I, Books 11-12, Alexander the Great*, Oxford 1997, 20 have excluded one of Seel's fragments of Trogus found in Ampelius, because the latter used Oxydracae "the form used by Arrian".

[243] Manuscript *Athous Vatop.* 655; this is despite the fact that all the main manuscripts are believed to have derived from a single, relatively late prototype.

[244] Strabo 15.1.6 (*Hydrakai* after Megasthenes); Pliny, *NH* 12.24 (*Sudracae* in modern texts, but just *Sydra* in the *Codex Moneus*); Stephanus Byzantinus s.v. *Oxydrakai*; Ampelius 35.2 (*Oxydracae*).

arose later.[245] Again it must be concluded that there is no sound basis to question the Cleitarchan nature of the *Metz Epitome*.

The *Metz Epitome* also has some things we might expect to have been in Cleitarchus, but which are absent from Diodorus and Curtius. For example, Alexander's interrogation of the ten gymnosophists is exactly the type of tale that would have appealed to Cleitarchus and would certainly have been known to him, since it originated with Onesicritus.[246] Furthermore, Arrian, *Anabasis* 5.2.3 tells as a story that when Alexander asked Acuphis, chief negotiater on behalf of Nysa, to surrender a hundred of his "best men" to him, the Indian retorted that he could more readily spare two hundred of his worst people. When Arrian tells such "stories", it usually means that he found them elsewhere than in his two main sources, Ptolemy and Aristobulus. Exactly the same story occurs in the *Metz Epitome* 36-38 and a slightly curtailed version is given by Plutarch, *Alexander* 58.5. These circumstances make it very likely that Acuphis' quip was in Cleitarchus, one of whose fragments relates to the Nysa episode. Nysa is mentioned in the contents list of Diodorus 17 but falls in the great lacuna in his text. Curtius would appear to have cut any mention of Acuphis from his account of Nysa, although he records that its citizens gave themselves up to Alexander. Perhaps Curtius' omissions of certain Cleitarchan episodes in India were motivated by his need to develop his theme of the deterioration of Alexander's character.

Merkelbach has analysed the sources of the *Metz Epitome* and agrees that much of the material in Sections 1-86 is essentially Cleitarchan in character.[247] However, he further supposes that the epitomiser interpolated two letters to Alexander and also the exchange with the Gymnosophists from a separate ancient collection. This is curious, since it presupposes that Cleitarchus did not himself quote from letters sent to Alexander, whereas there are in fact many indications that he did (as noted in item 22 under Cleitarchan Style and Themes above). In fact the letter from Porus in *Metz Epitome* 56-58 is reported in summary at Curtius 8.13.2: the parallels are so close that it is overwhelmingly likely that the two accounts are based on the same source, who is almost certainly Cleitarchus. It is transparent that Merkelbach is simply wrong in this instance at least. Furthermore, as already noted there is nothing surprising in the possibility that the exchange with the Gymnosophists was recorded by Cleitarchus, since it probably originated with Onesicritus, who was one of

---

[245] It is feasible that by the early Roman imperial era both *Oxydrakai* and *Sydrakai* existed in manuscripts of Cleitarchus: we could imagine that, when the copiest had multiple orders for this popular work, he might have recited the text to a group of scribes; the corruption of *Oxydrakai* to *Sydrakai* is among a range of observed errors that would fit this scenario.

[246] Jacoby, *FGrHist* 134 F17a-b = Strabo 15.1.63-65; Plutarch, *Alexander* 65.

[247] Reinhold Merkelbach, "Die Quellen des Griechischen Alexanderromans," *Zetema Monographien zur Klassischen Altertumswissenschaft*, Heft 9, Munich 1954, 118-121.

Cleitarchus' main sources. It would seem to be superfluous to believe that the otherwise distinctly unsophisticated epitomiser chose to adulterate his episodic Cleitarchan gleanings with letters from an entirely separate document.

There seem to be good reasons to suppose and no good reason to doubt that Sections 1-86 of the *Metz Epitome* were relatively directly derived from Cleitarchus. Baynham agrees that it was based on early historical sources and notes strong parallels with Cleitarchus.[248] It has too few parallels with Arrian to have been substantially derived from Aristobulus and it appears to have been adapted from too conventional a history to be based directly on the book entitled *On the Education of Alexander* by Onesicritus (which seems itself to have been modelled on the *Cyropaidia* of Xenophon), for Strabo 15.1.28 described Onesicritus ironically as the Chief Pilot of Marvels. In the context of the reconstruction of Cleitarchus the *Metz Epitome* is primarily important as a control on Curtius within the great lacuna in Diodorus 17. By an *ad hoc* extension of the *Einquellenprinzip*, wherever the *Metz Epitome* agrees with Curtius in matters of detail, then we can be reasonably confident that Curtius is following Cleitarchus. The secondary importance of the *Metz Epitome* lies in its mentioning a few Vulgate stories that are absent from Curtius and Diodorus and would therefore otherwise be difficult to associate with Cleitarchus and in clarifying the Cleitarchan version of some episodes, notably events at the Rock of Ariamazes and at Mazaga.

Cleitarchus in Plutarch

The use of Cleitarchus by Plutarch is probably more extensive than has generally been realised, perhaps especially on the events of Alexander's youth, although Heckel & Yardley note cogently that Plutarch's "basic narrative of Alexander's campaigns is the same as that used by Diodorus, Trogus and Curtius."[249] Hammond concludes that Plutarch used many early writers on Alexander, but that Cleitarchus, Aristobulus, Onesicritus and Chares exerted an especially strong influence upon his work.[250] Among these, as we have seen, only Chares is unlikely to have been an influential source for Cleitarchus. Hammond's attribution of material in Plutarch's *Life of Alexander* to Cleitarchus therefore represents a minimalist viewpoint, since some of the items attributed to other writers may in fact have been extracted from Cleitarchus, even when Plutarch explicitly cites another source. For example, as argued above in discussing the contents of Cleitarchus' first book, there are indications that Plutarch took some of his information on Alexander's birth from Cleitarchus,

---

[248] Elizabeth Baynham, "An Introduction to the *Metz Epitome*: its traditions and value", *Antichthon* 29 (1995) 60-77.

[249] Yardley & Heckel, *Justin – Epitome of the Philippic History*, 35.

[250] Hammond, *Sources* 149-151.

though he only mentions Hegesias as a source, presumably therefore following Cleitarchus in doing so. Nevertheless, it is difficult to identify Cleitarchan material unambiguously, since Plutarch evidently mixed together information from various early authors. However, Hamilton has usefully identified a shortlist of instances where Plutarch was very probably following Cleitarchus in his *Life of Alexander*.[251]

Plutarch's essays on the *Fortune or Virtue of Alexander* in the *Moralia* are also regularly imbued with Cleitarchan character. For example, at 343D and 344D Alexander leaps down inside the walls of a town in the country of the Oxydrakai and is rescued by Ptolemy amongst others, which is the version of Cleitarchus. However, at 327B Plutarch had noted that the event occurred among the Mallians, in agreement with Arrian and sourced from Ptolemy and/or Aristobulus. Plutarch actually cites Aristobulus, Onesicritus, Ptolemy, Chares, Duris, Anaximenes and others as sources for various stories in these essays, but never Cleitarchus. Consequently, it is relatively difficult firmly to attribute material in them to Cleitarchus, except where there are strong connections with Cleitarchan stories known from elsewhere. Even in these cases, the rather rhetorical and opinionated character of the essays clouds our ability to discern exactly what Plutarch had read in his source.

There are also important mentions of Alexander's career in other parts of the *Moralia* and in various other of Plutarch's *Lives*. A few of these may be associated with Cleitarchus' work.[252]

Other Anonymous Fragments

In addition to material from the ancient texts dedicated to the history of Alexander, stories pertaining to the King that would appear to have been inspired by the Cleitarchan Vulgate appear frequently in a host of other ancient sources. Prominent among these are Polyaenus, Athenaeus, Aelian, Pausanias, Cicero, Pliny the Elder, Frontinus, Ampelius and Valerius Maximus. Many Greek and Roman writers between the 1st century BC & the 4th century AD seem to have been familiar with Cleitarchus and this is often reflected in their works. Cicero, Athenaeus, Aelian and Pliny are sources of named fragments of Cleitarchus, but they also mention Alexander's career in other contexts, and, in general, it is productive to seek further fragments of Cleitarchus in authors known to have read his work.

For example, St Augustine *De Civ. Dei* 4.4.25 cites a lost passage of Cicero, *The Republic* 3.24 describing Alexander's interrogation of a captured pirate (Aristonicus of Methymne) at Alexandria, which is likely to have been sourced

---

[251] J. R. Hamilton, *Plutarch, Alexander: A Commentary*, Oxford 1969, lix.

[252] E.g. Plutarch, *Life of Themistocles* 27.1-2.

from Cleitarchus.[253] Additionally, Pausanias is especially interesting, because he combines the Cleitarchan story of Ptolemy rescuing Alexander in the town of the Oxydrakai with details of the arrival of Alexander's corpse in Egypt.

Conversely, the 4th century epitome known as the *Itinerarium Alexandri* is generally recognised to be derivative from Arrian in its character[254] and some Hellenistic authors seem to use other first generation sources: for example, Polybius appears to use Callisthenes, Hieronymus and Demetrius of Phalerum.[255]

The Character and Value of Cleitarchus

The key tension in the ancient source traditions of Alexander historiography is the contrast between the sensationalism of the Cleitarchan Vulgate versus the censorial attitude of Arrian. The latter exudes worthiness and appears to be sincere in his pursuit of the unadorned facts in most circumstances, nevermind how prosaic and dull this may render parts of his text. But he is often economical with the truth: the destruction of the Branchidae is altogether missing, and, more seriously, there are clear indications that he suppressed information on Alexander's personal life. For example, he fails to mention Alexander's mistress, Barsine, and takes some trouble in avoiding naming Bagoas in the Anabasis, especially when referring to the hanging of Orxines. Trying to interpret Alexander's personality through the medium of Arrian's filtrations is sometimes scarcely more fruitful than attempting to formulate an impression of the character of a modern politician from a calendar of meetings, events and visits that he/she has attended (though it would be an exaggeration to suggest that Arrian is entirely devoid of information on Alexander's character.)

Conversely, Cleitarchus' attitude to Alexander's private life seems to have been downright prurient. Few rumours were too exotic to be incorporated. Consequently, it is possible to regard the two principal traditions of Alexander historiography as being substantially complementary to one another. As far as concerns the details of the events themselves, the Cleitarchan tradition is sometimes demonstrably inferior to Arrian, but it nonetheless provides a good control on the relative authoritativeness of Arrian's version of each episode. In a few cases of disagreement, it may be Arrian who is mistaken. We have seen that Cleitarchus probably treated the revolt of Baryaxes more thoroughly than

---

[253] Cf. Curtius 4.5.19-22; Arrian, *Anabasis* 3.2.4.

[254] The *Itinerarium Alexandri* was published by Müller in his *Fragmenta*; see Yardley & Heckel, *Justin – Epitome of the Philippic History* 34.

[255] See Richard Billows, "Polybius and Alexander Historiography" in *Alexander the Great in Fact and Fiction*, ed. A.B. Bosworth and E.J. Baynham, Oxford 2000; but Jane Hornblower, *Hieronymus of Cardia*, OUP, 1981, p. 236 is uncertain whether Polybius used Hieronymus.

Arrian. Another illustration that Cleitarchus is relatively more reliable than often suggested is the fact that he correctly stated that the River Pasitigris lay 4 days' march from Susa, whereas Diodorus (following Hieronymus?) wrongly gives the distance as a march of a single day. Furthermore, some of the deficiencies in the Vulgate may have been introduced by intermediaries and cannot safely be deployed to denigrate Cleitarchus: for example, it has been seen that Diodorus misrepresented the 440 talents from Thebes as deriving solely from the sale of prisoners and Curtius (or a transcriber of his work) inadvertently suggested that Cohortanus was the father of Roxane.

In many Western nations there exists today a similar dichotomy among daily newspapers: on the one hand the sensationalist, popular titles, which habitually focus on the ephemeral antics of celebrities and on the other the more sober publications (formerly "Broadsheets"), which seek to focus and deliberate on events and issues which they deem to have proper significance for our lives. Yet from the perspective of a future historian, it would be difficult to achieve a fully rounded comprehension of our society without examining examples of both types of journal. In the same way, the Cleitarchan reportage and Arrian's meticulous dispositions are both essential in formulating a relatively balanced, accurate and human portrait of Alexander.

Feasibility of Reconstruction

Wherever Curtius and Diodorus agree *in detail*, then the *Einquellenprinzip* establishes a confident basis for the reconstruction of Cleitarchus. A particular problem arises within the great lacuna between Diodorus 17.83 and 17.84, however we have seen that the *Metz Epitome* can largely be used as a substitute for Diodorus in this period. It validates a great deal of material in Curtius as Cleitarchan in its origin. The weakest area in the reconstruction must inevitably be the period between the beginning of Cleitarchus' account and the opening of the surviving books of Curtius. In this range it should be the best assumption on the basis of incomplete and inconclusive evidence that the early part of Book 17 of Diodorus is essentially Cleitarchan. Occasionally, Diodorus may be supplemented from Plutarch's Life of Alexander and Justin's Epitome of the Philippic History of Pompeius Trogus. Similarly, Curtius has many significant lacunae in the period 324-323BC, though it is better established that Diodorus was mainly relying on Cleitarchus for this part of Alexander's reign.

Naturally, it is not feasible to reconstruct the exact phraseology of Cleitarchus, except in a few limited cases. Since Latin authors, particularly Curtius, must provide much of the detail, the Greek is obviously irretrievable. Therefore the reconstruction must be confined to establishing the factual material, sense and flavour of Cleitarchus' account of each reconstructed episode. In view of this, there is little point in trying to recreate the work in its original Greek. Rather English is preferable due to its superior accessibility to a wide readership.

Plan for Reconstruction

Firstly, it is necessary to compose a table of references to all the material with any claim to a Cleitarchan pedigree. The references need to be grouped against each successive incident or episode of Alexander's career, together with a concise outline of the Cleitarchan version of the incident/episode. Where relevant, notes must be provided to justify and to guide the Cleitarchan interpretation of the information in the references. The episodes need to be correctly ordered and grouped into the appropriate Cleitarchan books. This document has been compiled and is presented in Chapter 7: Organisation & Sources. It provides a basic framework for the reconstruction, which is further supported by the detailed analyses in this section. In providing an organized listing of the source material and some discussion of special issues, this Table serves as a substitute for copious annotations of the reconstructed text, which would otherwise overburden the reconstruction with footnotes.

It is necessary to indicate a hierarchy of confidence within the reconstructed text to maximise its value as a source for historiography. This needs to be done in a way that is immediately interpretable by the reader and flexible enough to be reproducible as an element of any likely publishing format (especially the present book form.) In particular it needs to be readily presentable within the constraints of a textual pdf file in standard black and white or greyscale fonts. In the light of these considerations and constraints the following range of six textual gradations has been adopted:

<u>**Underlined bold text for Fragments**</u>

Bold text where there is overwhelming evidence

Bold italic text where there exists direct/firm evidence

Normal text where direct/weak evidence applies

Italic text where the evidence is conjectural

Grey text for connecting passages, if Cleitarchus' version is indeterminate

Finally, the chapters/sections within the reconstructed books need to be enumerated in a logical and self-consistent fashion, so as to facilitate referencing of episodes. I have adopted a simple single-level section numbering system, which permits referencing of items down to the level of their paragraph.

Conclusions

This analysis suggests that Cleitarchus compiled his history *Concerning Alexander* some time around 280BC and that it comprised thirteen books, one for each year of Alexander's reign. Echoes of the *termini* of at least four of Cleitarchus' books have been discerned in Diodorus' seventeenth book. The first book of Cleitarchus opened with some details of Alexander's birth and ancestry. The last book probably extended to note Alexander's entombment at Memphis and seems briefly to have alluded to attempts by Antipater and Cassander to suppress rumours that they had poisoned Alexander. Perhaps it closed with the transfer of Alexander's corpse to Alexandria – a recent event at the time of compilation. It appears that Diodorus' seventeenth book is essentially solely an epitome of Cleitarchus' work, despite modern speculation that he incorporated a significant admixture of a second early author. Conversely, Cleitarchus himself, though he did not accompany Alexander's expedition, nevertheless based his account on the works of Onesicritus, Nearchus, Callisthenes and others, who had been eyewitnesses of the events.

It has also been found that Megasthenes wrote at the beginning of the third century BC and was probably a source for Cleitarchus. Furthermore, there are strong reasons to suspect that the *Metz Epitome* (sections 1-86) is essentially a crude and incomplete but nevertheless direct epitome of Cleitarchus.

This investigation has shown that it is generally inadequate to pursue a single strand of evidence in addressing the key problems presented by Cleitarchus, for such strands are almost invariably individually inconclusive. Nevertheless, progress has often been possible, where multiple independent strands of evidence can be recognised as intersecting and reinforcing when an apposite interpretation is adopted. The salvation of the Cleitarchan tradition relies on the agglomeration of disparate hints, clues and fragments into concrete foundations.

It has already been possible to cast some light on the full extent and magnificence of Cleitarchus' work. Whereas he frequently incorporated and even magnified the faults of his sources, thus leaning towards sensationalism and uncritically accepting embroideries of the original facts, Cleitarchus also gave a better rounded and more chronologically ordered version of Alexander's career than any other ancient author. An example is the discovery that he probably treated the revolt of Baryaxes in its correct chronological sequence within his work. It has also been seen that many faults and discrepancies in the Vulgate tradition are not due to Cleitarchus himself, but have been perpetrated by his disciples or have arisen through manuscript defects.

Finally, the key conclusions of this analysis are firstly that a relatively complete and generally accurate reconstruction of Cleitarchus' work is entirely feasible on the basis of the extant material, and secondly that such a reconstruction should be a valuable and useful document for scholars, despite necessary imperfections. Much stands to be learnt simply from the process of its creation and this has already been amply vindicated through the reconstruction of the Cleitarchan version of Alexander's campaigns in India, which is presented over the next three chapters.

TABLE 2.1a: The Books and Fragments of Cleitarchus (1-7)

BK	START	END	FRAGMENTS
1	SPRING 336BC Alexander's birth & ancestry Philip sends a vanguard under Parmenion & Attalus into Asia	AUTUMN 335BC Alexander's visit to Delphi	F1* - the wealth of Thebes was just 440 talents
2	WINTER 335-4BC Alexander's preparations for the invasion of Asia	JUNE 334BC Battle of the Granicus	F7 – 820 years between invasion of the Heracleidae and Alexander's invasion
3	JULY 334BC Alexander's advance down the Ionian littoral to Magnesia	JUNE-JULY 333BC Alexander cuts the Gordian Knot Digressions on Death of Memnon & Darius' preparations for war at Babylon	F33 & F34 – Themistocles at the court of Xerxes (the context is Alexander's visit to the tomb of Themistocles at Magnesia)
4	JULY 333BC Alexander's advance into Cilicia	JULY 332BC Balonymus appointed king of Tyre Ends with "Now we have described things concerning Alexander…" Diodorus 17.47.6	F2* - Death of Sardanapalus (the context is Alexander's visit to his tomb at Anchiale near Tarsus) F8 – Battle of Issus (November 333BC) F9 – Tyrian sacrifice of a boy
5	AUGUST 332BC Agis conquers Crete – digressions leading up to siege of Gaza	JUNE 331BC Alexander returns to Byblos after Egypt Digression on the rebellion of Agis in Greece	F3* - Story of Theias Byblios F4* - 50 Spartan hostages given to Antipater
6	JULY 331BC March to the Euphrates	JULY 330BC Pursuit & death of Darius "That was the situation in Asia" Diodorus 17.73.4	F10 - Description of Babylon F11 – Razing of Persepolis
7	JULY 330BC Advance to Hecatompylus	JUNE 329BC First crossing of the "Caucasus" (actually Paropamisus – modern Hindu Kush) "These were the concerns of Alexander" Diodorus 17.83.3	F12 – Caspian Sea equal to the Euxine F13 – Flooding of isthmus between Euxine and Caspian F14 – a wasp in Hyrcania F15 & F16 - Visit of Thalestria, Queen of the Amazons F32 – Castration of man (spouse of an Amazon?) for adultery

*Fragment with the book number in Cleitarchus

TABLE 2.1b: The Books and Fragments of Cleitarchus (8-13)

BK	START	END	FRAGMENTS
8	JULY 329BC Digression on quarrel of Bessus & Bagodarus at a banquet	AUTUMN 328BC Capture of the Sogdian Rock	
9	AUTUMN 328BC Scythian king offers Alexander his daughter in marriage	MAY 327BC Marriage to Roxane	
10	JUNE 327BC Preparations for the invasion of India. Alexander orders the formation of the Epigoni	JUNE 326BC Re-instatement of Porus as king following his defeat at the Hydaspes Report of the revolt of Baryaxes in Media	F20-22 – Indian processions with trees drawn on carriages and tame birds in their branches F17 – Ivy of Dionysus at Nysa F5* - Only the Persian king may wear the tiara upright (the only likely context at this juncture is the revolt of Baryaxes, whom Arrian notes wore the tiara upright)
11	JULY 326BC Foundation of Bucephala & Nicaea Digression on wonders of India and Alexander's geographical objectives	SPRING 325BC Treatment of the Mallian wound by Critobulus Digression on the revolt of the Greeks in Bactria	F18 –16 cubit serpents F19 – Troops of monkeys and an entrapment technique F28 - A salt mine F24 – Ptolemy saves wounded Alexander at the Mallian town
12	SPRING 325BC Surrender of Mallians & Oxydracae Contest between Coragus & Dioxippus	JUNE 324BC The arrival of 30,000 Epigoni at Susa "These were the concerns of Alexander" Diodorus 17.108.3	F25 – 80,000 Indians slain in the Kingdom of Sambus F23 – Mandi women bear children at 7 and are old at 40 F26 – Tidal bore in Indus Delta F27 Oroitae & Ichthyophagoi F29 – Nearchus & Onesicritus arrive with stories of the Ocean F6* - Gymnosophists scorn death
13	JULY 324BC The extravagance of Harpalus & his flight to Athens	JUNE 323BC (Epilogue 280BC?) Death of Alexander Suicide of Sisygambis Entombment in Alexandria?	F30 – The courtesans of Harpalus F31 – Roman Embassy at Babylon

*Fragment with the book number in Cleitarchus

TABLE 2.2: Sources of Cleitarchus

SOURCE	DATE	EVIDENCE	PROBABILITY
Onesicritus	Before 310BC	Amazon Queen; Indian salt mines; suttee & Indian beauty; departure & return of fleet; wonders of Hyrcania; Banyan; monkey capture; Delphic oracle; interview with gymnosophists; death of brother of Lysimachus	99%
Deinon	Father of Cleitarchus	365 Persian concubines; sirens & Indian birds; Themistocles; story of Sardanapulus; Euergetae; details of Persian history	99%
Nearchus	Before 310BC	Oreitae/Ichthyophagoi make bread from fish; 16 cubit snakes; trumpets to scare whales	95%
Callisthenes	After 336BC Before 327BC	Sea withdrawal in Pamphylia; visit to tomb of Sardanapalus at Anchiale; crows *en route* to Siwa & oracle responds in nods & signs	95%
Timaeus	Late 4th to early 3rd century BC	Invasion 820 years after Heraclidae; terms to describe anthredon; date of Alexander's birth; follows Timaeus' use of language	95%
Holcias(?) *Liber de Morte*	317BC Heckel or 308BC Bosworth	Poisoning of Alexander by a conspiracy instigated by Antipater and perpetrated by Cassander & Iollas	90%
Megasthenes	c.290BC	Mandi & Pandaea; Gymnosophists; River Iomanes & details of the Ganges region	80%
Hegesias	Early 3rd century BC	Siege of Gaza; Asianic rhythms; fire in Ephesian temple at Alexander's birth	75%
Polycleitus	Late 4th – early 3rd century BC	Confusion between Aral Sea and Sea of Azov; sweet water and sea serpents in the Caspian; Amazon Queen	70%
Herodotus	Early 5th century BC	Parallels between Darius/Charidemus/Amyntas and Xerxes/Demaratus	65%
Theopompus	324-320BC	Mistresses of Harpalus	50%
Aristobulus	After 301BC	Visit to Anchiale; apes & monkey capture; Alexandria on Tanais; Rock of Ariamazes; Aristander's prophecies	40%
Patrocles	After 380BC	Common statement comparing size of the Caspian to the Euxine – but may have been originated by Onesicritus or Polycleitus	35%
Ephippus	Late 4th century BC	Death & funeral of Hephaistion Giant cup at final party Parallel descriptions of Alexander's dress	30%
Berossus	After 293BC	Semiramis did not build the Hanging Gardens in Babylon	30%
Demetrius of Phalerum	318-310BC	Cleitarchus' attention to Alexander's fortune may derive from Demetrius' *Peri Tyches*	30%
Chares	Late 4th century BC	Heroism at Aornus; Bucephalus died of wounds	20%
Hieronymus	Shortly after 272BC	Conspiracy of Antipater, Cassander & Iollas?	10%

TABLE 2.3: The *Einquellenprinzip*: close matches between Curtius and Diodorus 17

C=Curtius, D=Diodorus, J=Justin, S=Schwartz, H=Hamilton in Cleitarchus & Diodorus 17, cf.=vergleiche in Schwartz

C3.2.1=D17.30.7 S
C3.11.7-11=D17.34.2-6 S
C3.11.20,23-6=D17.35.2,36.5,2,4 cf.J11.9.11-12 S
C3.11.27=D17.36.6 H
C3.12.15-17=D17.37.5-6 H
C3.12.26=D17.38.2 H
C4.1.15-26=D17.47.1-6 H
C4.1.27-33=D17.48.2-4 S
C4.1.39-40=D17.48.1-2 S
C4.2.7=D17.40.4 S
C4.2.12=D17.41.3-4 S
C4.2.18=D17.40.5 S
C4.2.20=D17.41.1 S
C4.3.6,9,11-12=D17.42.5-6,43.3 S
C4.3.20=D17.41.2 cf.J11.10.14 S
C4.3.22=D17.41.8 H
C4.3.25-26=D17.44.1-3 S
C4.4.1-2=D17.45.7 S
C4.4.3-5=D17.41.5-6 H
C4.4.10-12,17=D17.46.2-4 S
C4.5.11=D17.48.6 S
C4.6.30–D17.49.1 S
C4.7.1,5,9=D17.49.2-4 S
C4.7.12-14=D17.49.4-5 S
C4.7.16-17,20-28=D17.50.3-51.3 S
C4.9.4-5=D17.53.1-2 H
C4.13.26-29=D17.57.1-4 S
C4.15.9-11=D17.59.6-7 S
C4.15.16-17=D17.58.4-5 S
C4.15.28-29,32=D17.60.2-4 S
C4.16.31-32=D17.61.3 S
C5.1.10-11=D17.64.3 S
C5.1.40-42=D17.65.1 S
C5.1.43-45=D17.64.5-6 S
C5.1.25-26=D2.7.3-4 (Jacoby F10) S
C5.1.34-35=D2.10.4,1 S
C5.2.1-7=D17.65.2-4 cf.D17.27.1-2 S
C5.2.8, 12-15=D17.65.5,66.2-7 S
C5.3.1.2,4-5,10=D17.67.1-2,4-5 S
C5.3.17-18,23&C5.4.2-4,10,12,18=D17.68.1-6 S
C5.5.2-4=D17.69.1-2 S

C5.5.5-9,12,23-24=D17.69.2-8 cf.J11.14.11-12 S
C5.6.1-5,8,9=D17.70.1-71.2 S
C6.2.15=D17.75.1 S
C6.4.3-6=D17.75.2 S
C6.4.18,22=D17.75.3,6 S
C6.5.11-12,18-21=D17.76.3-8 S
C6.5.24-26,30-32=D17.77.1-3 cf. J12.3.5-7 & Strabo11.5.4 S
C7.1.5-9=D17.80.2 S
C7.2.18=D17.80.3 S
C7.2.35-37=D17.80.4 cf. J12.5.4-8 S
C7.3.1,3=D17.81.1-2 S
C7.3.5-18=D17.82 S
C7.3.22-23=D17.83.1-2 S
C7.4.33,38=D17.83.4-6 S
C7.5.28-35 cf. Dκ S
C7.10.4-9 cf. Dκβ S
C7.10.15-16 cf. Dκδ S
C8.1.11-19 cf. Dκς S
C8.5.4 cf. Dλα, J12.7.5 S
C8.10.5-6 cf. Dλβ S
C8.11.2=D17.85.1-2, J12.7.12 S
C8.11.3-4=D17.85.4-5 S
C8.11.7-8,25=D17.85.3,8-9&D17.86.1 S
C8.12.1-3=D17.86.2 S
C8.12.4-10,14=D17.86.3-7 S
C8.14.3=D17.87.5 S
C9.1.1,3-4,6=D17.89.3-6&D17.90.1 S
C9.1.8-12=D17.90.4-7 S
C9.1.24-33=D17.91.4-D17.92.3 S
C9.3.10-11=D17.94.2 S
C9.3.19=D17.95.1-2, J12.8.16 S
C9.3.20,23=D17.95.3,5 S
C9.4.1-2,5=D17.96.1-3 S
C9.4.8-14=D17.97.1-3 S
C9.7.16-26=D17.100.2-D17.101.6 S
C9.8.4-8=D17.102.1-4 S
C9.8.13-15(Jacoby F25)=D17.102.6 S
C9.8.17-28=D17.103, J12.10.2-3 cf. Cic. de divin. 2.135 S
C9.10.5-11,17-18,27=D17.104.4-D17.106.1 S
C10.2.4,8-12,30=D17.190.1-2 S
C10.5.21-25=D17.118.3, J13.1.5-6 S
C10.10.14,18-19=D17.117.5&D17.118.2 cf. J12.13.10 S

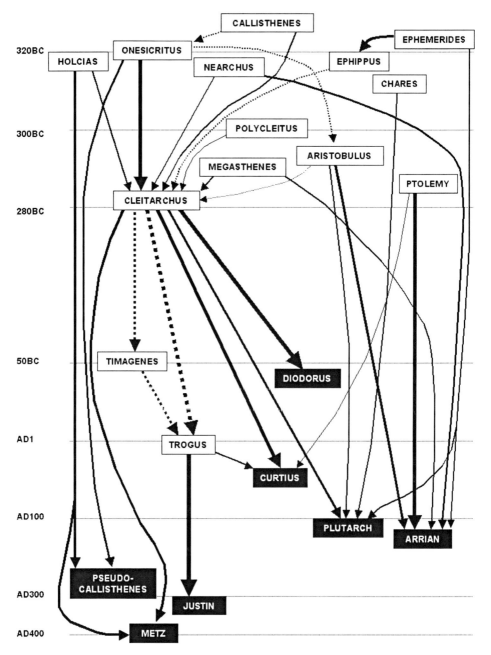

Figure 2.1. Relationships between ancient authors on Alexander's campaigns especially pertaining to Cleitarchus (white in black box = extant; and vice versa).

3. Book 10: June 327BC – June 326BC

The Invasion Of India, Nysa, Mazaga, Aornus And The Battle Against Porus

KEY
<u>Underlined bold text for attributed Fragments of Cleitarchus</u>
Bold text where there is overwhelming evidence
Bold italic text where there exists direct-firm evidence
Normal text where direct-weak evidence applies
Italic text where the evidence is conjectural
Grey text for connecting passages, if Cleitarchus' version is indeterminate

10.1 *At the outset of the tenth year of his reign,* **Alexander aimed to press on to India and thence to reach the Ocean** *in order to establish the ultimate ends of the Orient as the boundary of his empire.* And so as to hinder any threat to these prospects that might emerge in his rear, the king commanded that thirty thousand youths should be recruited from among all his satrapies and brought to him in arms to serve as both soldiers and sureties for the good behaviour of their compatriots. The king also despatched Craterus to tracks down Catanes and Haustanes, who had rebelled against his authority. Of these Haustanes was duly captured, whereas Catanes was slain in battle. Furthermore, Polyperchon brought the region known as Bubacenê into submission. Having thus set everything in order, Alexander was able to divert his attentions to his Indian campaign.

10.2 India was held to derive its wealth not only from its gold but also from gemstones and pearls. It was a land where the art of extravagance was better developed than the taste for elegant splendour. Those who were familiar with the place reported that its warriors glinted with chryselephantine accoutrements. Consequently, ***Alexander, in order that none should surpass him in distinction, embossed his troops' shields with silver,*** hence dubbing them "Argyraspides"[1]; and he also had their corselets either silvered or gilded ***and***

---

[1] "The Silver Shields".

gave golden trappings to his cavalry. A hundred and twenty thousand men-at-arms followed the king into that war.[2]

10.3 Most of India stretches out towards the east, since it is less extensive in latitude than in longitude. Those parts that face into the south wind rise up to an exceptionally tall ridge of land, but all the rest is flat and grants a smooth passage to numerous renowned rivers that spring down from this Caucasus range. The Indus retains an icier chill than the rest and conveys such waters as scarcely differ in their character from the open sea. The Ganges, greatest of all the rivers of the Orient, flows in a southerly direction, its unswerving channel grazing past the immense mountain ridges, until its course is deflected eastwards by cliffs that loom up in its path. The Ganges and the Indus too empty into the Erythraean Sea. The Indus carves away at its banks, dragging off many trees and great masses of soil. Its course is often obstructed by rocks, which cause it to meander this way and that. Wherever it encounters friable earth, its current slackens and it heaps up islands *of silt*. The Acesines is its tributary.

10.4 As it runs on down, the Ganges intercepts the Iomanes[3] and the confluence of these streams is quite turbulent, for the Ganges affords an uneven access to the influx, but the agitated waters are not held back. The Diardines[4] is less well discussed, since it flows through the ultimate extremities of India, yet it nurtures not only crocodiles like the Nile, but also dolphins[5] and other types of water-beast that are unknown to other regions. *Whilst at the near edge of India* the Ethymanthus,[6] often arcing and winding, is sapped for irrigation by those who dwell thereabouts. On this account, scarcely any of it reaches the area where it seeps anonymously into a sea. Besides these many other rivers partition the entire territory, but they remain obscure, since they flow through unexplored landscapes.

10.5 Moreover the parts of India that are nearer to the sea are raked by the north wind, but the interior finds shelter in the lee of the mountain ranges, thus attaining a lush and luxuriant mildness. But in that zone of the world the natural sequence of the seasons is reversed, such that India is cloaked in snow whilst other places bask in the heat of the sun. Conversely, elsewhere being frozen stiff, India languishes under stifling heat-waves. Nor is there any motive for this deviancy of Nature. ***Certainly the sea that laps India does not even differ***

---

[2] Cf. Arrian, *Indica* 19.5; Plutarch, *Life of Alexander* 66.2.

[3] The modern Jumna; note that *Iomanes* is an emendation of *in mare* by Hedicke.

[4] Seemingly the Brahmaputra; Strabo 15.1.72 calls it the Oidanes, citing the lost *Periplus* of Artemidorus of Ephesus (c. 100BC); probably the Doanas in Ptolemy's *Geography* 7.2.7,11.

[5] The Ganges River Dolphin or Susu.

[6] Possibly the Helmand: *Etymandros* in Arrian 4.6.6; *Hetoimandros* in Ptolemy 6.17.17; *Erymanthos* in Polybius 11.34.13; *Erymandos* in Pliny NH 6.25 – though McCrindle, *Invasion of India by Alexander*, p.184 queries this identification.

from others in the matter of its hue, despite that it is named after King Erythrus,[7] on which account naïve people imagine its waters to run to redness. But the land is bountiful in cotton, which garbs most of its inhabitants. And the bark of the trees is supple, so that it may be written upon exactly like papyrus. They have birds there that can be coached to parrot the human voice. In general their beasts are not found amongst other nations, except as exotic imports. Likewise, India spawns rhinoceroses, which are unknown elsewhere.[8] And *the Indian elephants are more powerful than those that are tamed in Africa: their size too matches their strength.[9] The rivers carry gold-dust,[10] which settles out of* the water *where it* flows sluggishly in a slack current. And the sea encrusts its shore with gemstones and pearls. They have no richer basis for their wealth than these, particularly since the dissemination of such corrupting merchandise among other nations. For, of course, lust fixes a high price for this vomit of the retching surf.

10.6 In India, just as everywhere else, the specifics of their environment influence the behaviour of the inhabitants. They wind linen sheets about themselves all the way down to their feet, which they shoe with sandals. They also bind linen around their heads and dangle precious stones from their ears. Those among the populace who are distinguished either by nobility or wealth also adorn their arms and wrists with bands of gold. They groom their hair more often than they shear it and the chin is never shaved, but they razor the rest of the skin of their jowls to apparent smoothness. *Yet the extravagance of their kings, which they themselves term splendour, excels all other peoples in turpitude.[11] When the king condescends to appear in public, his servants bring forth silver censers and waft perfumes along the entirety of his chosen route. He reclines upon a golden litter, which is hung all around with pearls, and he is dressed in a linen robe embellished with purple and gold. Men-at-arms follow close upon the litter, forming his bodyguard.*

---

[7] *Erythros* being Greek for red: this probably came from Nearchus (Arrian, *Indica* 37.2) and is repeated at Curtius 10.1.13, hence Cleitarchus is a very likely source for the latter.

[8] An anachronistic observation under the Roman Empire, which was aware of African Rhinoceroses, e.g. depicted on a quadrans of Domitian and mentioned by Martial. As Proconsul of Roman Africa, could Curtius have been ignorant of African Rhinos? Or is he simply failing to correct his source? (Note however that this is an emendation by Hedicke, whilst Yardley reads that the rhino was not indigenous to India, though any such suggestion would seem very odd.)

[9] This matches a fragment of Onesicritus in Strabo 15.1.43, probably via Cleitarchus.

[10] This was recorded by Megasthenes (Strabo 15.1.57) and by Onesicritus (Strabo 15.2.14).

[11] For a Roman who ascended to prominence under the Claudian emperors to attack the monarchs of India as the world's leading exponents of the vice of luxury/extravagance would have been disingenuous: more probably, Curtius transcribed views he found in Cleitarchus, for these sentiments harmonise with the ascetic philosophy of the early Greek Cynics, with whom Cleitarchus is associated.

10.7 In these festal processions, four-wheeled carriages trundle among the bodyguards, bearing broad-leafed trees, of which the branches serve as perches for a variety of tamed birds that have been trained to sing so as to divert the king from prosaic concerns. Among these songsters, Nature has made the Catreus, an indigenous species, outstandingly gorgeous in its polychrome plumage, being about the size of a peacock with the tips of its feathers tinged emerald green.[12] When it looks askance, the hue of its eyes is imperceptible. But you would judge they were vermilion, should it stare straight at you, except that the pupil has the colour of an apple; and its gaze is quite piercing. That region of the eye that is white in other species is pale yellow in the Catreus. The plush plumage of its head is azure, but there are also splashes like saffron, whilst its legs are a shade of orange. Its voice is mellifluous and pure like a nightingale's. The Indians raise these birds in order that they may feast their eyes upon loveliness, thus they can witness them in their purple or as red as unsullied flame. And they flock in flight such as to seem like clouds.

10.8 Besides these there is a flagrantly amorous species that is called the Orion: as large as the largest Herons and likewise sporting maroon legs, but dissimilar in having blue eyes. This Orion is instructed by Nature herself in the art of song, such that it warbles dulcet melodies like to bridal canticles or marriage madrigals in their charm and allure. Its arias reach such a pitch of perfection that it might be reckoned a sort of Siren, for we have the patter of the poets and the pictures of the painters to prove that Sirens were winged and maidens in myth with legs like birds.[13]

10.9 The king's palace has gilded columns twined about their length with a vine fashioned in gold and studded with silver effigies of birds, for they take the greatest delight in ornithology. When the king has his hair groomed and dressed, the palace stands open to all comers: at that time he responds to foreign delegations and that is the occasion on which he dispenses justice to his people. His sandals being discarded, his feet are anointed with perfume. His main exercise is hunting, which consists in archery against penned beasts to the accompaniment of the prayers and songs of his concubines. Their arrows are two cubits[14] long, but the effort of launching them outweighs their effectiveness, for a missile of which the efficacy depends upon slightness is handicapped by unwieldy weight. The king mounts a horse for his shorter journeys, but on longer expeditions he processes in a chariot drawn by elephants and the whole hide of each monstrous beast is gilded. Furthermore, in order that he need not desist from any of his decadent habits, a long column of

---

[12] Possibly the Monal Pheasant.

[13] Deinon, Cleitarchus' father, had suggested that there were Sirens in India (Pliny, NH 10.136).

[14] A cubit is about 45cm.

his concubines trails after him in golden litters. Though they are separated from the queen's column in the order of march, they enjoy an equivalent degree of luxury. Women prepare the king's meals and serve him wine, which all Indians imbibe copiously. As he sinks into a drunken torpor, his concubines convey him to his chamber, whilst performing a customary incantation to nocturnal deities.

10.10 Who would credit that there could thrive an appreciation of philosophy amid such decadence? But there does indeed exist a coarse and vulgar class of men that are called sages. These men consider it a splendid thing to anticipate their appointed end by ordering that they be burnt alive, should they be suffering from ill-health or the decrepitude of advanced age. To linger for the reaping they consider a stain upon their life and no respect is paid to the corpses of any who pass away from old age: they suppose the flame to be defiled, unless it receives them with the breath of life still in them. Those of them who live at public expense in the cities are said skilfully to observe the passage of the stars and to foretell the future. And they believe that a person shall not bring forward the day of his death, if he look forward to it without fear. They regard as sacred anything that they have begun to foster, and this is especially true of trees, injury to which constitutes a capital crime. They describe their month as comprising fifteen days, though they keep the year at its full duration. *This is because,* although they mark the passage of time by the phases of the moon, they begin their months at the threshold of its curvature into horns, rather than when it fills its face as most others do. Their months are consequently shortened *to half the usual length,* since their term is reckoned by *recurrences of* that *quarter* phase…[15]

10.11 All being readied, Alexander advanced into the countryside of *Bactria*. He passed *the encampment* and crossed the river *Oxus*. For *thirty* stades he led the army across an uninhabited region, then **he marched within the bounds of India** and reached *Drapis*, where he was met by King *Arines* with his young sons and the greatest quantities of supplies, which he divided up amongst the army. He presented Alexander himself with many barbarian vestments, three thousand horses and *fifty thousand* silver talents. When Alexander enquired as to his motivation, the Indian answered: "You are a great king, and I wish us to be friends." Alexander responded: "These monies passed to you from your father on his death and I hereby return them to you. The horses I shall use in my campaigns. Let you keep us in mind. The stewardship of this *region* shall be yours." [16]

10.12 From this place he advanced to *reach the River* Cophen, from which point it is nine days' voyage to the Indus. ***He was met by the minor kings of the neighbouring nations, who acceded to his governance. On witnessing***

---

[15] A lacuna in the reconstruction of Cleitarchus may be inferred at this point from Curtius' statement that he omitted further material describing India that was in his source.

[16] This derives from the Metz Epitome 32-3: the italicised figures must be corrupt, e.g. a stade is ~180m and a talent ~25kg. There is a possibility that Arines is Taxiles, cf. Arrian, *Anabasis* 4.22.6.

Alexander's arrival, they rejoiced, saying that according to tradition he was the third son of Zeus who had reached their lands. They knew of *reputed* visits firstly of Dionysus and secondly of Heracles, *but Alexander had actually manifested himself before their gaze. Gladdened by this, the king crossed the river, received the minor kings in a friendly manner and bade them be his guides in reaching the River Indus.*

10.13 *Moreover, when no more of the local potentates presented themselves before him, he sent Hephaistion and Perdiccas ahead with part of his forces to subjugate those who repudiated his overlordship.* His orders were that they should advance to the River Indus and there fabricate boats by means of which the army could be ferried across to the region beyond. *Since multiple rivers needed to be traversed, these commanders constructed ships which could be joined together to bridge each river, then disassembled and transported by wagon to be reassembled where required.*

10.14 After directing Craterus to trail after him with the phalanx, Alexander led forth the cavalry and the lightly armed troops *following the river. On approaching Silex, the first fortified town of India,* armed men issued forth to oppose him, but after a skirmish they fled back within their gates, whilst the army eagerly gave chase. *Then Alexander set the town's stockade alight, by which time Craterus had arrived.* In order to instil proper dread of Macedonian arms into nations that still lacked experience of such might, the king ordered Craterus to slay all the adult men. *Whilst Alexander was riding up to the walls, he was struck by an arrow. Nevertheless,* the town fell to him and having cut down all of its inhabitants, he further vented his fury in destroying its dwellings as well. *From there he progressed to lay siege to another fortified town, but in that instance he accepted hostages and installed a garrison.*

10.15 After having subdued an inconsequential clan, **Alexander** *advanced 230 stades through Nysaean lands and* reached the city of Nysa. By chance he encamped in the woods virtually before its walls, whereupon a most bitterly frigid night afflicted them with shuddering chillness, yet the opportunity was at hand to relieve their discomfort with fires. Hence they felled trees and set them aflame. However, fed by dead wood, the fire consumed the tombs of the townspeople. Constructed of aged cedar, these spread the incipient inferno over a broad area, until everything was razed to the ground. Initially the baying of dogs issued from the city, but straight afterwards the clamour of men was heard. And not until this point had *the unwary Nysaeans realised that their enemy had arrived*, nor had the Macedonians known that they had reached the city. So thereupon the king led forward his forces to besiege its walls and their missiles overwhelmed their enemies, who had sallied forth in an attempt to repulse them.

10.16 Then among **the Nysaeans**, some advocated surrender, whilst others favoured a trial of arms. When Alexander received word of their indecision, he held back from slaying them, ordering that they should merely be blockaded. And eventually, tired of the hardships of the siege, they **sent a delegation of elders to negotiate a peace with the king.** These men, *led by Acuphis,* managed through their entreaties to appease the king by pointing out that Dionysus had established their city of Nysa and the state of Nysaea at the extremity of his rovings and settled it with fifty thousand of his followers. They directed his gaze upon a mountain in the distance, which the god had called Meros, because he himself had sprung from the thigh of Zeus.[17] *And they attested to its exceptional delights. Then all at once they began to weep and to beseech him that the monument and good works of Dionysus should not be overthrown. In response Alexander granted the Nysaeans their freedom and returned everything to their care,* for he was pleased to believe not only that he had matched the exploits of Dionysus, but that he was even following in the god's footsteps. *And he ordained that Acuphis should govern Nysa, requesting that he should select a hundred of their most prominent men to accompany his expedition. But Acuphis* smiled and *retorted that no city could long survive, from which a hundred of its finest men had been abducted: "If you wish us to remain secure, let you lead away two hundred of the least worthy." Alexander recognised both the humour and the truth in this statement,* therefore he requested that Acuphis should send him both his own son and his daughter's son instead.

10.17 Afterwards Alexander *learnt the layout of the* sacred *mountain from the local people and sent provisions on ahead, and then he* climbed to the summit of Meros with his entire force. <u>The heights abound in</u> luxuriant vegetation with vines and <u>a variety of ivy, which they call "scindapsos",</u> growing wild, yet flourishing as though tended by unseen hands **and watered by numerous perennial springs.** There too thrive wholesome orchard fruits of diverse flavours, spontaneously sprouting forth from such of their seeds as chance to germinate in the rich humous. And copses of wild Laurel, Box and Myrtle burgeon among the rocky outcrops.

10.18 *The Macedonians were seized by the frenzy of the god, plucking the foliage to wreath themselves in garlands of the vines and the ivy, then cavorting through the groves in a Dionysiac comus. And the crags and the dells rang with thousands of yells as the revellers invoked the spirit of the place in adoration of its divinity.* As though in the midst of peace they reclined upon grass and fronds that they had heaped together. And the king was not at all averse to these fortuitous festivities, but most generously furnished the feasting with everything needed to immerse his army in the practices of

---

[17] In Greek μηρός is "thigh".

Dionysus for fully ten days. Who then could deny that fame and glory are more often gifted by fortune than gleaned through virtue? For neither in their feasting nor their sodden slumber did any enemy venture to assault them, being just as much intimidated by their holy howling as by the baying of their battle cry. Identical good fortune was to preserve the Macedonians in the course of their return from the Ocean, when they again drunkenly caroused before the faces of their foes.

Figure 10.1. Alexander's triumphal entry into Nysa (Antonio Tempesta, 1608)

10.19 Moving onwards, Alexander crossed the Daedalian Mountains, where the inhabitants had abandoned their homesteads and taken refuge among the remote and forested peaks. Therefore the king swept on past Acadira, which had likewise been wasted and forsaken due to the flight of its denizens. Hence Alexander was obliged to modify his conduct of the campaign. By splitting up his forces, he caused his warriors to appear in many places at once, and having thereby assaulted his enemies where they least expected, all who opposed him were thoroughly subdued in the slaughter. Ptolemy took most cities, but the largest fell to Alexander. Afterwards the king recombined his scattered forces for the onward march.

10.20 Now Alexander entered *the satrapy of* Assacena and *traversed the River Choaspes*.[18] *He left the siege of a wealthy city, called Beira*[19] *by its*

---

[18] Probably the modern River Swat.

[19] Arrian calls it Bazira, whilst Aurel Stein identifies it with Bir-Kot in the Lower Swat Valley.

inhabitants, in the charge of Coenus, whilst he himself descended upon the people of the fortified town of Mazaga.[20] Until recently this had been the realm of Assacenus, but he was lately deceased, so his mother Cleophis was ruling the city and territory *as regent* for *his young son. Amminais, brother to the late king, had incited 9000 Indian mercenaries to take up arms against Alexander and he had now brought them into the realm. The city was garrisoned by 38,000 infantry and was secured not merely by dint of its location, but also by a ring of fortifications.*

10.21 *On its eastern aspect a torrential river, either bank being so sheer as to stymie any approach from that direction, girds Mazaga. Towards the south and the west towering crags loom up forming a bulwark, seemingly by the design of Nature. And cavernous chasms plunge down from its base, eroded out over endless epochs. This abyss has been extended with* vast ditches *to* complete the dyke, within which a wall having a circumference of thirty-five stades encompasses the city. *Its lower courses are masonry, whereas its upper reaches are constructed in mud brick. This brickwork is mortared together by a mixture of stone and mud, such that the brittle material is reinforced by tougher stuff. Nevertheless, in order to prevent subsidence, robust logs have been embedded, upon which boarding was overlaid forming gangways, which also sheltered the structure.*

10.22 Alexander invested the city with a cordon of troops and prepared to launch an assault. He was encouraging his soldiers and surveying the fortifications - *being consequently undecided as to his plan of attack, since he could not bridge the chasm, save by filling it, and neither could he otherwise advance his siege-engines up to the walls* - whereupon someone loosed an arrow from the battlements. The missile chanced to strike the king in the calf of his left leg. *When* he wrenched forth its barb, *his wound bled copiously, yet he ordered that his horse should be led up. Mounting without troubling to bind his injury,* he refused to withdraw from the action, *but carried on as he had intended without tarrying. However,* he was increasingly afflicted with pain *as his leg drooped down and the wound stiffened after the flow of blood was staunched. Whilst he still exhorted his troops in the prosecution of the siege, he is said to have commented that, despite being dubbed the son of Zeus, he nevertheless suffered from the debilitation of bodily injury, quipping: "What issues from my wound is gore, not Ichor, such as flows in the veins of the blessed gods."*[21]

---

[20] Possibly Chakdara or Malakand in the Lower Swat Valley: it is Massaga in Greek sources, but the Latin sources have Mazaga (Curtius has "Mazagas" and the Metz Epitome has "Mazanan"), perhaps reflecting phonetic transliteration.

[21] The Ichor quote derives from Homer, *Iliad* 5.340, and is recorded by Plutarch, *Alexander* 28.2.

10.23 The king only returned to his camp after he had inspected the entire circuit and decreed what he wished to be done. Thereafter, in accordance with his orders, some of ***his troops*** demolished such dwellings as lay outside the fortifications and delivered enormous quantities of debris for heaping into the chasm, whereas others cast the boles and branches of great trees and masses of rubble into the gulf. And soon the level of the fill had risen up to the brink, so they **erected siege-towers** *ready for the assault*. **The Macedonians were ardent to avenge the injury inflicted upon their king,** so they had accomplished these labours by the ninth day.

10.24 Alexander ventured forth to inspect the results before his wound had scabbed over, and, having commended his soldiers, he issued orders that the siege-engines should be advanced. From these a heavy rain of missiles was poured upon their opponents. ***Then, their escorts having interlocked their shields above their heads, the siege-towers were trundled towards the walls.*** Their mobility was especially terrifying for folk who were ignorant of such contraptions. They believed that such massive structures, lacking help from perceptible exertions, were actually moved by supernatural forces. Similarly they were sure that mere mortal men could not have deployed the heavy bolts shot by the catapults and the javelins used against the walls.

10.25 *As the Macedonians surged towards her walls with scaling ladders, Cleophis surveyed a scene filled with a multitude of siege-towers advancing upon her city and a storm of projectiles fired from the slings of Alexander's catapults and scorpion engines. And she was panicked by the uncanny nature of the assault, for it seemed to her that the rocks hurled by the siege-engines were truly flying. Crediting Alexander with wielding supernatural powers, she called together* Amminais [22] *and her other friends, exhorting them to surrender the city to Alexander. However, the mercenaries were vociferous in their opposition: they grew obstructive and sought to foment a mutiny.* Nevertheless, the defence of the entire city seeming hopeless, its defenders withdrew into their citadel. From there, **on the following day** Cleophis **covertly despatched envoys to Alexander to negotiate terms of surrender and to seek his forgiveness for their behaviour,** *for they had been coerced by their own armed hirelings! Suspecting that such moves were afoot, the mercenaries themselves sent a delegation to treat with Alexander, seeking his permission to issue forth from the town bringing their possessions with them. The king granted the requests of both parties.*

10.26 As soon as the truce was concluded, Cleophis, marvelling at Alexander's magnanimity, sent him rich gifts and swore to follow his commands in every respect. And straightaway in accordance with their terms the mercenaries emerged from the town *gate with their wives, their*

---

[22] The Metz Epitome manuscript (destroyed in 1944) was read as "ariplicem".

offspring and their baggage and encamped upon a hilltop[23] at a distance of 80 stades from Mazaga, *oblivious of what was about to transpire.*

10.27 Alexander followed in the tracks of the mercenaries *with contingents of his lightly equipped troops, for he persisted in regarding these Indians as his enemies. Throughout the night, he held his forces in readiness and the following day he announced to his men that the mercenaries were all to be put to the sword. When* the Indians *realised what was underway, undaunted they* gathered their baggage and their families to their centre and arrayed themselves protectively in an armed ring, *prepared either to fend off the aggression or else steadfastly to give their lives in defence of their wives and children.* But initially they shouted out that the assault contravened their treaty with Alexander, invoking the gods *in whose names it had been sworn* to witness his impiety. In retort, Alexander yelled that he had given permission for them to come out of the city, but not for them to march clean away *as friends of the Macedonians.* And thereupon his onslaught began.

10.28 *The Indians were driven to mount a desperate resistance, drawing upon their combat expertise to make a robust and courageous stand, whereas the Macedonians feared to be bested by barbarians in the martial skills, and so the struggle caused carnage. They grappled hand to hand, every sort of injury and variety of death being dealt in their deadly contests. The Macedonians pierced through the flimsy shields of the mercenaries with their sarissas,[24] puncturing their lungs with shards of steel. The Indians in response cast their javelins into the densely packed ranks of their opponents at such close range that none could avoid its target.*

10.29 *Many mercenaries were disabled by wounds and quite a few lay dead, hence their women snatched up the weapons of these casualties, holding the line shoulder to shoulder with their menfolk, since the extremity of their plight and the ferocity of the fight forced them to feats of valour beyond their physiques. Some of them, fully armed, shared the shields of their husbands, whilst others leapt unarmed into the fray to seize the shields of their foes so as to hamper their assault. But in the end, despite their warrior women, the Indians were overwhelmed by superior numbers and cut to pieces, opting for glorious death rather than cowardly survival. Alexander rounded up the disabled, the disarmed and the remaining women and led them away in the custody of his cavalry.*

10.30 **The king returned to Mazaga and was met by Cleophis, who came** *down out of the citadel* **with a grand entourage** *of noble ladies, tipping*

---

[23] That Cleitarchus mentioned the hill is implied by Polyaenus 4.3.20 (cf. Arrian, *Anabasis* 4.27.3).

[24] A sarissa was the Macedonian pike-lance, which was over 4m long.

libations of wine from golden goblets. To signal their supplication, her leading citizens bore before them veiled produce and fronds of foliage. She herself placed her little grandson at Alexander's knees and elicited not merely a pardon, but also reinstatement in her former rank - as some say by virtue of the king's appreciation for her fair features. *But indeed, from her status and authority* among her people*, it was quite apparent that she was of noble breeding and worthy of regal power. Afterwards Alexander entered the citadel with a few of his retinue and tarried there for several days.* Furthermore, it is a matter of fact that Cleophis subsequently gave birth to a son, whom she named Alexander, whatever his paternity. *And it is said that Cleophis was thereafter called the Courtesan Queen by the Indians, yet her son eventually became a king among them.*

10.31 Polyperchon was sent hence with a task force against the city of Hora, where he triumphed in an engagement with a rabble of its citizens. Following on their heels when they fled within their walls, he soon subjugated the place. Numerous benighted towns, which had been abandoned by their inhabitants, now came into Alexander's power, but moving onwards he reached the citadel of *Bagasdaram.* Its natives together with **the surviving Indians from many** other **towns had snatched up their arms and fled to seek refuge on a pinnacle called Aornus, which was virtually impregnable. Indeed, Heracles in olden times was said unsuccessfully to have besieged this fortress crag, having been** *thrice* **forced to abandon the endeavour by a succession of earthquakes** *and other portents from the gods. When he heard this, Alexander was inspired by a keen yearning to outdo the deeds of his divine ancestor.*

10.32 The base of Aornus has a circumference of 100 stades and it soars to a height of 16 stades above the valley of the Indus, the greatest river in India, which flows between sheer banks beneath its southern flank. On its other sides it is hemmed by plunging gorges and towering cliffs. *Neither does the pinnacle itself reach its lofty elevation, as many others do, via a succession of moderate inclines, but rather it soars from its base in the fashion of an acute cone tapering to a sharp crest.* It gets its name from the observation that **it teems with birds that parrot the human voice,** a quite unbirdlike habit.[25] **On reconnoitring the obstacles Alexander was frustrated to find that a direct assault was impracticable, but thereupon an aged native came before the king with his two sons. He had long subsisted in penury in that neighbourhood, sharing a cave containing three rock-cut beds with his offspring. In consequence he had grown intimately familiar with every detail of the terrain. Explaining this, he now offered to guide Alexander up through the foothills so as to bring him to a spot that**

---

[25] The Greek ἄορνος is translated as "birdless", but it might mean "non-bird" in a name.

overlooked the crag occupied by the Indian defenders,[26] *provided it were made worth his while.* Alexander offered him a bounty *of eighty talents, and, retaining one of the young men as a hostage, he sent the father to shepherd a body of lightly equipped troops, led by Myllinas,[27] a royal scribe, in ascending a tortuous route to the summit, chosen to elude detection by the enemy.*

10.33 Following the guidance of the old man, Alexander's advance force soon occupied the only viable route from the summit of Aornus, hence cornering its defenders in a siege. However, a steep ravine separated the Macedonians from the pinnacle itself. *Alexander assessed that* this chasm had to be filled for the storming of the summit to be practicable. *A forest grew thereabouts, which the king commanded be felled and the trunks stripped of their branches, such that his troops might heave them into the ravine unhampered by the foliage. Alexander personally hacked the first tree and cast it into the gulf and the ensuing acclamation from the army announced their enthusiasm, for none could shirk a task that had been begun by the king.* Through seven days and nights they toiled ceaselessly at this labour, operating in relays *under enemy fire. Meanwhile the Indians kept yelling from the heights for Alexander to come on up, if he thought himself mightier than Heracles!* At first the defenders had the advantage of overlooking the Macedonian positions and they slew many who rashly sought to assault them. But before the seventh day was done, the causeway had risen to the brink of the ravine.

10.34 Now Alexander ordered the Agrianians and the archers to strive to scale the pinnacle. In addition he picked out thirty of the most resolute men from his own squadron, appointing Charus and *another* Alexander as their captains. The king urged the latter to recall their shared name *and therefore to be brave in conducting the mission.[28] This was faithfully promised by his eager captain.* Initially, in view of the patent perils, **the king** judged that he should hold himself back from the fray, but when the trumpet blared to signal the attack, that audacious dare-devil turned to his bodyguards, ordered them to follow him and **was the first to assail the crags,** *creeping upwards little by little.* Thereupon none of the Macedonians could restrain himself, but as one man they abandoned their stations and surged impulsively after their king. Many met a miserable end, for they slipped from the steep rock-face and were engulfed by the stream that cascaded down *the ravine.* It was a tragic spectacle even for those who watched from safety, but for those who were reminded of their own peril by witnessing

---

[26] Aurel Stein has convincingly identified Aornus with Pir-Sar: it is separated from a slightly higher peak to its west (Una-Sar) by the Burimar Ravine.

[27] Perhaps Myllenas son of Asander, honoured in an Eretrian decree together with Tauron son of Harpalus (*IG* xii.9).

[28] This is also mentioned by Plutarch, *Alexander* 58.3.

others perish, pity turned to dread. They did not mourn the dead, but their own predicament.

Figure 10.2. The assault on Aornus across the ravine (Antonio Tempesta, 1608)

10.35 By this point they had reached a situation, such that they could not return without catastrophe, unless as victors, for the barbarians were rolling massive boulders down among them as they clambered up. Their footholds being precarious and slippery, those who were struck went hurtling headlong downhill. However, Charus and that other Alexander, whom the king had sent ahead with his select band of thirty men, had now climbed onto the crest and were starting to grapple hand to hand with their foes, but since the barbarians were showering missiles upon them from yet higher ground, they were themselves smitten more often than they inflicted wounds upon the Indians. Alexander, remembering his name and his promise and consequently fighting with more passion than caution, was skewered from all sides and fell. When Charus saw him lying slain, oblivious of aught but vengeance, he hurled himself upon the enemy, transfixing many with his lance and slaying others with his sword. But when a host of foes assailed him, he collapsed lifeless athwart the corpse of his friend. *Sorely* distressed, as was natural, by the slaughter of these most valiant youths and by his other casualties, the king signalled a retreat. Then they preserved themselves by withdrawing gradually and avoiding panic. The barbarians, being satisfied at having repulsed their antagonists, neglected to harry them as they retired.

10.36 Although **Alexander** had decided to desist from the assault – for there seemed to be no prospect that he could seize the pinnacle – he nevertheless made an ostentatious display of persevering with the siege. He **ordered** the trails to be blockaded and **the siege-towers** *with the bolt-firing torsion-catapults* **to be advanced** with fresh troops replacing the weary. *When* **the king's persistence was recognised by the Indians,** *they were disconcerted,* but they staged a show of confidence, even of triumph, by feasting through two days and nights with a rhythmic percussion of drums, as was their custom. *Sensing a viable stratagem, Alexander cunningly removed his guards from a track, so that any Indians who wished might escape from the pinnacle.* Hence on the third night the beat of the drums was no longer heard, but instead the entire peak gleamed with the flame of torches, lit by the barbarians safely to light their flight across rocks that were impassable **in darkness.** The king sent Balacrus to reconnoitre, thereby confirming that **the summit was deserted and the Indians were scuttling away** *in fear of the fighting resilience of the Macedonians.*

10.37 Then Alexander signalled his soldiers to bellow in unison, thus striking terror into the Indians as they fled in disorder. Believing their opponents to be upon them, many perished through casting themselves headlong down slippery rocks and pathless, flinty crags. Others yet, disabled by injuries, were forsaken by those still sound in limb. **Thus Alexander** *used feints to outfox the Indians and* **took possession of the pinnacle.** Although he had conquered the place rather than its defenders, he celebrated the victory with sacrifices and thanksgiving to the gods, erecting altars to Athena Nike on the peak. **The contracted reward was faithfully paid to the trail-guides of his lightly equipped troops,** *though their assistance had accomplished less than they had promised. Finally,* the custodianship of the pinnacle and the surrounding territory was granted to Sisocostus, before *Alexander marched away.*

10.38 The king proceeded onwards to Ecbolima. **An Indian named Aphrices**[29] **was encamped nearby with twenty thousand men-at-arms** *and fifteen elephants. Discovering that this fellow was blockading a defile in his path, Alexander left the bulk of his forces marching at a moderate pace under the command of Coenus, whilst he himself forged ahead and deployed slingers and archers in driving off those who held the pass against him, thus opening the way for the force that followed. Either detesting their leader or seeking to ingratiate themselves with Alexander,* the Indians overthrew Aphrices *as he fled,* slew him and delivered his head *together with his panoply of arms* to the king. Being granted immunity from punishment for the deed, they preserved their lives, *but Alexander refused to condone such behaviour. He enrolled them in his*

---

[29] Arrian, *Anabasis* 4.30.5 speaks of a brother of Assacenus, whose elephants Alexander was pursuing at this time, but it is unclear whether he is Aphrices; that Aphrices might therefore be the Ariplex mentioned at Mazaga (Metz Epitome 42) is even more venturesome.

army and rounded up their elephants, which were roving about in the countryside.

10.39 Sixteen days after his departure from there, he reached the Indus, where he found that everything had been readied by Hephaistion *for the campaign beyond the river* just as he had directed: a fleet of triacontors[30] had been constructed and fully outfitted; a pontoon bridge *of linked boats* spanned the stream and a substantial stockpile of supplies had been accumulated. *The king rested his army for thirty days and offered up magnificent sacrifices to the gods.*

10.40 Mophis son of Taxiles dwelt beyond the river. Even prior to his father's death, whilst Alexander was in Sogdiana, he had persuaded Taxiles to place the kingdom of Taxila at Alexander's service in the conduct of his Indian campaign, since he was keen to ally their realm with the Macedonian, having been impressed by his accomplishments. After his father's demise, he sent a delegation to enquire of Alexander, whether he desired that Mophis should reign in the interim *at Taxila or else preferred to send a viceroy pending his own arrival? On hearing this, Alexander admired the remarkably fine sense and sensibility exhibited by Mophis. But* despite Alexander allowing that he should assume such a rule, he could not yet endure to exercise his powers, declining to adopt the royal raiment or the title of Taxiles, but *still* awaiting the arrival of Alexander. And although he had given a courteous reception to Hephaistion, freely issuing grain to his forces, he nevertheless had not met with him in person, not wishing to test the good faith of any save the king.

10.41 Alexander now *furnished provisions to his men and* conveyed his forces across the River Indus. *Receiving word of the king's approach,* Mophis was pleased to come forth with his army and elephants, *equipped as for war.* Whilst Alexander was yet at a distance of forty stades, Mophis, ensconced among his courtiers, arrayed his forces as if for battle, *the elephants being distributed among his formations of soldiers at measured intervals, giving from a distance an impression of castles.* Observing the approach of this vast and warlike host, Alexander immediately suspected that the Indian's pledges were deceptions in order that the Macedonians might be assailed in a state of unreadiness. He commanded the buglers to sound the call to arms *and deployed his cavalry to the wings. Though disturbed by this turn of events,* his troops confronted the Indians *in silence,* once they had reached their battle stations.

10.42 Mophis noted the agitated activity among the Macedonians and surmised its misconstrued cause. He ordered his men to raise their

---

[30] Thirty-oared galleys.

lances and to halt their advance, but spurred his own steed far forward escorted by a mere handful of horsemen. Alexander followed suit, considering himself safe whether he went to meet a friend or a foe: *by virtue either of the good faith of the Indian or else his own prowess in arms, for he reckoned himself to be a match for Mophis in single combat. But* they met in a spirit of friendship *insofar as their expressions could tell, though they could not converse without an interpreter. When one had been fetched and* Alexander asked why Mophis had mobilised, the barbarian explained that he had brought his army to meet Alexander, so as to place all the men under his command at the king's immediate disposal, *without tarrying whilst heralds delivered pledges of safe conduct. He was yielding up his person and his realm to him whom he understood to be pursuing glory in arms; to him who was most wary of staining his reputation with treachery.* Much relieved *and gratified by the candour of the Indian,* Alexander proffered Mophis his right hand as a token of friendship and fidelity and restored him to the rule of his kingdom.

10.43 Mophis relinquished fifty-*six* elephants into Alexander's hands together with teeming herds of prodigiously proportioned livestock and three thousand bulls bedizened as for sacrifice; such cattle being prized in that region and considered worthy of the prestige of potentates. *When Alexander queried whether his yeomen outnumbered his troops,* Mophis observed that he had more work for soldiers than for farmers, since he was at war with two kings. *Alexander asked the identity of these marauding monarchs. Mophis answered that* they were Abisares, whose abode lay among the mountains across the River Hydaspes, and Porus, who ruled over the plain on the far bank of the same waterway. Of these Porus was the more powerful, but both had determined to test the fortunes of war against any who bore arms. Then Alexander endorsed the assumption of the royal insignia by Mophis, as well as his adoption of his father's name in accordance with the custom of his nation. Thenceforth he was known as Taxiles by the people, for such was the title inherited by their sovereign.

10.44 *Then Taxiles hosted Alexander as his guest, whilst the king rested his army* at Taxila *for three days.* During his stay Alexander sent Onesicritus to converse with the Indian sages near this place and one of them, who was called Calanus, consented to follow Alexander and did so to the end of his days.[31] *Thereafter, on the fourth day Taxiles announced the tally of grain that he had furnished to Hephaistion's forces and gifted golden crowns to Alexander and each of his Friends, as well as bestowing eighty talents of minted silver upon*

---

[31] It is virtually certain that Cleitarchus mentioned the self-immolation of Calanus in his twelfth book; he also used material from Onesicritus' *On the Education of Alexander,* who in turn told that he met Calanus near Taxila (Strabo 15.1.63-64), so Cleitarchus may have introduced Calanus here.

them. He even made presents of several strange jungle beasts. Being extraordinarily delighted by his generosity, **Alexander** *gave back what had been given with the addition of a thousand talents from such spoils of war as he had brought with him, plus* **many gold and silver banqueting vessels, numerous Persian vestments** *and thirty of his own steeds, caparisoned as when he himself rode them.* Though it placed the Indian under a debt of gratitude, Alexander's largesse deeply shocked his Friends. Among them, Meleager, being the worse for wine, offered Alexander his congratulations on having in India at last identified a person worthy of a thousand talents! Not having forgotten the depth of his remorse over slaying Cleitus for his rash tongue, the king curbed his temper, but commented: "People who allow themselves to be consumed by envy subject themselves to torment." *And indeed,* **just as iron is eaten by rust, so are the envious corroded by their own characters.**[32]

10.45 *The next day* a delegation arrived from Abisares, *led by his brother. They had been mandated by Abisares to concede Alexander's suzerainty and* to negotiate friendly relations *with him. They gave pledges of good faith and in turn received similar assurances from the king, who sent them back to Abisares accompanied by Nicocles as his own emissary.*[33] Reckoning that Porus might also be coerced into submission *by the notoriety of his reputation,* Alexander sent him Cleochares as his envoy. *Both embassies were* to seek to arrange the payment of tribute and the surrender of hostages to the king, *whilst* Cleochares also conveyed a demand that Porus should meet Alexander in person at his frontier.

10.46 *Abisares prevaricated, since he* **did not wish to send the king's envoys back to him. But, on hearing Alexander's demands,** *Porus was seized by fury and inflicted a gory scourging upon Cleochares. Concurrently, he composed the following letter and had it delivered to the king:* "Porus, *Monarch of India,* says this to Alexander: *whosoever you may be – and I have heard it said that you are a Macedonian – I suggest that you steer clear of me and contemplate your own wretchedness, rather than look ill upon another.* The fate of *Darius does not disturb me: therefore, moron, do not presume to give me orders! If you but set one foot upon my land in enmity, then you shall know me as ruler in India, for none save Zeus can call himself my lord. And Porus swears by the great* ball of *fire that governs the skies, if I should apprehend any man of yours in my territory, then I shall slake my lance with his blood and I shall spread the spoils among my slaves, for I am already replete with spoils. One thing alone that you*

---

[32] This is Fragment 48 of Cleitarchus (Maximi, *Eclogae* LIV 962 A), considered doubtful by Jacoby, but it might be fitted to this context.

[33] Probably Nicocles the son of Pasicrates of Soli, a Friend of Alexander (Arrian, *Indica* 18.)

command, I shall enact. I shall stand ready to meet you where you enter my realm, but I shall stand in arms."

10.47 *On reading this letter, Alexander was incensed and considered it settled that he would traverse the River Hydaspes.* But at this juncture Barzaentes, who had fomented an insurrection among the Arachosians, was led before Alexander in chains and thirty elephants captured at the same time accompanied him. The latter were opportune reinforcements against the Indians, since their hopes and strength were vested more in these monstrous beasts than in their soldiery. Samaxus, king of a meagre portion of India, was also delivered in fetters, since he had been in league with Barzaentes. Having secured the traitor and the minor king in his custody, **Alexander approached the near bank of the Hydaspes in the company of Taxiles,** to whom he had handed over the thirty elephants. **From there they observed that Porus' forces had occupied various defensive positions in the plain on the opposite bank in order to thwart any crossing by his opponents.**

10.48 On enquiring of Taxiles as to the nature of the forces in the enemy camp, Alexander was told that Porus had arrayed eighty-five exceptionally mighty elephants against him, with three hundred four-horse chariots and over thirty thousand infantry backing them up.[34] *Archers who shot cumbersome two-cubit Indian arrows were interspersed among the foot soldiers. Porus himself rode upon an elephant that loomed above the rest of those monstrous beasts. His armour, chased with silver and gold, clad an almighty physique, for he stood five cubits tall and the girth of his chest was twice that of his warriors. His spirit matched the stature of his body and he was as wise as anyone to be found among ignorant people. But notwithstanding Taxiles' disclosures, Alexander began fervently to investigate where he might cross the river.*

10.49 The Macedonians were not only deterred by the spectacle of the enemy forces, but by the proportions of the river that they must traverse. It spread over a breadth of four stades with a deep bed and no sign of any fords, giving the appearance of a desolate sea. Nor was the impetus of its current slackened by the width of its channel, but, as though pinched by its banks into a narrow course, it swept past in a roiling torrent, and in many spots rebounding billows betrayed the presence of rocky shoals. Yet more forbidding was their prospect of the far bank, which was packed with men and steeds. There too stood a huge mass of monstrous hulks, which, when purposely goaded, trumpeted hideously, such as to exhaust the ears. The river and their foes between them suddenly set their hearts to trembling in breasts that could usually embrace optimism and

---

[34] The precise agreement between Curtius and the Metz Epitome on these figures confirms that they were in their common source (very probably Cleitarchus); Diodorus has larger numbers (50,000 infantry, 3000 cavalry, 1000 chariots & 130 elephants), but he cites them in a context such that they may be rounded-up combinations of the forces available to Porus and Abisares.

had often seen it justified. For they now believed that their rocking rafts could neither be steered to the bank nor protected during the landing.

10.50 The middle of the channel was crowded with islets, to which both Macedonians and Indians waded and swam, whilst holding their weapons over their heads. Here they engaged each other in skirmishes, and both kings sought to deduce from the results of these minor actions how the overall outcome would be settled. Conspicuous among the Macedonians for recklessness and daring were the noble youths Hegesimachus and Nicanor, who were spurred by their side's unending successes to scorn every peril. With naught but their lances for weapons, they led the most eager youths in swimming out to an island held by a throng of foes and thereupon slew many of the Indians, though armoured by nothing better than their audacity. They might have quit the scene with glory, if successful rashness were capable of showing discretion. But while they lingered with disdain, not to mention arrogance, to meet any who might come against them, they were encircled by Indians who covertly swam behind them and they fell beneath a hail of long-range missiles. Those who managed to elude the enemy were either swept away by the force of the current or engulfed by whirlpools. This clash greatly bolstered the confidence of Porus, who watched the whole thing from the riverbank.

10.51 In frustration, ***Alexander*** eventually ***devised*** such ***a stratagem*** as ***to fool his foe. There was an island in midstream*** that was more substantial than the rest. Being wooded, it was ideal for concealing a covert attack. Furthermore, not far back from the bank he held, there was a ditch of great depth, wherein not just infantry but also cavalrymen and their mounts might be hidden. Therefore, ***in order to avert his enemy's gaze from guarding this propitious place, he ordered*** Ptolemy with his entire troop of ***cavalry to ride to a point far downstream from the island and there to panic the Indians by raising a clamour and even to canter into the shallows, as though they were about to swim across the river.***[35] ***For many days*** Ptolemy's ***cavalry squadrons repeated these manoeuvres at various spots, and by this tactic Porus was driven to array his forces against the zone from which the feints were made. Hence the enemy's watch upon the island lapsed and Alexander further directed that his pavilion be erected on a part of the bank downstream from it. His personal squadron stood guard before it and all the royal paraphernalia were conspicuously flaunted before the eyes of the enemy.*** Attalus scarcely differed from Alexander in age, build and general appearance - at least when seen from a distance - so he was robed in the royal chlamys[36] and accoutrements and ordered repeatedly

---

[35] Their presence in Frontinus, *Strategemata* 1.4.9 & 1.4.9a tends to confirm that the cavalry manoeuvres and the island were in the Vulgate and therefore were very probably described by Cleitarchus.

[36] A Greek cloak of medium length.

to make excursions to the edge of the river with his retinue during daylight hours. *Thereby the king sought to convey the impression that he himself was directing operations from that spot and was not organising a crossing.*

10.52 *Now Alexander received word that Abisares was* encamped *just four hundred stades away* with his army, *so he determined to attack Porus forthwith, before his* potential *ally could unite with him.* **When darkness fell, the king assembled a select force of infantry and cavalry *and bade them follow him for 150 stades to a wild and wooded area* opposite the island, *having ordered Craterus to take the main army across the river as soon as he saw that Alexander's task force had occupied the far bank.*[37]** Alexander was at first delayed but then assisted in putting his scheme into effect by the occurrence of a storm, for Fortune even turned troubles to his advantage. As *he made ready to cross over to the island with the rest of his task force, whilst the enemy's attention was focussed on the riverbank downstream where* Ptolemy and *his cavalry had been manoeuvring,* there poured forth such tempestuous rains as were barely tolerable beneath shelter. Swamped by the downpour, the soldiers fled back onshore in panic, forsaking their boats and rafts. Yet the wailing of the wind masked the uproar of their tumult, so their foes could not hear them.

10.53 Then in a trice the rain ceased, yet such dense clouds blanketed the heavens as to block all their light, so that those who spoke together could not discern each other's faces. Such a night of blacked-out heavens would have unnerved any other commander, when he sailed upon an unfamiliar river and his enemies might have chanced to occupy the shore to which his blind and reckless course was directed. But **the king** reckoned on evoking glory from peril and deemed that the darkness that disconcerted the rest was his opportunity. Thus he **gave the signal for his forces to embark upon the rafts, which were fashioned from inflated hides with wooden decking,** and ordered that his own vessel should be launched first. *The bank for which they were making was empty of the enemy, since Porus' attentions were still fixated upon the zone where the cavalry* under Ptolemy *had made feints.* Therefore, apart from a single ship that was struck by a wave and stuck upon a rock, all the vessels got across unscathed. *On the far side Alexander ordered his soldiers* to take up their arms, then he deployed them for action and began *to advance upon the enemy.*

10.54 And now Alexander's forces were arrayed in a winged formation with himself at their head, whereupon **it was announced to Porus that armed men had occupied his own bank of the river** and that a crisis was impending. *Initially,* through that flaw in human psychology that entertains false hopes, *he*

---

[37] The distance of 150 stades (~27km) between the main camp and the island is given in Metz Epitome 59, but Arrian, *Anabasis* 5.11.2, precisely confirms it.

ventured to believe that Abisares was coming as his ally, as had indeed been agreed. But soon *enough,* as the dawning light of day unveiled his foe's formations, **he deployed *100 four-horse* chariots *and 4000 cavalry* against the oncoming ranks.** Those contingents that he sent forward were commanded by his brother, Hages[38], with the greatest threat being posed by the chariots, each having a complement of six men. Two of these bore shields and a second pair were archers, stationed on either side of the vehicle. The others were the charioteers, though not disarmed by their duties; for in close combat they would lay aside the reins and fling showers of javelins upon their enemies. However, on that particular day these squadrons were rendered virtually impotent, since the extraordinary cloudbursts of the preceding evening had left the fields slimy and impracticable for horse-drawn vehicles. The weighty and sluggish chariots became bogged down in the mud and the marshy patches. Conversely, Alexander with his wieldy and light-armed lines charged them with verve. The Scythians and the Dahae were the first to engage the Indians.[39] Then **Alexander unleashed** Perdiccas with **his cavalry against** the right wing of **the enemy.**

10.55 Now battle was joined right across the front, and those who drove the chariots began as the last recourse for their side to swerve their vehicles with unbridled speed into the midst of the mêlée. This was a two-edged blow that fell on both sides. Whilst the Macedonian foot were trampled in the collisions, the chariots in hurtling forward over slippery and uneven ground ejected those who directed them. In other cases the maddened steeds yanked their vehicles not just into the quagmires and the swamps but even into the river itself. A few, goaded by the missiles of their foes, plunged back through their own ranks as far as Porus, who was energetically invigorating *his men in* the fighting. *But* **soon all the chariots were out of action.**

10.56 *Craterus, who had been left in command at the Macedonian camp, saw that Alexander had crossed and was advancing upon the Indians. Therefore he conveyed his forces across the river on rafts and ships, of which he had a great fleet.* Porus, *perceiving that he was unexpectedly confronted by two armies* and seeing his chariots wandering driverless over the entire front*, determined to engage Alexander at close quarters. Hence he distributed his elephants* among those of his courtiers who were nearest to him. *Then, deploying his cavalry to either flank, he* spaced the monstrous beasts *between them* in a single rank at fifty-foot intervals*, so as to strike fear into his foes.* Himself he stationed with the leading elephant on his left wing. **His infantry were posted** *behind the elephants and* in the

---

[38] There appears to exist no manuscript authority in the Vulgate for Anspach's emendation of the name to Spitaces the Nomarch, who dies at the Hydaspes in Arrian, *Anabasis* 5.18.2, though Pittacus in Polyaenus 4.3.21 tries to ambush Alexander's advance for Porus and is his nephew.

[39] These were probably mounted archers (*hippotoxotae*), cf. Arrian, *Anabasis* 5.14.3.

intervening gaps *with the task of supporting them and impeding javelin attacks upon their flanks.* The archers were interspersed with the foot and so were the usual drummers; whose tattoos serve the Indians as substitute for the blaring of buglers; neither did this din bother the elephants, whose ears had long since been inured to the sound. An effigy of Heracles was borne before the ranks of the infantry, which was a sharp spur to these warriors: to forsake its bearers was a martial disgrace and death had been decreed for failure to fetch it back from the field of battle; for fear of this former foe had been sublimated into religious veneration.[40]

10.57 *For a little while the Macedonians were awed into halting not just by the monstrous beasts but also by the spectacle of their ruler. For* **the array of elephants resembled the towers and the troops between them the curtain walls of a fortified city,** *whilst Porus himself seemed almost superhuman, so great was his stature. And this impression was reinforced by the fact that* **the elephant Porus rode loomed over the rest of the herd by as much as he towered above his men.**

10.58 Surveying the Indian king and his forces, Alexander declared: "At last I behold a trial worthy of my spirit, since I am up against both monstrous beasts and warriors of prowess." He stationed his cavalry *with himself* on his right wing, *the rightmost* half of them being angled forward. He deployed his phalanx and the light infantry on his left with some *at the extreme left* bent away from the enemy. Gazing intently at Coenus, the king said: "When I, supported by Ptolemy, Perdiccas and Hephaistion, have charged against the enemy's left wing, and you see me embroiled in the midst of the fighting, yourself edge to the right, then bear down upon the enemy where they are in turmoil. Thereupon, you, Antigenes, and you, Leonnatus and Tauron will advance against the centre and engage their front. The length and strength of our sarissas will never prove more effective than against these monstrous beasts and their drivers: topple the riders and stab their steeds! The elephant is a two-edged type of weapon in warfare, which slashes more sharply against its own side; for it is goaded against the enemy by command, but against its own ranks by panic."[41]

10.59 This speech having been spoken, Alexander was the first to spur his mount and he led the cavalry hard to his right hoping to outflank the enemy's left wing. Porus moved to intercept him, but his beasts broke formation at many points, since Alexander's manoeuvre was unforeseen. When, as planned, Alexander drove into the ranks of the enemy, Coenus charged with great impetus into the Indian left wing, where gaps had emerged in their line. The phalanx *under Antigenes and the others* also broke through the Indian centre at their

---

[40] Possibly Heracles was equated with the Sanskrit term Heri-cul-eesh, meaning the Lord of the clan of Hari, i.e. Vishnu alias Krishna, or some such syncretism.

[41] Coenus, Ptolemy, Perdiccas & Hephaistion commanded cavalry, whilst Antigenes, Leonnatus and Tauron led the infantry; cf. Arrian, *Anabasis* 5.16.3 naming Seleucus instead of Leonnatus.

first onslaught. And indeed Porus ordered that the elephants should be goaded against Alexander's cavalry, when he realised where they were attacking, but such was the sluggishness and relative immobility of these animals that they could not match the speed of the cavalry manoeuvres.

10.60 Neither were even their arrows of any use to the barbarians. Since they were long and ponderous, unless the foot of the bow were braced against the ground, they could not be properly fitted and nor could the bow be readily drawn. As the soil was slimy, it hampered bow-bracing, so that whilst struggling to shoot they were overrun by their impetuous opponents.[42] Therefore the Indians spurned the orders of their ruler, as tends to happen, when fear begins to supplant leadership by issuing sharper commands to those in turmoil. And so there were as many generals as there were stray clusters of warriors: one voice would bid them to reform the line, another to dissolve it; some urged them to stand fast and others to ride around to the rear of their opponents. They lacked any cohesion. Meanwhile Alexander had virtually succeeded in bringing his cavalry against their rear.

10.61 *On observing his formations disintegrating into disorder* under the **Macedonian onslaught, Porus** *with a few of his men, whose honour conquered their fear,* **rallied his scattered soldiers and gathered about forty of his elephants that were still manageable. Instructing that these elephants be arrayed ahead of his massed troops and himself mounted upon the largest of the beasts, the Indian king led these combined forces against his foes. The monstrous brutes were trained to employ their size and strength to best advantage, so they instilled great fear and inflicted many casualties.** *Their strident trumpeting not only panicked the horses, which are naturally nervous of everything, but even threw the Macedonian warriors and their formations into turmoil.*

10.62 *Victors but a little while before, the Macedonians were now looking around for escape routes, whilst against the elephants Alexander unleashed his light-armed Agrianians and Thracians, since they were better at hit and run tactics than his close combat troops. These fighters cast great showers of missiles against both the beasts and their mahouts. Their* **javelins began to pierce the hide on the elephants' flanks, racking them with pain. And the Macedonians were coping manfully with the menacing crisis, as** *the contingents brought by Craterus entered the field so that* **the phalanx began relentlessly and tellingly to bring their sarissas to bear upon the maddened monsters and the Indians stationed beside them, evening out the contest.** *But some were so zealous in stalking the beasts, that they rounded upon them, incensed by their wounds. The*

---

[42] That the foot of an Indian bow was rested on the ground is confirmed by numismatic evidence; especially the Porus medallions of tetradrachm weight with the elephant & archer design.

elephants stomped their tormentors underfoot, so that they perished with

Figure 10.3. The phalanx attacks at the Hydaspes (André Castaigne, 1899)

their bones crushed and even their armour crumpled. **Many Macedonians were impaled upon the tusks and rapidly expired, being skewered right through their bodies.** It was an especially awful spectacle when they grabbed men and armour in their trunks and lifted them over the heads of their mahouts, then dashed them upon the ground, where they died a dire death. These horrifying examples served to teach the rest the merits of a more cautious approach.

10.63 Thus the tide of battle ebbed and flowed: now chasing the elephants, then being chased by them. And the protracted conflict remained indecisive until late in the day, when at last they began to hack off the beasts' feet with axes, such implements having been readied in advance. With the softly curving blades of kopis swords they slashed at the trunks of the monsters.[43] Fear familiarised them with novel types of torment, not only in meeting but also in meting out death.

10.64 Therefore the elephants, *overwrought by their injuries,* could no longer be curbed by their drivers, but veered about and careered into their own ranks, trampling friendly warriors. *And their mahouts too were flung to the ground and mangled underfoot. Hence like livestock, more panicked than aggressive, they were herded off the battlefield. But* Porus, *though forsaken by most of the other elephants, began to hurl spears from his copious cache upon those foes that now swarmed around his own beast. He* cast his javelins so forcefully, that they were scarcely less lethal than the bolts from the mechanical catapults. The Macedonians who were confronting Porus were astounded by his heroic defiance, but Alexander summoned his hippotoxotae and other light-armed troops, ordering them to concentrate a barrage of projectiles upon the Indian king.[44] *Despite wounding many at a distance,* Porus *himself* presented a substantial target to strikes from every direction, so few missiles missed.

10.65 By now **he** had **suffered** nine **wounds,** some to the chest and others to the back. **They bled profusely** and the javelins rather fell than were propelled from his enfeebled grasp. Though still uninjured, his own elephant had been incited to frenzy and charged into the Macedonian ranks with undiminished verve, up to the point at which the mahout noticed that his king had gone limp and had dropped his weapons, being barely conscious. Thereupon, he wheeled the monstrous beast into rapid flight with Alexander in close pursuit. But *Bucephalus, the king's steed, having been gored by many gashes, was on his last legs and collapsed from under Alexander, gently setting him upon the ground rather than throwing him.* Consequently the chase was briefly delayed whilst his attendants rushed to the king's aid and he swapped to another mount.

---

[43] A *kopis* is a single-edged Greek hacking sword, more commonly known as a falcata.

[44] *Hippotoxotae* = mounted archers (probably Scythians and Dahae).

10.66 Meanwhile, the brother of Taxiles, the Indian king, having been sent forward by Alexander, began to counsel Porus not to persist with his last stand and to give himself up to the victor. But he, though **his strength had been sapped with loss of blood,** was roused by the familiar voice to retort: "I know well that you are the brother of Taxiles, the betrayer of his sovereignty and his throne." It chanced that there was just one javelin he had not yet relinquished, which he now flung at Alexander's emissary, piercing the middle of his chest and emerging from his back. After executing this last deed of bravado, Porus accelerated his flight. But his elephant too had now received many missile strikes and was faltering. Therefore he ceased to retire and arrayed his foot soldiers against the posse of his foes.

10.67 By now the king had caught up with Porus and, recognising his stubbornness, Alexander forbade that any who fought on should be spared. Therefore flights of missiles hurled at both the Indian infantry and their monarch converged upon them from every direction. Hence **Porus finally slumped over and began to topple from his monstrous beast.** The Indian who directed the elephant supposed him to be dismounting and set the beast to crouching down on its knees in the usual fashion. *Then, not wishing to delay the surrender, he held his hands high asking for his life.*[45] When the king's elephant bowed down, the other beasts followed its example, in accordance with their training, and settled down upon the ground. By this deed both Porus and the others *still with him* were delivered up to the victors. Believing that Porus had perished, Alexander ordered that his body should be stripped of its appurtenances, and men were hurrying over to remove his cuirass and robe, when the elephant began to stand guard over him and to menace the despoilers, lifting his body and setting him back upon its back. Therefore the beast was overwhelmed by a hail of missiles from every quarter and, when it had been slaughtered, Porus was laid in a chariot.

10.68 *Word now spread that Porus was dead, so the Indians fled. Many were being slain in the rout, but then Alexander, being satisfied by his outright victory in the battle, ordered that the bugles should sound the recall.* **Over twelve thousand of the Indians had fallen,** *including the two sons of Porus and his generals and his most illustrious commanders.* **More than nine thousand Indians** *with their beasts of burden* **and eighty of the elephants were captured alive. The Macedonian losses were two hundred and eighty cavalry plus over seven hundred infantry** *and a multitude of them were wounded.* **In the aftermath Alexander instructed that the dead be given burial according to the customary rites:** *both his own men and the most valiant of his foes.*

---

[45] This phrase follows a lacuna in Metz Epitome 60, where it is unclear who performs this action.

Figure 10.4. Alexander receives the surrender of Porus (Charles Le Brun, 1673).

10.69 When Alexander saw Porus lift his eyelids, roused to pity rather than hatred, he enquired: "What awful folly was it that drove you to try the fortunes of war, in full knowledge of the fame of my deeds, when Taxiles was at hand as an example of my clemency to those who place themselves beneath my sway?" And Porus responded: "Since you ask, I shall reply with the same candour with which you have posed your question. I had considered that nobody stronger than I existed. Though I knew my own power, I had not yet tested yours. The outcome of the conflict attests that you are the stronger. But I am not too unhappy to be second to such as you!" **When Porus was** further **asked how he believed that the victor should treat him, he responded: "As advised by your conscience as a king** this day, on which you have witnessed the frailty of fair fortune." **Alexander promised that he would do so.** Indeed, Porus profited more by his cautionary advice, than if he had resorted to pleas, for the greatness of his spirit, neither cowed nor shattered by misfortune, moved Alexander to respond not merely with compassion, but even with respect.

10.70 The king had Porus' injuries cared for *just as if he had fought on his own side*, turning him over to the Indians for medical attention. When, against the expectations of everyone, he recovered, Alexander ranked him among the number of his Friends and not only restored his kingdom to him, but also thereafter extended his domains across adjoining territories. Truly, there was no more enduring and steadfast trait of Alexander's character than his admiration for genuine merit and glorious deeds. Yet he was more candid in his assessment of excellence in his opponents than in his countrymen, for he believed a fellow citizen might overshadow his own greatness, whereas it would beam forth more brightly, the greater were those whom he conquered.

10.71 *Also in that year, thinking Alexander safely distant in India,* a Mede called Baryaxes launched a rebellion back in Persia together with certain associates. **Although their tiara may be worn by any of the Persians, he ventured to wear it upright, which is the prerogative of their monarch** and indeed he styled himself King of the Persians and Medes. He was arrested by Atropates, Satrap of Media, and later delivered up to Alexander, who had him and his associates executed.[46]

10.72*These were the concerns of Alexander* in the tenth year of his reign.

---

[46] Cf. Arrian, *Anabasis* 6.29.3.

4. Book 11: July 326BC – May 325BC

Eastwards Through India, The Mutiny On The Hyphasis And The River Voyage To The Siege Of The Oxydracae

KEY
<u>**Underlined bold text for attributed Fragments of Cleitarchus**</u>
Bold text where there is overwhelming evidence
Bold italic text where there exists direct-firm evidence
Normal text where direct-weak evidence applies
Italic text where the evidence is conjectural
Grey text for connecting passages, if Cleitarchus' version is indeterminate

11.1 *As the eleventh year of his reign began,* **Alexander** was elated by his remarkable victory over Porus, which he considered to have laid open the uttermost east to his advance, so he **slaughtered various sacrificial animals as a dedication to the Sun, *in return for its gift of the Orient for his taking.*** Then he convened an Assembly of his troops in order to set their spirits upon the continued prosecution of his campaigns. After lauding their prowess, he asserted that any will possessed by the Indians to resist them had been broken in the recent struggle. The rest of the campaign would be fine plunder, since the prodigious opulence of the region towards which they were headed was universally famed. In comparison, the booty from Persia was mean and tawdry. There would be enough gems and pearls and gold and ivory not merely to cram their own houses, but to sate all Macedonia and Greece too. The soldiers were greedy for both riches and glorious deeds and neither had any prospect presented by Alexander failed to live up to his promises, so they dedicated themselves to the venture *en masse*, and were all buoyed up by great expectations, when the Assembly was dispersed.

11.2 Alexander intended to advance to the ends of India, so as to bring all the peoples of Asia beneath his rule, but afterwards he planned to sail downstream to reach the Ocean at the edge of the world. *He thought to voyage thence to the Red Sea and onward even as far as the Atlantic.* **To this end he commanded that a fleet of many vessels should be constructed on the river. This was facilitated by a plentiful supply of timber in the nearby mountains, including stately firs, abundant cedar**

and pine and other sorts of wood well suited for shipbuilding. *The first vessel was finished in just thirty-three days.*

11.3 In the course of felling the timber, the men encountered various curiosities among the mountain forests. There were innumerable serpents of exceptional length, some extending to sixteen cubits.[1] They also saw a great beast distinguished by a single horn protruding from its nose, which they consequently named "rhinoceros", but the Indians know it by a different name, though it is rare elsewhere in India.[2]

11.4 Also in these mountains the Macedonians found many species of monkey in a range of sizes. In one instance Alexander and his men suddenly came across a huge troop of the larger type confronting them and crowded into an array upon a group of bare eminences. The apes happened also to be standing erect when first seen, thereby conveying an impression of an army waiting in ambush. Therefore Alexander ordered his soldiers to prepare to defend themselves, but Taxiles was then with the king and was able to reassure him that these animals presented no real threat.

11.5 The Indians dispense with the use of nets or scent-tracking hounds in the hunting and snaring of these apes, *asserting that the beasts themselves have taught how they may be caught. They cannot readily be captured by brute force, due to their combination of brawn and wit, but they habitually mimic the antics of mankind. Thus,* if he should see a person dance, then the ape becomes a dancing animal, and he would play the flute too, if anyone were to teach him to blow it. Therefore in plain view of their quarry, which watches from its refuge among the boughs, the ape-hunters dab honey on their lower eyelids. They put on sandals and bind them around their ankles, and they hang hand-mirrors from thongs about their necks and admire their reflections. Afterwards they move well away having covertly swapped birdlime for the honey, having anchored the sandals by means of both weights and fastenings and having substituted a rugged slip-noose for the thong of the mirror. Then the ape fails to resist its urge to imitate the actions of its stalkers and thereby incapacitates itself, for its eyes become glued, its feet are held fast and its whole body becomes tightly leashed as it gazes in the mirror. Being thereby reduced to a helpless state, its capture is made easy.

11.6 Alexander now exploited a plentiful supply of labour by speedily founding two cities, the first sited on the western bank of the River Hydaspes opposite the island, where he had crossed with his troops in launching his attack on Porus; the other on the eastern bank at the field

---

[1] Probably pythons.

[2] This is the Indian Rhinoceros (a.k.a. Great One-Horned Rhinoceros), which is now an endangered species: it does indeed dwell among the southern foothills of the Himalayas.

of battle. He also rewarded those of his men who had performed well in this engagement. He presented a crown of gold and also a thousand gold coins to each of his commanders, and to all the rest he gave honourable gifts in proportion to their status in his entourage or to the merit of their services.[3]

11.7 *Alexander rested his army on the eastern side of the Hydaspes for thirty days, since supplies were plentiful in the kingdom of Porus.* By this time to the surprise of everyone **Porus himself had recovered from his many wounds,** *so the king commanded that he be brought before him. When he came, Alexander invited him to accompany him, when he set out for his own land. Porus replied: "O great Alexander, I would be willing to put aside half of my life in order to see your homeland, except that you cannot persuade me to appear as a captive before your countrymen. I have no desire to continue to defy death. If you wish to take me away to serve as an exhibit, then you can carry me off as a corpse." Hence Alexander assured him that nothing would be done against his will. Furthermore, in recognition of his virtuous excellence,* the king enrolled him in the fellowship of his Friends and **reinstated him as ruler of his former domains.** Indeed, Alexander subsequently extended Porus' realm quite considerably.

11.8 At this time Alexander received fresh envoys from Abisares, the king of the neighbouring realm, *who had had been allied with Porus, yet had also previously sent a delegation to treat with Alexander and indeed Porus had received no reinforcements from him.* Now he promised to do anything that Alexander might command, excepting only that he refused to appear before the king in person, *for he could not bear to risk the loss of his royal power or liberty.* Alexander sent back a threat, that If Abisares should persist in his reluctance to manifest himself, then he would undertake to visit Abisares *together with his army.* This resulted in the capitulation of Abisares.

11.9 Then Alexander led his army eastwards and, after crossing the river in Porus' realm,[4] he penetrated into *the heart of India through* a territory of exceptional fecundity. It was shaded by *vast forests of seemingly limitless extent and comprising* weird trees that reached a height of seventy cubits. The girth of their trunks could barely be encompassed by a ring of four men with arms outstretched and they spread to shade an area of three plethra. *Most of their branches dipped down into the soil, then reared up again from the earth, so that the impression was not of boughs, but rather of a tree risen up on its own roots.[5] The air was*

---

[3] It has been suggested by Frank Holt (AtG & the Mystery of the Elephant Medallions, p.148) that this was the occasion of the issue of Alexander's Porus Medallions (see front cover image).

[4] Perhaps the Acesines.

[5] The banyan tree (1 plethron is an area of 30m square, i.e. 900m²).

temperate and salubrious, for the forest canopy filtered the intense sunlight and streams gushed forth from a profusion of springs.

11.10 In this region they again encountered a multiplicity of snakes, but quite distinctive from those seen in the mountains, being far shorter in length and having brightly coloured skin of many hues, as though their scales had been daubed with dyes. Some of them resembled bronze wands decorated in bands all the way from head to tail, whilst others were silver-tinged and still others were ringed with red.[6] A few even glinted with a golden sheen. The worst of them displayed broad hoods.[7] Their bites were most deadly and mortality was swift. The victims were wracked with agony and exuded bloody perspiration. The Macedonians were greatly plagued by snake attacks, so they resorted to slinging hammocks between trees and maintaining vigilance throughout the night. Eventually, however, they learnt from the local people of the curative usage of a plant root, which *functioned as an antitoxin and relieved them from incessant anxiety.*

11.11 *As Alexander marched on, he received intelligence that another king named Porus, who was cousin to him he had already subdued, had forsaken his realm and sought the protection of the people of Gandara. This so incensed Alexander that he delegated Hephaistion to lead an army into his territory with the objective of transferring those lands into the governorship of the Porus who had become his ally.*

11.12 Proceeding onwards through stretches of desert, they arrived at the River Hiarotis,[8] which was fringed by water meadows and woodland glades with shady trees of a type that they had not seen elsewhere and the clearings were crowded with peacocks. Having moved his camp beyond the river, ***Alexander campaigned against the local people who were called the Adrestians, and gained control of their towns, sometimes through force of arms, but often through negotiation.*** He surrounded and besieged their city[9] not far from the Hiarotis, inducing the surrender of the inhabitants, and afterwards imposing tribute payments and seizing hostages.

11.13 Next he entered the country of the Cathaeans, who are notable for their custom that the wives are cremated together with their husbands, if the latter should die.[10] This law had been enacted following an incident in

---

[6] Perhaps kraits and coral snakes.

[7] Cobras.

[8] Hydraotis in Arrian, the modern Ravi.

[9] Probably Pimprama.

[10] Suttee – Cleitarchus is evidently following Onesicritus: cf. Strabo 15.1.30.

which a wife was found to have poisoned her husband, because she had fallen in love with a younger man.

11.14 Alexander advanced upon Sangala, **the largest and best-fortified city of the Cathaeans,** since it was defended by a marsh as well as its ramparts. The barbarians came forth to give battle in wagons that had been yoked together, casting javelins and brandishing pikes. They would vault athletically from vehicle to vehicle, whenever they needed to reinforce their compatriots. Initially, these alien tactics intimidated the Macedonians, since they were taking casualties at long range, but soon they learnt to scorn such cumbersome conveyances and hemmed them in from either side, slaying any who fought back. Alexander ordered that the lashings that linked the wagons should be slashed, in order that they might be encircled and picked off individually. Hence the Cathaeans suffered 8000 casualties and the survivors scuttled back into their city. But the very next day its walls were taken in an assault with scaling-ladders propped simultaneously against every stretch, and so *the city was sacked and razed to the ground.*

11.15 A few rescued themselves by their quick reactions, and, on realising that their city had been obliterated, waded through the swamp and petrified all the settlements in the vicinity by avowing that an invincible host, undoubtedly composed of divine beings, had come among them *to wreak havoc.* In consequence, the Indians spread an adverse report that Alexander's forces fought savagely and viciously. On receiving word of this, Alexander began to look for opportunities to moderate his reputation with the native peoples. Nevertheless, the king sent forth Perdiccas with a mobile task force to ravage the surrounding territory, though he also assigned a detachment of his troops to Eumenes with the mission of persuading the barbarians to submit.

11.16 *Alexander himself led the deployment of the rest of his army to invest a well-fortified city,* whither the inhabitants of other towns had fled to seek refuge. The citizens sent a delegation to plead with the king, though without slackening their preparations for resistance. For a dispute had broken out, which had split the populace into two factions: one party deemed any alternative preferable to surrender, whilst the other believed that they could not defend themselves effectively. Neither did it prove possible for them to reconcile their conflicting views, but instead the party advocating surrender opened the gates to admit their enemy. Although Alexander could reasonably have punished the members of the faction that had wished to fight him, he chose rather to pardon everyone and to arrange a treaty, under the terms of which *he received hostages from them.*

11.17 *Then the king moved his camp to the next* hostile *city,* which was large and populous. *As the army advanced towards its walls, the hostages,* who included old men, women and children, *were sent forward ahead of the phalanx.* From their ramparts *the defenders recognised that the hostages were members of their own tribe,* so they invited them to parley and learnt of

Alexander's leniency, and of his invincibility too! Interpreting also the release of the hostages as conciliatory behaviour, **the populace** *opened their gates to the king and* welcomed him by waving suppliant branches, *so he aborted his assault. Afterwards, news of Alexander's clemency quickly spread throughout the region, such that the rest of its cities were readily induced to place themselves under his protection as well.*

11.18 Alexander next moved against the cities that were governed by Sopeithes. **His realm has the reputation** among the Indians **of being wisely ruled in accordance with high moral principles. In particular, the administration directs its policies towards the acquisition of moral eminence and physical perfection is esteemed above all else.** *For example,* from the moment of their birth the fate of their children is *relinquished by their parents and* consigned to the discretion of examiners, who determine the physical condition of the infants. Those who are handsome, healthy and vigorous, they select for rearing, but any who are crippled or who exhibit any conspicuous bodily defect, they subject to infanticide, considering them unworthy of raising. *Furthermore,* they arrange their marriages without consideration of dowries or the wealth and prestige of their families, but rather with the objective of breeding beautiful and athletic children from especially comely couples. *By virtue of such practices most of the denizens of these cities rejoice in a prevalent sense of their superiority among the Indians.*

11.19 *Alexander arrayed his army before the town occupied by Sopeithes himself, since its gates were closed against him. Observing that its walls and towers appeared deserted, the Macedonians supposed either that its citizens had abandoned the place or else that they lay in hiding to take them by surprise. But suddenly a portal was flung wide and the Indian king emerged, flanked by his two adult sons.* He was a paragon of physical attractiveness *and further surpassed his countrymen in height, being over four cubits tall. His raiment, which draped his entire body down to his ankles, was embellished with gold and purple and he was shod with bejewelled and gilded sandals. Pearls adorned his arms from wrist to shoulder and huge gemstones of dazzling lustre dangled from his ears. His golden sceptre, which was garnished with beryl, he yielded to Alexander with an invocation that good fortune should attend its transfer. Thereby* he surrendered himself, *his offspring* and his kingdom*, but through the benevolence of his conqueror he was immediately reinstated in his former rank and responsibilities. With corresponding beneficence, Sopeithes entertained Alexander's entire force royally for some days.*

11.20 Alexander was pleased to receive numerous grand gifts from Sopeithes, including 150 large hunting dogs of a *famously* valiant and relentless breed. *They are reputed also to refrain from barking when they sight their quarry and they are especially aggressive towards lions.*

Sopeithes was keen to demonstrate their strength and quality to Alexander, so he had a full-grown lion brought into a ring-fenced arena and set two of the least impressive dogs upon it. As the lion began to prevail over this pair, Sopeithes released two more of the hounds into the fray. Now *the advantage was shifted in favour of the dogs and* the lion showed signs of succumbing, so Sopeithes sent in an expert handler *who sought to restore the evenness of the match* **by yanking a dog off the lion by its right leg. But the animal refused to release its jaws from its opponent, so** the handler hacked away its leg with a curved knife. Alexander protested vociferously at this, and his guards rushed forward to stay the hand of the Indian, but Sopeithes *craved Alexander's indulgence,* promising three fine replacements for the maimed beast, which still would not relax its grip on the lion. *Hence the handler resumed his attack, slicing elsewhere at the dog, and, when it yet kept its teeth clenched upon its foe, slashing indiscriminately* until it fainted and died from loss of blood athwart the lion without having uttered the merest yelp or whimper *for fear of lessening its hold.* Such is the passion for the chase that Nature is reputed to have cultivated in these beasts.[11]

11.21 *The king enquired as to the secret of the tenacious bravery of these dogs. Sopeithes replied that* it was rumoured that they had inherited a strain of tiger blood, *for in that region this animal is most extraordinarily fierce and powerful with a great turn of speed. It gets its name from its swiftness, for the Persians call an arrow "tigris". On the same basis the River Tigris derives its name from having the most rapid of all currents. It was the custom to truss the bitches, which were forbears of these dogs, and to leave them out overnight in the woods, such that some of them were slain by the tigers, whilst others were impregnated.*[12] *From the offspring of these matings,* **a most exceptionally fierce breed of dog was spawned, as had been demonstrated.**

11.22 At this time Hephaistion brought his army into camp to recombine with Alexander's forces, having *successfully* fulfilled his mission by subduing another **great** region of India, *including the lands of the rebel Porus,* **by force of arms. Alexander was pleased to commend him on his victories.**

11.23 Leaving Sopeithes in control of his realm, Alexander marched his forces on to the River Hyphasis. Phegeus, the king of that region, *had commanded his subjects to carry on working in their fields as normal when the Macedonians arrived, so* the inhabitants greeted their *actual* appearance with alacrity. Phegeus himself came to welcome Alexander

---

[11] Curtius thought this might be a shaggy dog story, but Pit Bull Terriers exhibit similar reluctance to unclamp their jaws from their victims, so it may be an injustice that this story has been used to impugn the probity of Onesicritus, its probable ultimate source (cf. Strabo 15.1.31).

[12] Cf. Isidore of Seville, *Etymologiae* 12.2.28.

with numerous presents and placed himself under the king's authority. Consequently, Alexander endorsed the governance of this nation by Phegeus, who generously entertained the Macedonians as his guests for two whole days. On the third day Alexander planned to cross the River Hyphasis *near the citadel of Altusacra,* although it was a great barrier, being seven stades wide, six fathoms deep *and strewn with rocks* with a treacherous current *flowing between them.*

11.24 Accordingly, the king sought information from Phegeus regarding the territory beyond the far bank of the river. Phegeus confided that a journey of twelve days through desert wastes would bring Alexander before a still greater river, which was 32 stades in breadth and deeper than any other stream in India. It was called the Ganges and beyond it lay the lands of the Prasii and the Gangaridae, whose king was Xandrames. He had barricaded the highways with an army comprising 20,000 cavalry, 200,000 infantry, 2000 chariots and, so Phegeus believed, up to 4000 elephants caparisoned for war, *the latter constituting a particular source of dread for the Macedonians.* Alexander was dubious of the accuracy of these figures, so he sent for Porus, *who was near at hand,* and asked whether he could confirm their validity. Porus firmly endorsed the information on the numerical strength of Xandrames' forces, but he disparaged their ruler as a lowly and mediocre serf. For he was said to be the son of a barber, who had barely scraped a living through this trade, but had traded more profitably with his good looks by seducing the queen. *She had promoted him into a close companionship with the king, her husband, whom he had proceeded foully to murder, seizing a regency of the kingdom on the pretext of protecting the succession of the dead king's offspring. But instead he had slaughtered the legitimate heirs and sired Xandrames, who was reviled and despised by his people on account of a disposition better suited to his father's humble origins than his royal status.*

11.25 *Alexander was troubled by Porus' corroboration on several counts. Although he felt only disdain for the enemy and his monstrous warbeasts,* he *nevertheless* realised that a campaign against the Gangaridae would be arduous, *for he especially feared* the defensive advantage afforded by *the terrain with its fast-flowing rivers. It would be a tough task to hunt down and extricate people who dwelt virtually at the edge of human existence. Conversely, his feverish thirst for glory and his ever-burning desire for fame would not allow him to brook any obstacle nor to consider anything beyond his reach.* Therefore he was not downhearted, for he had faith in the prowess of his troops, and he believed the promises of the oracles that had forecast his triumph. He recalled that the Delphic Pythia had dubbed him invincible and that Ammon had granted him the rule of the entire Earth.

11.26 *However, the king was also concerned about the willingness of his soldiers to advance further, for* he was well aware that they were showing signs of fatigue from the rigours of the campaign. They had endured nearly eight years of unremitting toil and peril. *Many had grown aged, whilst traversing vast tracts of the Earth in Alexander's service.* It would be vital to lift their morale with a rousing exhortation, if they were to be motivated to march against the Gangaridae. *Else he worried that they would rest content with the piles of plunder that they had already garnered instead of exhausting their lives in pursuit of ambitions no longer compatible with their own.*

11.27 *Whereas the king continued to covet the dominion of the world, his troops wished to settle down to enjoy the fruits of their endeavours as soon as practicable.* Many of their comrades were already dead, and no respite from *the toll of* warfare was on offer. The ceaseless trekking had ground thin the hooves of their steeds. Their weapons and panoplies had become dilapidated and not a thread survived of their original Greek vestments. They had resorted to adapting foreign clothing: for example, tailoring Indian garments to suit. Unfortunately too, this was the monsoon season of relentless rains, which had been drumming down for seventy days with the accompaniment of continual percussions of thunder and lightning.

11.28 Recognising all these impediments to the undertaking, Alexander realised that the only hope of fulfilling his aspirations would be specially to ingratiate himself with his troops. *Therefore he permitted them to forage through the land alongside the river, which was crammed with all kinds of bounty.* Whilst the soldiers were occupied with their pillage in the ensuing days, the king assembled their wives and sons. He awarded a monthly grant of provisions to the women and he announced a cadet bursary commensurate with the service records of their fathers for each of the youths. Then, when his veterans returned to camp sated with the spoils of their expedition, he called an Assembly and delivered a rousing oration concerning the campaign against the Gangaridae.

11.29 "Soldiers, I am well aware that worrying rumours have been spread about by the Indians in recent days with the aim of demoralising you. I know too that you are familiar with the tricks of such propagandists. For the Persians sought to deter us with grim accounts of the passes of Cilicia, the fields of Mesopotamia and the Tigris and Euphrates rivers, though we readily forded one and bridged the other. Reputations are invariably inflated: all such hearsay exceeds the truth. Even our renown, though founded on solid deeds, grows greater in the telling. Who, even now, would believe the tales of us tackling monstrous beasts arrayed like turreted ramparts in breaching the defences of the Hydaspes and all other such reports that embellish upon reality? By Heracles, we should long since have fled from Asia, if we could be intimidated by fables."

Figure 11.1. The Mutiny at the River Hyphasis (Antonio Tempesta, 1608).

11.30 "Are you so credulous as to believe in a hoard of elephants in India more numerous than the oxen of other *armies*, despite the rarity of these beasts and the difficulties presented by their capture and training? The same mendacity imbues the rumours of our opponent's strengths in cavalry and infantry. Consider too that wide rivers run smoothly, for it is the narrowing of their channels that induces torrential currents in order to balance their flow. And, besides, the true danger lurks at the further bank, where the enemy stalks us as we land our craft. Hence no matter what breadth of river confronts us, the risk does not alter, since it awaits our coming ashore. But suppose the rumours are true: need we allow the enormity of our enemy's war-beasts or his vast hosts to discourage us? Regarding elephants, we have witnessed their propensity to inflict more harm on their own side, when we hacked their gargantuan hides with our axes and kopis swords, whereupon they launched a frenzied charge back into their own ranks. What does it matter, whether they have as many as Porus or even 4000 such, when you know from recent experience that all will panic and flee, if but one or two be maimed? Furthermore, even small numbers of elephants can only be directed and coordinated awkwardly. If thousands were aggregated *in battle*, they would trample one another, being neither able to stand their ground nor to bolt. I myself had the use of these animals *after Arbela*, but, being contemptuous of their utility in warfare, I refrained from deploying them, knowing well that they would prove fratricidal."

11.31 "You may say that it is our enemy's myriads of horse and foot that saps your confidence. Should I suppose it your custom only to fight little battles, whereas now shall be your first experience of holding the line against an immense rabble? In fact the invincible robustness of the Macedonians in the face of hostile hosts is well-attested by the river of blood at the Granicus and the flood of Persian gore in Cilicia, and also by Arbela, whose fields are filled with the bones of those we routed. It is a bit late to begin to quantify the enemy's legions, when you have already emptied Asia through the destruction of your foes. The time to worry about the sparseness of our forces was when we first sailed across the Hellespont. Now Scythian warriors follow our lead, Bactrian auxiliaries campaign at our side and confederates from the Dahae and Sogdiani serve in our ranks. Yet I do not rest my faith in those throngs, but rather I place myself in your hands. In your valour lies the surety of my success. Grant me, therefore, your spirits filled with eager faith and, so long as you stand by me in the fight, I need count neither my allies nor my foes. We stand not at the outset of our endeavours, but rather at their culmination. We have reached the birthplace of the Sun and the Ocean. Provided dispiritedness does not hold us back, we shall win control of the ends of the Earth, before returning thence to our homeland as famous victors."

11.32 "Do not like lazy peasants let slip the ripe fruit through sloth, for the rewards exceed the risks, since the country is both prosperous and peaceable. Thus I lead you rather to riches than to glory. It is right and proper that you should salvage the pearls that are washed up on the shore of the Ocean and convey them to our homeland, for no opportunity *for profit* should elude you or be relinquished through timidity. For the sake of yourselves and your glory, which ascends beyond the ceiling of human achievement, and in the name of the favour I have shown to you and the matching favour you have shown for me, I implore you not to forsake your protégé and comrade (I will not mention king) as he approaches the boundary of human existence. All else I have commanded, but in this matter I shall place myself in your debt. It is I that asks this of you; I, who has always been at the forefront of any peril to which I have exposed you; I, who joins your battle line with interlocked shield. Do not snap the palm frond that I grasp in order, if Nemesis be assuaged, to emulate Heracles and Dionysus. O grant my entreaties and shatter your delinquent silence. Where's the clamour that signifies your enthusiasm? Where's that Macedonian countenance of old? I do not know you anymore, soldiers, nor perhaps do you know me. You closed your ears to me some while ago and I have sought in vain to inspire broken and cowering spirits."

11.33 Yet each Macedonian obstinately kept his peace and locked his gaze upon the soil at his feet, so Alexander continued: "Have I in some unsuspected manner wronged you, that you refuse even to look me in the face? It is as though I were alone in a wasteland. No one answers me, yet neither does anyone refuse me. With whom do I speak? What do I propose? It is your power and glory that I strive to defend. What has become of the men that erstwhile vied for the privilege of bearing the body of their wounded monarch? Now I am abandoned, forsaken and betrayed to the enemy. Nevertheless I shall march onwards all by myself. Consign me to the rivers, the monstrous beasts and those peoples whose very names make you quake. Though deserted by you, I shall find fresh followers. The Scythians and Bactrians will be with me. Though they were our foes but a little while ago, now they are my *loyal* soldiers. Glorious death is preferable to a mutinous command. Go and skulk back to your homes! Go glean what acclaim you can, having forsaken your king! For here I shall stay either to win the victory of which you despair or else to find a place to die with unblemished honour."

11.34 Even these words failed to coax any speech from the troops, who deferred to their senior commanders in the thankless matter of responding: their message being that, grown haggard through relentless toil and scarring wounds, they did not deny their duties, but were no longer capable of performing them. Yet their officers, being frozen with trepidation, still kept their gaze fixed upon the earth. Then an initially barely audible whisper spontaneously erupted to beset their ears with groans and sighs, as gradually their dolorous mood was openly expressed in floods of tears, which soon indeed dissolved the king's anger into a corresponding effusion of compassion. For Alexander himself, though he fought back against a wave of emotion, failed nevertheless to keep his eyes dry. At length, when **all at the Assembly were weeping** uncontrollably and despite his fellows persisting in hanging back, Coenus alone dared to approach the rostrum signalling his wish to be heard. As soon as the troops saw him doff his helmet, which is the custom when addressing the monarch, they petitioned him insistently to plead the army's cause with the king.

11.35 So Coenus began to speak: "Let the gods forfend that we should think rebellious thoughts, and surely they do forbid them. The sentiment of your soldiers is as it has always been: to go whither you command; to fight and to encroach upon danger *on your behalf*, to vaunt your name to posterity written in our blood. Hence, if you ultimately insist upon it, we shall still traipse after you wherever you may lead us, though we be disarmed, disrobed and bled white *from our many wounds*. But if you are prepared to listen to heartfelt truths, rent from your soldiers' mouths by force of circumstances, then lend a compassionate ear to those who have most diligently enacted your orders and respected your guidance and will forever do so, wherever you may go."

11.36 "My king, through the immensity of your deeds, you have not merely triumphed over the enemy, but over your own soldiers as well. Insofar as human beings could withstand the rigours, we have done your bidding. We have journeyed across lands and seas, such that their geography is better understood by us than by their inhabitants. Now we are convened virtually upon the far edge of the Earth. You are about to enter and explore a different world, another India that is mysterious even to the Indians. You will strive to extricate from their dens and lairs people who lurk among serpents and brute beasts, so that you may cleanse by your conquests more lands than the sun beams down upon.

It is an entirely fitting ambition for your exalted spirit, but it soars above ours. For your courage will expand indefinitely, but our strength is now almost spent. Just **examine our bodies,** which are bled white, **fissured with wounds and decayed by so many scars.** Many of us are grey-haired with barely enough lifespan left to get ourselves back to our homes, for, alone in your army, we Macedonians have served successively under both your father, Philip, and yourself. If any of us should die before our homecoming, then we beg only that you should return our remains to the tombs of our fathers."

11.37 *"Our weaponry is blunted and our armour is decrepit. We have sunk to adopting foreign ways and donning Persian attire,* having long been beyond the reach of supplies from our own country. How many of us still have a corselet or a steed? Let it be admitted how few of us retain their servants and how little is left to us of the booty from our campaigns. Though we are victors over all, we lack every comfort. Nor does the explanation for our destitution lie in profligacy, but rather it is warfare and the tools for warfare that have swallowed our wealth. So will you place this lovely army defenceless before monstrous beasts? Though the barbarians must deliberately have exaggerated the number of their elephants, their lies would not be plausible unless the true number were substantial. But if your intent to drive on deeper into India remains firm, consider that the southerly expanse of this continent is less vast and, when the intervening territory has been subdued, you may still run down to that great sea with which Nature has bounded human affairs. What's the point of stretching your luck by going the long way round, when a shorter southerly route to the Ocean lies open to you? Unless you would wish to wander for the sake of wandering, we have reached the point from which your best fortune leads you back."

11.38 "I have chosen to speak these truths to your face, rather than foment dissension behind your back. It is not my purpose to ingratiate myself with the army, but that you should hear the voice of those who *seriously* debate these matters, instead of the mere moans of grumblers." As Coenus concluded his oration a clamour arose in every quarter pierced with wails of lamentation: "O king", "O father", "O lord" yelled a cacophony of voices. Then, finally, Coenus' pleas were endorsed by the other commanders, especially the elderly for whom it was more respectable to ask to be relieved and whose views carried more weight.

11.39 *Alexander* could neither bring himself to rail against their intransigence nor to relax his own resentment at their stance. In a quandary, he leapt down from the rostrum, **ordered the royal quarters to be sealed and denied admission to all but his retinue of attendants. Two days were spent in ill temper, but on the third** the king emerged and issued orders that twelve altars of dressed stone, each fifty cubits high, should be erected *along the river* in honour of the twelve Olympian gods as a lasting memorial of this limit of his campaign. He further directed that the perimeter of their camp should be extended to thrice its original dimensions and that a ditch should encompass it, measuring fifty feet wide by forty deep, the earth being heaped up on its inner margin to form a formidable rampart. The infantry were required to construct huts containing pairs of bedsteads each five cubits in length; the cavalry, additionally, had to erect pairs of mangers at double their usual height *and even to scatter about bridles with bits of extraordinary weight, as if made for massive mounts.* Similarly, everything that they left in that place, *also including outsize shields and weaponry,* was scaled up in proportion. The king's purpose was to fabricate evidence for an encampment of heroes of giant stature and phenomenal strength as a wonder to deter the defiance of the native peoples and to amaze posterity.

11.40 *The men undertook the enlargement of the camp with alacrity. Then, after the conduct of propitious sacrifices,* the expedition retraced its steps and encamped in the vicinity of the River Acesines. There by the hand of fate Coenus fell sick and died. Though Alexander was grieved by his death, he could not resist commenting that Coenus had given a lengthy speech to gain but a short span of days *homeward bound,* as if *Alexander supposed* Coenus alone had wished to see Macedonia again! **Alexander found the fleet, which he had commissioned before marching eastwards, afloat in the river awaiting him.** *These ships he arranged to have fitted out for the voyage downstream, whilst he had still more vessels constructed.* At this juncture, reinforcements arrived in camp comprising allied and mercenary troops from Greece *and elsewhere* led by various commanders. *Memnon had brought* over 5000 cavalry *from Thrace, whilst Harpalus had dispatched 7000 of the infantry, who totalled over 30,000 men.* They had escorted a consignment of 25,000 splendid panoplies *inlaid with silver and gold* together with 100 talents of medicaments. Alexander distributed the supplies and the armour to the soldiers, *ordering that their worn-out battle dress should be burnt.*

11.41 It was Alexander's intention to row downriver to the southern Ocean aboard his fleet, which now incorporated over a thousand ships including 800 bireme-galleys and *300* cargo vessels. *As reward for their aid in building his armada, he left Porus and Taxiles as kings of separate realms, but reconciled with each other through a marriage alliance,* for they had been reviving their former rivalry and feuding. **He also gave names to the two cities that he had earlier founded either side of the river near the site of his battle against Porus, calling one Nicaea in commemoration of his victory and the other Bucephala as a memorial to his horse,** who *had borne him to victory in all his battles, but* had perished in that engagement. *Indeed Alexander suffered another personal bereavement at this time, when his little son by Roxane died. After the funeral and the performance of sacrifices,* having ordained that the bulk of the army *with the elephants and the baggage train* should march down the banks under the command of Hephaistion and Craterus, Alexander himself embarked *upon his flagship* accompanied by his Friends and sailed *his fleet* downstream *with its multicoloured sails unfurled.* However, he advanced only about 40 stades each day in order that he might frequently put task forces ashore at convenient spots.

11.42 Not long after the start of their voyage they reached the kingdom of *another* Sopeithes. The most remarkable feature in this region is a mountain made entirely of salt, sufficient to supply the whole of India. Not the least wondrous feature of the mines that exploit this resource is the way in which **the salt-rock is naturally replenished within the excavations over time.**[13]

11.43 When the fleet reached the confluence of the Acesines and Hydaspes, Alexander disembarked his troops opposite to Eleumezen **and marched them against the Sibians, who occupied the country around the unified river. It is recorded that these people claimed to be descendants of the army deployed by Heracles during his unsuccessful siege of Aornus. The lion-caped club-wielder had been forced to settle their forbears in this vicinity,** *since they had been incapacitated by sickness. Their origins were betokened by their garbing themselves in the skins of savage beasts and their brandishing of clubs as weapons as well as many other vestiges, although proper Greek customs had died out among them.* Alexander *advanced for 250 stades, ravaging the country so as to induce its inhabitants to flee, until he* invested an illustrious town and its leading citizens emerged to treat with him. They presented him with splendid gifts and recalled their common descent from Heracles, vowing therefore to assist his expedition by every means in recognition of their shared ancestry. The king graciously welcomed their support for his cause and pronounced that their cities should retain self-rule.

11.44 Alexander proceeded against the next nation *downstream,* **who were called the Agalasseis, and found them drawn up in a strength of 40,000 infantry and 3,000 cavalry** *on the opposite bank of the river.* **Alexander** *crossed the river and* **launched an assault, mowing down the greater part of their forces and driving the survivors to seek refuge within the walls of the nearby towns, but these were besieged and stormed.** The males of fighting age were killed, but the remainder of **their inhabitants were sold into slavery.** *Others among the natives had also congregated to oppose him,* **leading the king to attack another substantial fortified city, where 20,000 people were sheltering. The Indians fought back manfully from barricades in their streets, driving back the Macedonians and slaying a significant number of Alexander's men.** But when the onslaught was resumed, the Indians abandoned all hope of successful resistance and began to set light to their houses, roasting themselves within them together with their

---

[13] Probably the ancient salt mines at Khewra 15km north of the Hydaspes in the Salt Range.

spouses and offspring. Ironically, therefore, the aggressors found themselves fighting to extinguish the flames, whilst the defenders sought to spread the conflagration in a perverse inversion of normal fighting conditions. **Most of the inhabitants were incinerated, but three thousand had escaped to the citadel. These waved fronds in supplication and were pardoned by Alexander.**

11.45 The king occupied the citadel of this great stronghold with a garrison of his sick and injured troops, before sailing on past **with his fleet to the** *nearby* **confluence of the conjoined Acesines-Hydaspes with the Indus river,** for this city had been protected on its northern side by the latter stream as well as on its southern margin by the former.[14] *These are the mightiest rivers in India with the exception of the Ganges, so* the turbulence at their union is *correspondingly* intense, generating surges and deadly vortices *like a stormy* sea. *Boats may only pass via constricted channels, since the riverbed is heaped with numerous banks of viscid sludge, which are constantly shifting about through the action of the current. The fleet met these shoals at speed whilst under sail,* causing many vessels *to be buffeted by successive violent swells and* to career out of the control of their helmsmen *before their canvases could be furled. Some of the ships collided and* two of the galleys were sunk whilst all looked on. Many of the vessels of a lesser draught *were also rendered unmanageable by the wild waters, but* were driven aground *intact at the riverbank.*

11.46 Alexander's flagship was swept headlong into the most dangerous area of rapids, *which twisted it sideways-on to the current, such that its pilot could no longer steer it. The king had stripped with the intention of throwing himself into the torrent and his Friends were ready to swim beside him in order to rescue him* from drowning, *but it seemed just as risky to take to the water as to press on in their careening vessel. Therefore they set to their oars in a concerted strenuous effort, and fought against the surges that sought to overwhelm them with as much force as humans can exert. It seemed as if the waves were rent asunder and the eddies retreated before them. When finally their ship was extricated from the maelstrom, they could not manage to dock it at the bank, but rather grounded it on the nearest sandbar.* On getting safely to shore, Alexander sacrificed to the gods for his deliverance from dire danger, *erecting altars in equal number to the channels of the divided watercourse and* comparing his battle with a river to that of Achilles.

11.47 *Meanwhile Indian philosophers, natives of this region, who made do with a folded over cloak and no other clothing, dispatched the following letter to Alexander: "From the Indian philosophers to Alexander of Macedon,* Greeting. *We have heard that your Friends are*

---

[14] Probably therefore located in the vicinity of modern Sitpur.

endeavouring to persuade you to make war against us and our region, so as to bring it into your hands, though not even in their sleep have they dreamt of our mode of life; if you attempt to follow their advice, you will only be able to herd our bodies around, for our spirits can neither be led astray nor made to do anything unwillingly, though you bring the greatest force to bear upon us; nay, no more than you would be able to make rocks or trees converse with you.[15] *We can inflict the greatest pain and the greatest injury upon ourselves, for* our living bodies can triumph over fire: we walk upon it of our own volition and a part of our bodies *ascends in the flames.* No king or prince throughout the land has the power *ever to succeed in compelling us to do what we do not choose to do.* That which is actually bestowed through divine inspiration is most of all in the hands of god. We strive hard fully to comprehend that which we hold dear and consider to be profitable in life and we have the free use of other men's property. We are gladly praised, since investments *made by others* end up proving worthless. And we are not at all like the philosophers of the Greeks, who are only mighty in their speeches: when we venture to speak, our actions always correspond to our words. Hence the greatest value is vested in us, for we embody the truth and liberty of our most ancient past. Therefore refrain from applying force in this matter, since nothing can be taken away from us against our will. But if, nevertheless, you direct yourself against us, it will be seen as unjust and foreign to that virtue, which good men strive to cultivate."*

11.48 *Being disturbed by this letter,* Alexander *advanced with his army for* **thirty stades and** entered upon the lands of the Oxydracae and the Mallians. Both were bellicose, teeming tribes, who traditionally fought each other, but at this time, in view of their mutual peril, they had formed an alliance *to oppose Alexander.* In order to cement this pact, they exchanged **10,000 virgin brides between them. United, they fielded** *the most powerful* **army in the Indus River region, comprising 80,000 infantry** *recruited from* **their younger men and 10,000 cavalry with 700 chariots besides.**

11.49 But when the Macedonians, who had believed themselves relieved from deadly duties, learnt that that they were confronted with renewed campaigning against the most ferocious people in India, they dreaded this unforeseen peril and rounded on their king with seditious recriminations: their leverage had but shifted the battle-ground from the River Ganges and beyond rather than ended the war. They were being put up against fiercely independent natives, so that their blood would clear a path to the Ocean. They were being drawn beyond the Sun and the stars and driven to approach that which Nature herself had concealed from mortal gaze. Again and again new enemies were manifested to meet their refurbished arms. And even if they routed and dispersed all of these,

---

[15] Perhaps this quip, inferred from Philo, Every Good Man Is Free 96 and St Ambrosius, Letter 37.35, was the inspiration for the story in the Romance about Alexander's conversations with trees in India.

what recompense awaited them? Glooming darkness and eternal night extending to cloak a sea swarming with schools of gargantuan monsters and channelling irresistible currents, via which expiring Nature is swept away.

11.50 Not for his own sake, but stimulated rather by his soldiers' anxiety, the king convened an Assembly, reassuring his men that those they dreaded were irresolute warriors. After them no other tribe obstructed their traversal of wide-open country to reach the end of both their travails and the world itself. As a concession to their fears, he had forsaken the River Ganges and the populous nations that lay beyond its torrent. He had turned aside to lead them whither undiminished glory might be won with less peril. Before them lay the prospect of the Ocean. Already the taint of the sea blew upon the breeze. Let them not begrudge him his quest for renown. They would surpass the limits set by Heracles and Dionysus, thereby assuring their king of everlasting fame at scant risk to themselves. Let them permit him simply to withdraw rather than flee from India.

11.51 All crowds are easily swayed, and crowds of troops especially so; hence an outbreak of sedition may be cured as trivially as it was instigated. Never before had such a joyful clamour resounded among the ranks of the army. They called upon him to lead them onwards and, with divine favour, to match the glory of those in whose footsteps they trod. Buoyed up by their acclamation, Alexander straightaway broke camp and deployed against the enemy. These were the mightiest nations of the Indus region and they were making strenuous preparations for war, so they had picked a man of proven valour from the Oxydracae as their commander. He had chosen to establish his base among the foothills of a mountain,[16] distributing his campfires over a wide area, so as to convey an impression of a vast host. Furthermore, the Indians sought to instil fear by means of their customary bellows and war cries, though to no avail in the face of the resilience of the Macedonians. Then, as day was dawning, a blithely confident and optimistic Alexander issued the order for his cheery troops to take up their arms and advance to battle. *Yet the barbarians spontaneously took to their heels, fleeing into the nearby cities* or taking inaccessible refuge among the peaks, ostensibly **due to a quarrel regarding the leadership,** *else perhaps inspired by terror of the Macedonians, when their commander, whose name was Sambus, happened to be transfixed through both his thighs by a three-foot bolt from a Macedonian catapult.* The king captured their baggage train during the pursuit, but failed to overtake the bulk of their forces.

11.52 Next Alexander approached *and surrounded* **the principal city** *of the Oxydracae wherein many of the enemy had sought refuge, though they trusted in its walls no more than in their weapons.* **Alexander was on the verge of launching his attack, when one among the seers, a man**

---

[16] Perhaps Gendari Mt.

named Demophon, came forward and announced to the king that many omens had foretold a great danger to Alexander's life from a wound he would sustain in the action. He besought Alexander to abandon the operation or at least to divert himself elsewhere for the time being. *But the king glared at the prophet, challenging him: "If someone were thus to interrupt you, whilst you were intent upon your craft and busied with interpretation of the signs, I do not doubt that you would regard that person as a tactless irritant." And when Demophon conceded that it would absolutely be so,* he rebuked the seer for having disconcerted the soldiers, *inquiring: "When I have before my gaze weighty matters, rather than animal offal, could anything be a greater nuisance than a soothsayer obsessed with superstitions?"*

11.53 Loitering no longer than needed to dismiss the seer, *Alexander deployed his forces and personally led the advance, being keen to capture the city in this assault. His war engines lagged behind, but he battered down a side gate and led the break-in, felling many opponents and chasing the rest into their citadel. Therefore he ordered scaling ladders brought up and,* since the rest of the Macedonians were dawdling *in the attack upon the wall,* he himself seized a ladder, propped it against the rampart of the citadel and clambered up to its parapet, *whilst holding a rimless shield[17] over his head. He moved so quickly, that he gained the parapet before the defenders could oppose him. Due to the crest of the wall being narrow and lacking in crenellations, but obstructed by a continuous breastwork, the king clung there precariously,* raising his shield to parry a rain of arrows and javelins flung at long range *from the various towers of the citadel,* for the Indians did not dare grapple with him hand to hand. At first his soldiers were impeded from supporting him by a storm of missiles, but shame vanquished their *sense of* peril, as they perceived that Alexander was being given up to the enemy through their hesitation. Whilst the king staggered under the onslaught, they raised two ladders and surged up them, but in such numbers that both collapsed, causing all upon them to plummet to the ground.

11.54 Hence Alexander stood utterly alone upon the battlements; isolated, though in plain view of his vast army, and his left arm bearing his shield was already tiring from the continual need to fend off the enemy's projectiles. *His Friends below screamed for him to leap down into their waiting arms, but* it seemed to him quite at odds with his reputation for valorous victory that he should impotently retreat from even so dangerous a predicament. Instead, he had the astonishing temerity to vault down within the ramparts of the citadel with naught but his armour to protect him from his seething opponents. *Had he stumbled in landing, he might*

---

[17] Λ πελτη.

instantly have been overwhelmed and captured, but by good fortune he alighted upon his feet, poised to defend himself. Fortune had *also* thwarted his encirclement, for an ancient tree was rooted upon his right close by the wall, *its branches thick with foliage, as though designed for the purpose of securing his flank.* Thus he ensconced himself between the huge girth of its trunk and the wall, blocking every bolt hurled by the Indians and putting up such a courageous resistance as befitted a king with so many illustrious deeds to his name. *His fame was itself a kind of haven, since none of his foes dared approach him, all being content merely to fling missiles from afar.* Despairing of his safety, he remained resolute that his final feats should secure him a supremely glorious death.

11.55 *Though most of the enemy's projectiles were deflected by branches,* the king received a great many strikes upon his shield and his helmet was battered and dented by stones. *As he wearied under the relentless pressure, he sank to his knees, thereby tempting his less cautious assailants to close in upon him. Two of these he slew with his sword, leaving them slumped lifeless at his feet. This sapped the courage of the rest, who again kept their distance, but persisted in pelting him with missiles from a safe range. Despite everything he maintained a stout defence, until* at last an Indian archer shot an arrow two cubits long so well aimed that it pierced his cuirass and lodged just beneath his breast *slightly above his right lung* not far from his gullet. *A great jet of blood gushed forth from the wound,* the shock of which caused him to *lower his guard and* topple onto one knee *as if mortally injured. Vainly he sought to pluck the shaft from his chest with his right hand, on seeing which* the archer sprang forward eager to despoil his victim. *But the indignity of the Indian's hands grappling with him revived* Alexander *sufficiently for him to* thrust his sword upwards into his enemy's exposed flank, inflicting a fatal gash.

11.56 *Now a triad of bodies were laid low around the king, whilst* most of *his surviving antagonists stood back in stupefaction,* but another Indian scurried out of a mill and thwacked Alexander's head from behind with a cudgel, leaving him dazed. Nevertheless *the king struggled to rise to his feet by using his shield as a prop, thinking to die fighting, ere he drifted into unconsciousness. Yet lacking the strength to get upright,* he grabbed with his right hand for support from the branches hanging over him. *Even so he could not manage to stay on his feet, but sank once more to his knees,* gesticulating defiance at his assailants and daring them to take him on hand to hand.

Figure 11.2. An overloaded ladder breaks at the siege (André Castaigne, 1899).

Figure 11.3. Alexander's lone defence within the Indian citadel (anon. 1696)

11.57 At this juncture, Peucestes, one of the hypaspists, arrived in Alexander's footsteps to raise his shield over the king, having used a

ladder to surmount a section of wall *that he had swept clear of defenders. Alexander looked to him rather for camaraderie in death than for preservation of his life, allowing his exhausted body to slump over his shield. But shortly afterwards more Macedonian guardsmen appeared: Limnaeus next, then successively Leonnatus and Aristonous. Nevertheless, word of Alexander's plight within their walls had spread to the other Indians, who now abandoned the defences in other sectors and sped to join the assault upon his handful of protectors. Of these, Limnaeus suffered many injuries in the course of a magnificent fighting stand and eventually perished in the onslaught. Peucestes, despite being gouged by three javelins, persisted in holding his shield over the king, rather than protect himself. Leonnatus valiantly repelled the frenzied charges of the barbarians, until he was gravely stricken in the neck* and pierced through his right thigh, *collapsing semi-conscious at the feet of the king. As Peucestes, enfeebled by many gashes, permitted his shield to droop, their sole hope of salvation rested in Aristonous, yet he too had received severe wounds and could no longer resist such an aggressive hoard of opponents.*

11.58 *In the interim a rumour had reached* the Macedonians *that Alexander had perished. Though this news might have deterred another army, it drew an incensed reaction from the Macedonians. Insensible of any peril, they hacked their way through the defences with pick-axes,* even adapting their swords to the task. **Having broken open a gateway, they surged into the citadel <u>with Ptolemy to the fore</u>,** *whereby he merited his later title of "saviour"*[18] Hardly any of the Indians stood their ground in the face of so many invaders, but instead they fled in panic, *including those surrounding Alexander.* Considering that any of the occupants might have been complicit in the wounding of their king and seized by a fury of vengeance, the Macedonians slew all they found, sparing neither the women, nor the aged, nor even the very young. **Only when they had filled the city with corpses** and levelled its buildings over them *did they feel that their righteous malice had been sated.*

11.59 Alexander was conveyed to his pavilion, where the medics sliced off the wooden shaft of the arrow embedded in his body, whilst avoiding disturbing its head. *Thereby they were able to remove his breastplate, which had been pinioned to him.* With his body bared, they determined that the arrowhead was barbed; hence it could not be extracted without massive trauma to the body, unless the wound were surgically widened. But they were fearful that they would be unable to staunch the haemorrhage from the surgery, for the arrowhead was enormous, *perhaps three finger-widths broad and four in length,* and it appeared to have penetrated through to the internal organs. The doctor, Critobulus, though he was a

---

[18] I.e. "Soter" in Greek; see Arrian, *Anabasis* 6.11.8 – perhaps actually awarded by the Rhodians.

paragon of the physician's art, was yet horrified by the magnitude of the risk. He dreaded engaging upon the task, lest the consequences of his skills proving inadequate should rebound upon his own head. Noticing that Critobulus was tearful and turned deathly pale with anxiety, Alexander asked: "What are you waiting for? Why not release me from this agony as soon as possible, even if it mean my death? Why should you fear any blame, if I have received a mortal wound?" At length, having set aside his fear or at least concealed it, Critobulus implored the king to allow himself to be held down, whilst he withdrew the point, since even a slight shift of his body could be harmful. After having assured the doctor that no restraint was needed, Alexander kept still as instructed, without the least flinching.

11.60 Therefore the wound was enlarged and the arrowhead was extracted, whereupon a copious effusion of blood induced the king to lose consciousness. With darkness veiling his vision, he lay supine as if at the verge of death, whilst the medics sought in vain to stem the flow of blood with poultices. All at once Alexander's Friends began to wail and lament, believing that their king had expired. But eventually the haemorrhaging ceased and Alexander gradually regained consciousness, becoming aware of those gathered around him. Throughout that day and the ensuing night the army invested the royal quarters in battle dress, acknowledging that all of them survived through their king's inspiration. Nor were they persuaded to depart, until they ascertained that he had been sleeping comfortably for a little while, whereupon they returned to camp with good hopes for his recovery.

11.61 After seven days of care and convalescence, his wound had not yet scarred over, but Alexander heard tell that exaggerated rumours of his death were spreading among the Indians. Therefore he instructed that two ships should be fastened alongside each other with his tent erected so as to be conspicuous in the middle. Hence he could show himself alive to those who had believed the false reports that he had perished. And being thus manifested before the eyes of the inhabitants, he dashed the misconceived hopes of those who opposed him. Afterwards he sailed on downstream, keeping a short space ahead of his fleet, in order not to disturb the tranquillity essential to his recuperation with the incessant beating of the oars.

11.62 During the fourth day after setting out, Alexander reached an area that had been evacuated by its natives, but was plentifully stocked with grain and cattle. The place appealed to him for resting both himself and his troops. It was customary for the leading Friends and the Bodyguards to stand watch in front of the royal lodgings whenever the king was in poor health. Since this practice was being observed at that time, they were all of them able to enter his bedchamber together. And since they all entered at once, Alexander was concerned in case they intended to impart some grave tidings, querying whether the enemy had launched a surprise attack? However, Craterus, who had been appointed spokesman for supplications from the king's Friends, responded thus:[19] "Do you suppose that we could be made more anxious by the approach of the enemy, even if they now stood before our palisades, than we already are through our duty of care for your well-being, which you deem inconsequential? However great a strength every nation may join in fielding against us, though they cram the world with arms and men and strew the sea with their fleets, even if they goad alien monsters into harrying us,[20] you stand as guarantor of our invincibility. Yet what divinity may promise that this pillar and Star of Macedon will endure, when you rampantly expose your person to manifest perils, oblivious to having thereby dragged so many of your countrymen to the brink of disaster? Who among us, indeed, would be either desirous or capable of surviving your death? Following your guidance and your commands we have reached this place, whence none of us can return without you to lead us back home."

Figure 11.4. The wounded Alexander sails past troops (André Castaigne, 1899).

11.63 "Were you still disputing the rule of Persia with Darius, though none of us would wish it, nobody would be astonished by your readiness to deal audaciously with every hazard. For when the prize is equal to the peril, not only are the fruits of success more honourable, but there is also nobility in defeat. Yet who could bear that the taking of a humble hamlet should cost you your life? Not even those among the foreigners that recognise your greatness, let

---

[19] Arrian, Anabasis 6.13.4, mentions that Nearchus recorded the ensuing admonition of Alexander by his Friends; if so, then Curtius probably found it in Cleitarchus, since his Fragments strongly suggest that Nearchus was one of his sources.

[20] "Alien monsters" (invisitatas beluas) is of course a reference to elephants, yet these beasts are unlikely to have been unfamiliar to Curtius, who was probably Proconsul of the Roman Province of Africa in the mid-first century AD: this terminology therefore hints that Curtius is paraphrasing an early source, most probably Cleitarchus.

alone your own soldiers! My spirit quails in recollecting the drama, which we witnessed a little while ago. I fear to speak of how those most cowardly hands might have tarnished the armour stripped from your invincible corpse, had not Fortune taken pity on us and brought about your rescue."

11.64 "We're just a gang of villains, a bunch of deserters, all of us who were unable to catch up with you. Branding all your soldiers to signal their disgrace would be entirely justified and none will shirk his punishment for the offence, even though none had any chance of forestalling it. However, I beg you to allow us to become your villains in its other sense. Wherever you direct us, we shall go. Abject perils and ignominious skirmishes we crave for ourselves. Let you reserve yourself for matters suited to your eminence. Nothing is more disreputable than wasting a reputation where it cannot be flaunted, for fame fades fast in fighting filthy foes!" Ptolemy too spoke in this vein and the rest of them likewise. By then a jabber of voices were bewailing Alexander to refrain from becoming a glutton for glory and to take due care of his welfare, which was identical with the security of the state.

11.65 The king was gratified by the devotion of his Friends, being moved to embrace them individually with special fondness. Then, having invited them to be seated, he began nobly and reflectively to address them: "Particularly to you, my most loyal compatriots and truest companions, I offer my sincere gratitude, not just by virtue of your concern this day for my welfare above your own, but also because you have stinted me neither pledges nor proofs of your goodwill towards me since the outset of our campaign. So much so that I confide that I have never before held my life so dear as henceforth: in order that I may take protracted pleasure in your friendship. Yet my views are at odds with those who wish to die in my stead, for I actually judge that it is through my valour that I have merited your continuing goodwill. Though indeed you may aspire to long-lasting benefits through me, perhaps even perpetual profits, it is not the length of my life by which I measure myself, but rather by the endurance of my fame.[21] It was an option for me to have been satisfied with my father's realm, idly lurking within Macedonia's bounds pending an obscure and dishonourable dotage. Yet even the unadventurous cannot prescribe their fates, for premature death often seizes those who suppose length of days to be the only true blessing. But I, who count my victories rather than my years, if Fortune's favours be rightly reckoned, have already lived a long while."

11.66 "Starting out with Macedonia, I have retained the dominion of Greece; I have subjugated Thrace and the Illyrians; the Triballi and the Maedi obey my commands; from the Hellespontine shore to the Red Sea surf, Asia lies in my possession. And now I am not far from the end of this world, upon going beyond which I plan to open up another Nature, a different Earth. I once

---

[21] This is "The Choice of Achilles", cf. Iliad 9.410-416.

passed from within the confines of Europe across to Asia in a single hour.[22] Having become the conqueror of both sides of the continental divide[23] in the ninth year of my reign and the twenty-eighth of my life, can you conceive of my relinquishing the pursuit of fame, which has been the sole object of my existence? I'll not deviate from my true path, and wherever I may fight, I shall consider that I am performing within the theatre of the entire Earth. I shall grant distinction to wretched places and I shall open up to all peoples lands which Nature has set apart."

11.67 "To lose my life in these enterprises, as chance may have it, would be a splendid way to go. I am sprung from such a lineage that I am bound to seek a crowded life rather than a long one.[24] I implore you to ponder upon our having reached a territory where a woman is famed for her gallantry. Semiramis founded such cities, brought so many nations beneath her sway and accomplished such great deeds! Are we already nauseated by a surfeit of fame, when we have still not matched a woman in renown? If the gods be willing, even greater feats lie before us. Yet those future accomplishments shall never be ours, unless we reckon nothing trivial, in which there is actually scope for great glory. Therefore let you but preserve me from perfidious plots and court conspiracies and I shall confront the crises of war and Ares himself undaunted."

11.68 "Philip was better guarded in battle than in the theatre: he often dodged the clutches of his enemies, but could not escape those of his own subjects. Also, if you review the deaths of other monarchs, you will count more who were slain by their own people than by foes. Aside from this, I'll take this opportunity to air a matter that I've long been turning over in my mind. I shall obtain the greatest gratification from my labours and exertions, if my mother Olympias should be accorded divine honours upon her demise.[25] If I get the chance, I shall personally put this into effect; but if fate should forestall me, recall that I have laid this onus upon you all." Then he excused his Friends, but he kept camp in that place for many days thereafter.

11.69 Whilst these things transpired in India, **the Greek troops whom Alexander had recently settled around Bactra *and in Sogdiana, received***

---

[22] Curtius has *Ex Asia in Europae terminos*, but surely this should be reversed?

[23] Curtius is rather ambiguous, but this looks like a reference to Alexander's crossing of the Hindu Kush into India in 327BC.

[24] A clear reference to his putative descent from Achilles.

[25] Curtius 10.5.30 also notes Alexander's wish that Olympias be accorded divine honours, hence this request is probably historical and Alexander truly made it in the aftermath of his near-death experience, perhaps seeking to bolster his own claim to divine honours through inheritance. Curtius 10.5.11 records that the Macedonians had refused such honours to Alexander himself, whereas it appears that Philip had received divinisation prior to his assassination in the light of Diodorus 16.92.5 & 16.95.1 (Philip's statue paraded with the Olympians) and M. N. Tod, Greek Historical Inscriptions 191.6 (altars erected to "Zeus Philippios" at Eresus on Lesbos).

word that the king had died of his wounds. Disgruntled by their life among foreigners, they hatched dissension among themselves. After they *heard that the king yet lived,* **they launched a full rebellion against the Macedonians,** though more from fear of castigation than from animosity towards Alexander. For, having slaughtered some of their fellows, the dominant faction began to look to their weaponry. Then, having seized the citadel of Bactra, which had been guarded somewhat negligently, they managed to compel the barbarians to defect to their cause. Their leader was Athenodorus, who actually assumed the title of king, though not so much because he coveted power, as to provide himself with the authority to lead his countrymen back to their homeland. However, jealousy inspired hostility towards him in a fellow Greek, named Biton, who concocted a plot whereby Athenodorus was invited to a feast by Boxus, a Bactrian, and slain in the course of the entertainment. During the ensuing day, Biton convoked an assembly and persuaded most of the Greeks that Athenodorus had in fact been conspiring to take his life; but others felt that Biton was deceiving them and little by little the suspicion began to spread to more of them. Hence the Greek soldiers took up their arms, intending to kill Biton at the earliest opportunity. However, the rest of the leading men managed to quell the anger of the crowd.

11.70 Despite having been snatched from impending peril, much against his apprehensions, just a little while later Biton authored a conspiracy against his deliverers. But when his treachery was detected, they arrested both him and Boxus. The rest of the leadership were satisfied to have Boxus executed straightaway, but Biton they chose to torture to death. And they were already instigating his torments, when the Greeks, as if driven mad (for their reason is uncertain), rushed to take up their arms. With the roars of the mob resounding in their ears, those assigned to contort Biton let him go, fearing that the tumult was directed at inhibiting their task. When their victim, stripped naked as he was, appeared before the Greeks, the pitiful figure of the condemned man inspired them with forgiveness, so they issued orders for his release. In this fashion Biton was once again reprieved from due punishment, so he returned to Greece with **a band of three thousand men** who *abandoned the colonies founded by Alexander and* **underwent great hardships during their homeward trek.** Such were the events in the vicinity of Bactra and the marches of Scythia.

11.71 *These were the concerns of Alexander* in the eleventh year of his reign.

5. Book 12: June 325BC – June 324BC

Southern India And Its Ocean, The Kedrosian Desert And The Return to Persia

KEY
<u>**Underlined bold text for attributed Fragments of Cleitarchus**</u>
Bold text where there is overwhelming evidence
Bold italic text where there exists direct-firm evidence
Normal text where direct-weak evidence applies
Italic text where the evidence is conjectural
Grey text for connecting passages, if Cleitarchus' version is indeterminate

12.1 *As the twelfth year of his reign began, Alexander completed his recovery from the chest wound that had so nearly proved fatal.* **When the king had been made better,** a delegation of **the Malli and Oxydracae** a hundred strong presented themselves before him. They all arrived in chariots and were powerfully built men with an air of proud dignity. Their dress was of linen, chased through with threads of gold and purple. They **conceded the subjugation of** their towns, their lands and **their persons to Alexander's authority**, thus relinquishing their accustomed liberty and placing their faith in the king's protection and good government. They asserted that it was an oracle of their gods that had motivated their submission, for their strength in arms remained undiminished. Alexander took counsel with his Friends before granting them his protection in exchange for their fealty. He further directed that a tribute, which these nations had paid to the Arachosii, should instead be delivered to him and he ordered that they should furnish 2500 cavalrymen to augment his forces. These commands were faithfully performed by the Indians.

12.2 ***Alexander sacrificed to the gods for his salvation and arranged a sumptuous banquet for his Friends and the Indian envoys and magnates.*** A hundred golden couches were arrayed side by side, each draped about with purple tapestries glinting with strands of gold. ***After much wine had been drunk at this magnificent feast, there transpired a notable incident.*** **There was present one of Alexander's Companions, a Macedonian called Corragus of great bodily strength and a gallant veteran of numerous battles. Spurred by the alcohol he challenged Dioxippus of Athens to a**

duel, *saying he should agree to meet him in armed combat if he were a man.* The Athenian was a renowned athlete, who had been crowned as victor in the boxing contest at the Olympic Games. Naturally the drunken guests encouraged their rivalry; therefore Dioxippus accepted the challenge, *contemptuous of the soldier's bravado. On the following day the king sought to dissuade them, yet their resolve had hardened, so* Alexander fixed a date for the contest.

12.3 When the appointed day came tens of thousands of men turned out to witness the spectacle. Many of the troops, especially the Greeks, backed Dioxippus, but Alexander and the Macedonians favoured Corragus, because he was their countryman. The pair progressed to the field of combat, the Macedonian arrayed in his costly panoply and bearing a shield and his usual weapons: a sarissa in his left hand, a javelin in his right and a sword slung from a strap, as if he were up against a whole team of opponents. But the Athenian came naked and gleaming with oil, garlanded and carrying a purple drape in his left hand, whilst bearing a well-proportioned club in his right. Both exhibited splendid physiques and their bodily strength was regarded with wonderment. The crowd looked forward to a battle of the gods, for the Macedonian by his bearing and his shining armaments evoked trepidation as though he were Ares, whilst Dioxippus through his surpassing strength and fitness and particularly on account of the club bore close comparison with Heracles. *The audience was thrilled with keen anticipation by the disparity, since it seemed not merely rash, but actually insane for a nude man to confront an opponent in full armour.*

12.4 As the two closed the Macedonian, believing that the Greek could be dispatched at range, hurled his javelin, but Dioxippus dodged its impact with a slight twist of his torso. Then Corragus charged, whilst swapping his sarissa into his right hand, but the Greek too leapt forward and shattered the shaft of the sarissa with a single blow of his club. Having suffered twin setbacks through the loss of both of his spears, Corragus was forced to resort to his sword. But even as he sought to draw it, Dioxippus grasped the Macedonian's right wrist with his left hand and pushed with his own right to cause his foe to lose his balance, then tripped and butted Corragus, so that he tumbled to the ground. Snatching away the sword, the Greek set his foot upon the Macedonian's neck, as he lay recumbent. Finally, he raised his club poised to crush his defeated adversary and looked to the spectators to decide Corragus' fate.

12.5 The crowd was in tumult at the paradoxical and overwhelming nature of the Greek's skill, but the king signalled that he should release Corragus, and then ordered the gathering to disperse. Alexander was clearly displeased, for the spectacle had exposed the Macedonian reputation for valour and prowess in arms to ridicule in full view of the barbarians. Yet Dioxippus freed his fallen foe and departed the scene of his triumph bound about with ribbons by his fellow Greeks, who basked in the reflected glory from their countryman. But Fortune curtailed his opportunity to brag about his victory.

12.6 Alexander grew increasingly hostile to Dioxippus, for his ears were opened to the resentful lies of his Friends and other Macedonian courtiers. A few days later these men persuaded one of the attendants at a feast to conceal a golden cup beneath the pillow of Dioxippus' couch. During the banquet the staff reported its loss and the Macedonians pretended shock at its discovery, accusing the Greek of its theft. Thus Dioxippus was placed in a shameful and embarrassing quandary. Perceiving that the Macedonians were united against him, he could not endure the stigma of theft, so he quit the banquet.

12.7 A little later on reaching his personal quarters he composed a letter to Alexander exposing the ruse of which he had been the victim. This he placed in the hands of his servants for delivery to the king. Then he took his own life by running himself through with his sword. Though he had been indiscreet in accepting the challenge to single combat, it was downright foolish of him to commit suicide in these circumstances. For many who had despised him, now mocked his folly, joking that it was hard to live with his fate of being endowed with great bodily strength, but a tiny mind. <u>Let us learn from this not to allow the body's strength to become the soul's weakness; let us consider wisdom to be the soul's strength.</u>[1]

12.8 Alexander read the letter and was moved to grief and anger by Dioxippus' death, *which he recognised to have been inspired by indignation and despair rather than guilt.* Afterwards, he frequently mourned the virtues of the man whom he had neglected in life, but whose death he now regretted. Only when it was futile did he appreciate the excellence of Dioxippus contrasted with the calumny of his detractors.

12.9 The Indian envoys were given leave to return home *to report the success of their mission,* but they returned a few days later bringing tributary gifts for Alexander. These comprised 300 cavalrymen, 1030 chariots each drawn by four horses abreast, a substantial amount of linen cloth, 1000 Indian shields, 100 talents of white iron, remarkably large lions and tigers, but all trained for handling, and also the skins of gargantuan lizards and the shells of tortoises. *Afterwards Alexander issued orders to Craterus to march the main army downstream, whilst maintaining contact with the river. But those who*

---

[1] This is Fragment 39 of Cleitarchus (Maximi, *Eclogae* II 734 B), considered doubtful by Jacoby, but it might be fitted to this context.

had been escorting him in the fleet he re-embarked and sailed with them towards the Ocean through the territory of the Malli.

12.10 The king next reached the lands of the Sambastae, a people who were the equal of any in India in numbers and breeding. Their cities were ruled in a democratic fashion and hearing of the approach of the Macedonians, they gathered an army of 60,000 infantry, 6000 cavalry and 500 armoured chariots, *which they placed under the command of three generals, distinguished in the conduct of warfare. Yet the folk in the fields on the banks of the river, inhabitants of a multiplicity of villages, watched amazed as the entire sweep of the stream within their gaze became crammed with vessels each scintillating with the arms of innumerable troops. Astounded by the novelty of the scene, they believed they saw a heavenly host led by a new Dionysus, a god whose name was hallowed among those nations. And so the bellows of the soldiers and the thrashing pulse of the oars and the sailors' chant of mutual exhortation flooded the ears of the natives filling them with terror. They fled to their own men at arms shouting that they were mad to seek battle with so many divine and invincible heroes.* The Indian troops being thus intimidated and the elders of their nation also counselling against a risky fight, the Sambastae dispatched an embassy of fifty of their chief men to Alexander to seek favourable treatment from him. The king praised them for the wisdom of their submission to his authority **and concluded a peace treaty with them, being heaped with lavish presents and heroic honours in return.**

12.11 *Four days travel downstream tribes living on either side of the river, who were called the Sodrae and the Massani, submitted to Alexander.* At this place the king founded a city, Alexandria beside the river, and designated ten thousand persons as its populace. Afterwards he entered the lands of **King Musicanus,** *at which juncture he held a trial for the satrap Terioltes, due to charges laid against him by the people of the Paropanisum range, of whom Alexander had made him the governor. Finding him guilty of many acts of avarice and tyranny, the king ordered his execution. Yet Oxyartes, leader of the Bactrians, was not merely absolved of guilt, but was thereby granted the rule of more extensive territories among the Parapanisadae, due to his bond of affection with Alexander.* A campaign was undertaken to complete the subjugation of the Musicani and the king left a garrison to secure their principal town. *Also at this time Alexander sent Craterus and Polyperchon back to Babylonia with a great part of the army, whilst he himself sailed on downstream towards the shore of the Ocean with select regiments.*

12.12 Alexander next launched an invasion through the forests to a wild part of India, where lay the kingdom of Porticanus. He stormed and captured two cities, allowing his troops to ransack their dwellings prior to setting them ablaze. Porticanus together with a great section of his population ensconced themselves in a fortified city, but Alexander overwhelmed its defences after a siege lasting three days. Porticanus retreated to its citadel *and sent out envoys to seek terms of surrender from Alexander, but, before they had a chance to treat with the king, two towers collapsed with a resounding boom and the Macedonians surged across their ruins into the stronghold.* After its fall, Porticanus was slain as he made a last stand with a few loyal followers. *Having demolished the citadel,* Alexander *sold those captured into slavery, and then* went on to capture the other cities of the kingdom, razing them all and thereby inspiring much fear of him throughout those lands.

12.13 Afterwards Alexander ravaged the realm of King Sambus, where many towns submitted to his authority, but the strongest city of the nation was taken by digging beneath its ramparts. *The barbarians were ignorant of military engineering tactics, so it seemed to them a supernatural horror when armed men rose up out of the earth near the centre of their city, since they had not noticed any prior sign of the mining operation.* Most of the cities of this region were obliterated and the king sold their inhabitants at auction, though <u>more than 80,000 of the Indians were cut down</u> *in the fighting. The sect known as the Brahmins shared in this catastrophe, but their survivors came before Alexander as suppliants waving fronds of foliage, so he absolved them, punishing only the worst culprits. King Sambus himself abandoned the struggle and escaped with thirty elephants into the territory on the other side of India.*

12.14 At this time the Musicani launched a rebellion. Alexander entrusted Pithon with the task of suppressing their revolt, which he accomplished by capturing its leader: King Musicanus himself. Pithon arraigned his prisoner before Alexander, who had the man crucified, before rejoining his fleet, where it lay moored upon the river.

12.15 Three days later whilst travelling downstream Alexander reached a town at the far end of the kingdom of Sambus. *He had reached Harmatelia, the last city of the Brahmins, whose citizens were so confident of its invulnerability and so proud of their own valour that they* forswore the submission of the realm and *closed their gates against the king.* But Alexander sent a force of five hundred of his fleet-footed Agrianians to assault the ramparts, considering that their sparse numbers would be deemed contemptible. Their orders were to lure the enemy into an engagement beyond their walls, then steadily to retreat once they had been counter attacked. Around 3000 fighters spewed forth from the city, whereupon Alexander's contingent *turned their backs and* rushed away in feigned flight. The barbarians leapt after them in a hot pursuit, but were subsequently intercepted and surprised by forces led by Alexander himself. Charging furiously into the fray, the king's troops slew 600 of the barbarians and captured 1000 more, the remnants being chased back within their defences.

12.16 *Yet this was not so splendid and joyful a victory as at first appeared, as events went on to show.* Those among Alexander's forces who had suffered wounds were now exposed anew to mortal danger. The Brahmins had smeared their weapons with a deadly toxin, which indeed had been the basis of their confidence in joining battle. The potency of the poison was derived from a species of snake, which was hunted down and its carcass placed in the sun. The scorching radiance melted the flesh of the creature such that it sweated moisture and through this liquefaction the animal's venom was gleaned. By its action the bodies of the wounded at first became numbed, then little by little sharp pains developed and the victims were racked by shivering and convulsions. Their skin became clammy and grey and they began to vomit bile, whilst a dark spume seeped out of their gashes, which started to putrefy. The gangrene spread rapidly to overwhelm key parts of the body, thus inflicting a wretched death upon the sufferer. Whether the wound was great or small or even just a scratch, the outcome was the same. *The physicians were perplexed and confounded.*

12.17 *It had been the hope of the barbarians that the rash and fearless Alexander could thus have been eliminated, but though he fought in the thick of the action, the king came through unscathed. However* Ptolemy, the future king, had been injured *in the left shoulder, and, though the wound was slight, as the casualties began dying,* Alexander was greatly upset, since this man ranked high in his affections. He was a close relative and some said he was a son of Philip: indeed it was known for sure that he was the son of a woman who had been one of Philip's mistresses. *Furthermore, he was one of Alexander's elite Bodyguards and a most resolute warrior, but even more accomplished and illustrious in the arts of peace than in military crafts. Temperate and courteous in his manner, notably generous and approachable, he had adopted nothing of the arrogance of royalty. Hence it was dubious whether he was more popular with the king or the people, for* his virtues were appreciated by all.

12.18 *So great was the concern of the Macedonians for Ptolemy's well-being that it was as if they had foreseen his later enthronement.* But indeed on this occasion he received a just reward for his many kindnesses, some said through the intervention of divine Providence. For when Alexander came to visit Ptolemy, *exhausted by the battle and fatigued by worry, he commanded that a bed should be fetched for his own use and he slipped into slumber as soon as he lay down upon it.* On awakening he told of a serpent that had visited him in his dreams gripping a plant between its jaws and of how it had taught him the curative properties and the habitat of this herb. *The king gave out that he would know this plant were it brought before him. Therefore many joined the search that tracked it down.*

12.19 Alexander ground a poultice from the herb and smeared it on Ptolemy's wound. *The pain was eased straightaway and soon a scab formed over the gash.* The king also brewed a tea from the leaves and had Ptolemy drink it, thus restoring him to health. Now that the virtue of the remedy had been vindicated by Ptolemy's recovery, the therapy was extended to all the afflicted troops and they were similarly cured. Then Alexander renewed his preparations to assault and subjugate Harmatelia, notwithstanding its formidable defences. But its inhabitants, *being thwarted in their hope of inflicting a decisive blow upon the Macedonians,* emerged waving branches in supplication and surrendered.

12.20 *At this same fortified town* **Alexander captured ten of the Indian** naked **philosophers, who had done most to encourage the resistance of King Sambus.** They were reputedly adept at producing witty and concise retorts to all manner of queries. Alexander therefore challenged them: *"Since, Indian philosophers, your enmity to us is manifest, and your lives are therefore forfeit,* it would be best to pay attention to what I say. *I will question you one by one, and you will respond as best you can.* The first man who gives a wrong answer, I shall put to death, and then according to quality of response **the rest of you shall die.** One among you I shall appoint to judge the replies, and if his adjudication be correct, then he alone shall be granted his life." **Then the chief of them requested whether each of them might be permitted to add explanations to their responses. This Alexander allowed.**

12.21 *Alexander proceeded to pose the question to the first of them of whether the dead or the living were greater in number. The Indian responded: "The living, of course, for those who do not exist cannot have any number."*

12.22 *Alexander asked the second whether the beasts of the land or the sea were more numerous. The Indian responded: "Of the land, of course, for the land contains the sea."*

12.23 *Alexander asked the third: "Which is the most cunning animal?" The Indian responded: "That, of course, which has appeared to no man up until now."*

12.24 *Alexander asked the fourth: "For what reason did you counsel King Sambus to make war against me?" The Indian responded: "So that he might either live or die with his self-respect intact."*

12.25 *Alexander asked the fifth: "Which of night or day was born first?" The Indian responded: "Night was born before day by one day." Alexander was dubious about this response, but noticing this the Indian explained: "Riddling questions will usually elicit riddling answers."*

12.26 *Alexander asked the sixth: "What must a man do in order to make everyone happy?" The Indian responded: "If, being powerful, he looks after them, without being seen to be severe with them."*

12.27 *Alexander asked the seventh, "On what basis can a man seem to be a god?" The Indian responded: "If, whilst being mortal, he does what no man can do."*

12.28 *Alexander inquired of the eighth whether life or death were greater in strength? The Indian responded: "Life, for this reason, that life makes things to exist out of nothing; whereas death makes nothing out of these things."*

12.29 *Alexander asked the ninth: "How long is it beneficial for a man to live?" The Indian replied: "So long as he himself does not perceive death to be more beneficial than life."*

12.30 *Next Alexander asked the last of them, which of those who had spoken appeared to have responded worst, at the same time conjuring him not to exhibit any favour for their cause in his judgement. And he, unwilling to voice his judgement of which of them should perish, said that each of them had answered worse than the others. Alexander retorted: "It is thus clear that all must die including you their chief, who has judged so badly." The chief Indian responded: "But, surely, Alexander, it is not kingly to lie, for you said: 'Whichever of you whom I command to judge, if he judge correctly, he will be set free.'* I said that each answer was worse than those already given, so I judged myself to have given the worst answer of all, which you have agreed. It was* not therefore false, but true judgement. It is not in fact fair to condemn any of us through my judgement. None of us therefore according to your rules should meet with death, for indeed *to avoid* unjustly killing us, not so much to us, but to you is providential." ***When Alexander heard all this, he judged them to be wise, so he ordered*** gifts and ***garments to be given to them and let them go.***

12.31 *It is said that* **Heracles sired** but **one daughter and named her Pandaea. He granted her the rule of the southernmost part of India stretching as far as the Ocean and he divided up** <u>the inhabitants</u> **of her realm to** <u>dwell among 365 villages</u>**. He commanded that one village should pay a tax to the queen on each day of the year, his purpose being that those that had recently paid this tribute would support Pandaea in claiming from those whose payment was about to fall due.** <u>The people of this region are called the Mandi and the females of their race are mature enough for bearing children at just seven years of age whereas the males do not live beyond forty.</u>

12.32 *Alexander commanded his forces to re-embark upon the ships and ordered them regularly to observe the constellations in order to resolve whether the river Indus issued into the Atlantic and thence into the*

Erythraean Sea.[2] *When they had voyaged onwards for some days, they came to the distinguished city of Patala and its island. It was governed in a fashion resembling the constitution of Sparta: the heads of two leading dynasties inherited a joint-kingship from their fathers, which accorded them the leadership in military matters. Conversely, a council of elders was responsible for the civil administration.* One of the kings, whose name was Moeris, had lately evacuated his city to seek refuge in the hills. Therefore Alexander occupied the town *and ordered that it be fortified.* Through pillaging the fields, he amassed a great plunder of grain, flocks of sheep and herds of cows, which *he took onboard* as *provisions together with guides, who were familiar with the river. Then he sailed to the island, which arose in mid-stream, being formed by the branches of the Indus Delta. In that region on the right-hand branch of the river dwelt the Bigandar, whilst living upon the left were the Mamalces.*

12.33 Due to the laxity of their guards, the guides managed to escape. *The island appeared deserted, but Alexander ordered that, if anybody existed in that place with knowledge of the area, they should be rounded up. Eventually, when nobody could be found,* his burning ambition to reach the Ocean and visit the limits of the world persuaded him to consign his own fate and that of his many brave warriors to a mysterious waterway without guidance. *After praying together to god, they departed from the island,* sailing on into the unknown, in ignorance of the native tribes, the distance to the sea and the navigability of the channel for the warships. Conjecture was their blind, two-faced augur and their sole solace lay in the perpetual good fortune of their king.

12.34 *Already they had hastened on for 400 stades, when suddenly they sensed sea air, a thing of which they were not ignorant. Hope inspired the king and filled him with joy,* so that he urged the oarsmen to row with renewed vigour, declaring: "The avowed objective for which we have all striven is at hand; now nothing shall sully our glory nor stain our valour; the world shall fall to us without further bloodshed or intercession from the God of War; Nature herself cannot advance further and, shortly, things unknown to any save the immortals shall be revealed." *And so between them they all encouraged one another, whilst rowing ever onward with the sea not far away.*

12.35 *Then,* when they spied natives wandering about, *Alexander ordered boats to be sent to the bank, having instructed them to seek out informants on the region. Searching all day, they finally discovered several peasants* skulking in their huts. *These they led before the king, who asked, how far away the sea lay? They denied any knowledge of the sea, but said that three days' further sailing would bring them to polluted waters. It was clear that this was a reference to seawater by persons ignorant of its nature. Their spirits lifted, the army rapidly embarked, so*

---

[2] By the Erythraean (or Red) Sea is meant the Persian Gulf (and the Arabian Sea by extension).

as to reach the sea as soon as possible. So the sailors rowed on eagerly as the consummation of their hopes drew near and each successive day the fire in their souls burnt brighter. *By the third day* they had reached salt waters and *they began to notice tidal undulations,* which were at first quite gentle.

12.36 Now they edged towards another island in the middle of the stream, their progress being retarded by a contrary flow. Mooring the fleet on its shore, they rushed off to garner provisions in blissful ignorance of the calamity that was about to befall them. At approaching the third hour, the Ocean in its habitual alternation began to swell and surge against the current. The flow of the stream was first arrested and then reversed with escalating force, generating a torrent with more impetus than a cascade in spate. The common soldiers lacked experience of the temperament of the sea, so they imagined that they were witnessing a portent of divine displeasure as *the surge of salt water streamed into the fields, rapidly flooding* a vast expanse of erstwhile well-drained land.

12.37 The ships were buoyed up *and they felt the force of the flow tugging upon them and wrenching them into violent motion,* such as to cause the entire fleet to be dispersed. Those onshore were aghast at this malign turn of events and so from every quarter they raced frantically back to their vessels. Yet in the face of panic even haste is tardy: thus some sought to punt their ships along, whilst others obstructed the deployment of the oars by squatting down in a mass. Some rushed to set sail without their full complement, thus incapacitating their vessels, which wallowed laboriously, whilst others crammed multitudes onboard. Hence both under-manning and overcrowding undermined their expedition. Here and there some yelled that they should hold back and others clamoured for departure, so that their contradictory cries confounded the ears and compounded the confusion that lay before their eyes.

12.38 Nor could the pilots rescue the situation, since their voices were drowned in the tumult and the sailors were anyway in such a state of consternation that they were uncontrollable. And so the ships began to collide, each obstructing the course of another and shearing off whole banks of oars. You might have supposed them to be two fleets engaged in battle, rather than a single army embarked upon its own vessels. Prows crashed against sterns as ships, which struck those before them, were themselves assaulted in the rear and angry words even led to fistfights.

12.39 And now the tide had inundated their entire panorama with just a few slight mounds protruding like miniature islands, whither many swam vigorously, being driven by terror to abandon the ships. One part of the divided fleet floated on a great depth of water, where before there had been depressions in the landscape; another part was stranded among shoals created where the flood had barely covered uneven stretches of higher ground. At this point a fresh source of even greater alarm was visited upon them: the sea began to ebb away with a huge dragging force as the waters returned to their former channels, draining the submerged terrain. Hence some ships were left high and dry, tilted onto their prows or leaning upon their sides. The fields were strewn with baggage, arms and fragmentary oars and planks. The troops feared either to land or remain aboard, since they anticipated that further and worse calamities might strike at any moment. They could scarcely trust their own eyes as they witnessed ships wrecked on dry land and the sea vanishing into streams.

Figure 12.1. Disaster strikes Alexander's fleet during the journey to the Ocean.

12.40 Nor was this the end of their suffering, for, since they were ignorant of the fact that the sea would shortly return to re-float their ships, they expected hunger and dire deprivations to ensue. Vile sea-beasts deposited by the flood were roving around and night was fast approaching, so that even the king was grieved by the desperation of their plight. Yet *these troubles could not* so *overwhelm his invincible spirit, but* that *he* kept watch throughout the night and *stationed cavalrymen at the river mouth* in order that, on perceiving a resurgence of the sea, they might race back ahead of it. Furthermore he issued orders that the damaged ships should be mended and that those which had been capsized by the flow should be righted, and that all should remain vigilant against a recurrence of the flood tide. When the whole night had been spent in watchfulness and exhortation, <u>all at once the cavalry pickets came charging back, and yet the swelling flood following on their heels came close to cutting them off from the fleet.</u>

12.41 Then as the water began to seep beneath the ships, they were each lifted afloat and when the fields were entirely inundated, the whole fleet was freed to sail on. The riverbanks echoed with the unrestrained cheers of the soldiers and sailors as they joyously hailed their unexpected deliverance. Whence had the sea returned and whither had it sped hence the day before? They could only wonder at this natural phenomenon, which sometimes obeyed and sometimes breached the constraints of time. However, the king conjectured from its recurrences that the surge was due after sunrise each day, so he set off down the river with a flotilla in the middle of the night to reach the estuary ahead of the tide. *Escorted by his Friends,* he sailed out 400 stades **into the Ocean,** *where he encountered two islands.* **Here he performed opulent sacrifices,** *having set up altars to Tethys and Oceanus,* **the gods who presided over the sea.** *Pouring libations from many a golden cup, he also cast these chalices into the waters, proclaiming his campaign to have achieved its end,* the objective of his prayers.

12.42 *After rejoining the main fleet, Alexander headed back upriver towards Patala.* On the second day of the return journey his ships were moored near a briny lake, the innocent appearance of which deceived those who rashly bathed in its waters. They contracted an itchy mange, which proved communicable to others, but oil was found to cure it. Since the route by which Alexander intended to lead the army passed through an arid region, Leonnatus was sent in advance to dig wells along the line of march. The king held back with his main contingents *waiting for the monsoons to abate,* whilst taking the opportunity to found several cities.

12.43 As the stormy season drew to a close, **the king burnt such of his ships as were damaged or unserviceable and placed the most seaworthy vessels from his fleet in the hands of Nearchus** *and Onesicritus, who were master navigators.* **He ordered them to voyage out into the Ocean** *as far as safety permitted,* **taking careful note of everything they saw. They were to seek to meet him at the mouth of the Euphrates,** or alternatively, *if that were impossible,* to sail back to the Indus and rejoin him from there. *Alexander himself got the army underway on a march across vast tracts of land, befriending friendly natives, but vanquishing any who opposed him.*

12.44 *After marching for nine days* the army entered the land of the Arabitae and after *nine more* they came to the territory of the Kedrosii. These independent nations decided *in council* to accept Alexander as their overlord, *but the king, whilst welcoming their allegiance, asked nothing of them but the provisioning of his forces. On the fifth day thereafter, he crossed a river known locally as the Arabus. Beyond its further bank* he entered a wide stretch of virtual desert, which having traversed, he arrived at the frontier of the Oreitae. At this point, the king divided the lightly armed contingents between Ptolemy, Leonnatus and himself. *Leaving the bulk of the army in the care of Hephaistion,* he ordered Ptolemy to raid the coastal areas and Leonnatus to plunder the central region, whilst his own party pillaged the upland districts and the hills. Hence the entire country was simultaneously laid waste and every settlement was lit with flame and carpeted with corpses, for the death toll climbed to tens of thousands. But the troops garnered vast spoils and the devastation intimidated the neighbouring tribes, so that they proffered prompt submission. In the same region Alexander conceived a desire to found a seaport. Discovering a sheltered harbour in the vicinity, *called Rhambacæ,* he constructed an Alexandria *and populated it with citizens from Arachosia.*

12.45 *Alexander advanced further into the land of the Oreitae via the passes and speedily subdued the whole territory. For the most part these people share the customs of the other Indians, save in one peculiar and incredible respect. Relatives of their deceased disrobe, then, when completely naked and brandishing spears, they bear away the body and deposit it in one of the copses scattered around their countryside. They similarly divest the corpse of its clothing, exposing it to the depredations of wild beasts. After sharing out these robes of the dead, they offer sacrifices to their Heroes in the Underworld and celebrate by holding a feast for their friends.*

12.46 Thence the king moved into Kedrosia, marching with the sea on his flank and encountering a primitive Indian race, *who dwelt along a vast and desolate stretch of the coast,* where only a few palms and a kind of thorn bush and tamarisk grew. *Complete isolation from their neighbours had made this people* hostile and aggressive towards visitors. But indeed they are savage and brutish in their very nature, for their nails become talons, through never being trimmed from birth to senescence and they allow their hair to grow shaggy and to become matted like felt. Their complexion is seared black by the radiant sun, though they drape themselves in the hides of beasts. <u>Their sole fodder is fish</u> and the flesh of beached whales, <u>which they are wont to shred with their talons and to dry in the sun,</u> then to grind it in whale vertebrae and mix in a little flour, <u>so as to make a sort of bread.</u> They *fabricate and* decorate the walls of their dwellings using oysters and other **shells and anything suitable that may drift ashore. The roof beams of these huts can span up to eighteen cubits, being formed from the ribcages and tiled with the scales of gargantuan whales,** whose jaws serve as portals.

12.47 A scarcity of provisions *among the fish-eaters* began to place the supply of the army in jeopardy, but Alexander led them on into a region of sterile desert, where shortage became famine and hunger turned to starvation. *Though they had sweet water from the wells Alexander had ordered dug by advance parties, the lack of food meant that* the Macedonians were soon reduced to grubbing up the roots of palms, the only tree that continued to flourish in their path. When eventually even this meagre sustenance failed, they were compelled to slaughter their beasts of burden, not even sparing the cavalry mounts. Bereft of any means to transport their baggage further, they simply burnt the gorgeous plunder stripped from their opponents, so that all the rich rewards for their campaigns in the uttermost east were merely fuel for the conflagration. And illness stalked their famished condition, for the noxious succulence of their revolting nourishment together with the exhaustion from the march and the mental stress of their plight combined to spread sickness among their ranks. Their deadly dilemma was that lingering meant starving, whereas progress risked debilitation and a surer death.

12.48 Therefore their tracks across this landscape became strewn with their incapacitated comrades more so than their stoical dead, since even mild infirmity sufficed to cause men to fall behind in the forced marches. For the army advanced at the fastest pace that the healthy could maintain, as they felt impelled to pursue their hope for safety with all their vigour. But those whose energy had failed appealed desperately for aid to their friends in the column and to strangers also, yet neither to any avail. There were no more beasts to bear the infirm and the marchers were challenged even to manage to carry their arms. Indeed, the pathetic sight of their fallen fellows was a constant reminder of their own peril. Hence, despite frequent entreaties, they looked away from the dropouts as fear conquered their compassion. Those abandoned called upon the gods to be their witnesses and invoked the sacred bonds of fraternity and the duty of care owed to them by the king. But in the end, realising that their breath was wasted on deaf ears, despair made them utter irrational curses that those who had refused them succour should suffer as cruel a fate as theirs and with equally faithless friends.

12.49 Thus starvation claimed many victims and the army was greatly dispirited. Alexander himself experienced a mixture of dolour and anguish, *also tinged with shame, since his personal leadership had brought about the disaster.* **It seemed a detestable irony that men who had surpassed all in the art and practice of warfare should perish ignominiously for want of basic rations in an empty land. Therefore the king took action by dispatching fleet emissaries to** *Phrataphernes, Satrap of* **Parthyaea and to Drangianê and Aria and to all his provinces bordering on the desert. The governors were commanded with the utmost urgency to send racing camels and other trained beasts of burden to him via the passes of Carmania, each to be loaded with cooked food and other essentials for the relief of his forces. These messengers were swift to reach their objectives and the response of the satraps was equally expeditious, such that large quantities of supplies soon arrived at the specified rendezvous. Therefore the army was rescued from hunger, though not without losses,** *and came through to a more fertile region of Kedrosia. Alexander encamped for some time at that place in order that his traumatised troops might gently recuperate.*

12.50 *There he received a letter from Leonnatus, describing a victory won against* the Oreitae. *They* had attacked Leonnatus' brigade *in a strength of 8000 infantry and 400 cavalry,* but the Bodyguard had forced them to flee back to their own country, though he had suffered significant casualties in the battle. News also reached him from Craterus, that he had subdued Ozines and Zariaspes, Persian aristocrats who had fomented a rebellion, and clapped them in irons. Menon, the satrap of Kedrosia having lately died, Alexander appointed Sibyrtius to the office in his stead, before advancing into Carmania, where the satrap was Astaspes. There were suspicions that this man had sought to revolt whilst Alexander had been in India, but the king suppressed his anger in greeting his governor pleasantly and retaining him in his office, pending an opportunity to investigate the accusations properly.

12.51 Following further orders from Alexander, the provincial governors now requisitioned huge stocks of cavalry steeds and beasts of burden from throughout their domains, so that Alexander was able to replace the chattels of those who had lost them *in the desert.* This included armaments as magnificent as those that had been discarded, for the entire wealth of conquered Persia was now at the king's disposal. He therefore conceived an ostentatious extension of his rivalry with Dionysus. In a spirit of ascending above and beyond the mere imitation of the god's triumph over the subject nations, **Alexander decided also to emulate the festal procession and carousal for which Dionysus is especially renowned.** To this purpose he arranged that his path through the villages *of Carmania* should be carpeted with blossom and hung with garlands. Cauldrons and even vats of wine were set upon the threshold of every dwelling on his route *to fuel the festivities* and he had carriages extended to accommodate large parties of soldiers, enclosed beneath canopies formed from dazzling white sheets or precious *purple* fabrics, *richly embroidered, or else shaded by fresh green fronds.*

12.52 Alexander himself led the pageant in the company of his close friends and the rest of the royal party, each of them crowned with a wreath woven from a diversity of flowers. To one side the flautists trilled; on the other strummers plucked melodies from their lyres, *so that the air was filled with music and song.* Trundling in their tracks came the rest of the army conveyed by *innumerable* wagons garnished with displays of their most impressive weaponry. The king's own chariot was *drawn by eight horses, being* particularly heavily laden, for it bore basins and beakers of solid gold as well as his personal guests *and a lofty dais, on which he banqueted day and night.* **In this state of revelry, feasting and intoxication the entire army progressed for seven days,** virtually defenceless against any among the local inhabitants who might have summoned the courage to attack. Yet none dared, for Fortune, whose gift is fame, turned even this militarily imprudent behaviour to glory. And now it is considered a wonder that Alexander paraded a drunken army through lands not yet purged of enemies and that the barbarians mistook his rashness for invulnerability.

12.53 But the executioner stalked at the tail of this Dionysiac comus, for shortly afterwards it was ordered that Astaspes, the governor of Carmania, should be put to death. Indeed **at this time Alexander discovered that many of his officials had abused their powers and committed serious crimes** *in his absence,* **and so he inflicted punishment upon a number of his satraps and generals.** *For example,* around this time Cleander and Sitalces, and Heracon accompanied by Agathon joined the king. These were the officers who had assassinated Parmenion at Alexander's behest. They brought with them a force of 5000 infantry and 1000 cavalry, but complainants from the provinces that they governed also followed on their heels. Although the king was greatly appreciative of the service, which they had rendered by eliminating Parmenion, this could not compensate for the numerous offences that they had since perpetrated. Having despoiled everything in the temporal sphere, they failed to exclude even sacred things from their depredations. Virgins and noblewomen, whom they had raped, came *before Alexander* to bewail the defilement of their bodies. The grasping and libidinous misbehaviour of these men had blighted the reputation of the Macedonians among the native peoples. Yet Cleander excelled the rest in lechery, for after having forcibly deflowered a virgin of noble family, he consigned her to become the harlot of his slave.

12.54 It was not so much these accusations of atrocities as remembrance of their slaughter of Parmenion that influenced a large number of Alexander's Friends against these men, though this might privately have favoured their cause with the king himself. The courtiers were glad that the king's wrath had recoiled upon the instruments of his wrath, so that no power acquired through acts of infamy should prove lasting. After considering the case, Alexander pronounced his judgement: "The prosecution has overlooked the greatest treason, and that was the abandonment of hope for my safe return. For it is inconceivable that the accused should have lapsed into such misconduct, if they had either believed or desired that I should come back unscathed from India." Accordingly, he had them fettered and ordered that 600 of their soldiers, who had been the agents of their ferocity, should be put to death. On that same day the captured leaders of the Persian rebellion, Ozines and Zariaspes, who had been brought in by Craterus, paid the price with their lives. *As the news spread that Alexander was righteously disciplining his delinquent commanders, many of his generals were disturbed by recollections of their own extravagant or criminal behaviour. Some instigated insurrections with the backing of mercenary armies, whilst others absconded with substantial hoards of treasure. When Alexander ascertained these reactions, he dispatched letters to each of his generals and satraps in Asia, commanding them instantly to disband their private armies.*

12.55 At this time Alexander was resting in a city called Salmous, not far *upriver* **from the sea. He was presiding over stage contests in the theatre, when the fleet was brought into the** *nearby* **harbour by its officers, Nearchus and Onesicritus. They immediately came** *into town* **to greet**

Alexander in the theatre and to report upon the progress of their mission, for the king had ordered them to explore the sea-lanes and the coastal waters on the Ocean route from India back to Persia. The Macedonians were overjoyed by their deliverance from the perils of their voyage and welcomed them with a rousing ovation, so that the whole arena resounded with unrestrained jubilation.

12.56 *The mariners told of wonders they had themselves witnessed and of others that were merely rumoured.* They had observed astounding ebbs and surges of the Ocean waters, so that many great islands were unexpectedly revealed along the coast by the former, only to be submerged by the latter with a vigorous landward flow, its surface white with roiling foam. <u>They described an island opposite the mouth of the river that was rich in gold but wanting in steeds, for which its inhabitants would pay a talent apiece to anyone who ventured to ship them from the mainland. Another island had a sacred mountain, which was shaded by a grove of trees that exuded a marvellously dulcet perfume.</u>

12.57 They said that their most extraordinary experience was an encounter with a multitudinous school of unbelievably huge whales, *each of them the size of the largest of ships. They drifted with the flow of the current,* converging upon the course of the fleet. The crews were terrified and fearful for their lives, believing that the beasts were about to dash their vessels to smithereens. But when they all yelled in unison, striking their shields to generate a great cacophony and when this was further augmented with the trumpeting of their bugles, then the beasts were discomfited by the strange din and promptly dived into the depths of the Ocean *with a great crashing of the waves as they closed over them, just like the roar of a foundering ship.*

12.58 *They also recited a legend of the natives that the Red (or Erythraean) Sea did not take its name from the hue of its waters, as was commonly supposed, but was called after a King Erythrus. The grave of this king was to be found on an island not far offshore in the centre of a dense palm forest at a site marked by a lofty column with an inscription in the native alphabet. It was added that merchant-venturers, pursuing their pilots' reports of a golden treasure, had sailed to the island, but had never been heard of again.*

12.59 *All these stories enthused the king to complete the exploration of the sea-route.* He *therefore* requested that his fleet should continue its voyage by navigating a coastal course to the mouth of the Euphrates *and thence upriver to Babylon.*

12.60 *At these same contests in Carmania, after wine had warmed the mood, it is recorded that Alexander's lover, Bagoas the Eunuch, won the prize for singing and dancing, whilst the king presided. Decked in his festal adornments, the champion quit the stage and went across the theatre to sit down right next to Alexander. On seeing this, the Macedonians clapped their hands and shouted for the king to kiss the victor, until their persistence was rewarded by the spectacle of Alexander embracing the eunuch and kissing him passionately.*

12.61 Having brought all the eastern coastal regions beneath his sway, the king conceived plans that were unbounded in their ambition. He intended to cross from Syria into Africa in pursuit of his animosity towards the Carthaginians for their aid to Tyre *during his siege.* Thence he would trek through the wastes of Numidia, directing his course towards Gades, for it was widely reported that the Pillars of Heracles lay thereabouts. Next he aimed to cross to Iberia, named after its eponymous river. Afterwards he would march up to the Alps, but detour around them along the coast of Italy, whence it is but a short voyage to Epirus *and his homeland.* To these ends he issued commands to the governors of Mesopotamia to fell timber on Mount Lebanon and to convey it to the Syrian city of Thapsacus; there to lay the keels of 700 ships, all septiremes[3], for delivery to Babylon *via the Euphrates.* The kings of Cyprus were ordered to supply the requisite bronze, hemp and sails. Whilst Alexander concerned himself with these matters, letters from the Indian kings, Porus and Taxiles, were brought to him, advising that Abisares had ailed and died and Alexander's viceroy, Philip, had perished from a wound, though the culprits had been punished. Accordingly, the king appointed Eudaemon, a commander of the Thracian troops, in Philip's stead and endorsed the inheritance of Abisares' kingdom by his son.

12.62 Afterwards the king arrived at Parsagada, where the people are Persians. Their satrap was Orsines, pre-eminent among all the inhabitants due to a combination of noble ancestry and wealth. His family were descended from that Cyrus who had once reigned over the Persians. He had inherited the family fortune, which he had considerably augmented in the course of a lengthy tenure of the Satrapy. He showered gifts upon Alexander and purposefully directed his largesse upon the king's Friends as well. Herds of ready-broken horses trotted in his train, together with gilded chariots, magnificent furniture, flawless gems, massive golden vases, rich purple robes and three thousand talents of silver coin. Yet this immense profligacy of the barbarian was to lead to his death. For having bestowed presents exceeding all expectations upon the rest of Alexander's Friends, he conspicuously neglected similarly to honour Bagoas, the eunuch who had won Alexander's affection by making himself sexually available to the king. Orsines was actually cautioned by certain individuals that Bagoas was very dear to Alexander, but he quipped: "I wished to show my respect for the king's noblemen, rather than for his whores, for it is not the Persian custom to treat as men those who adopt the female sexual role."

12.63 On hearing of this, the eunuch *directed all his power and energy towards the downfall of the satrap. By making surreptitious enquiries he discovered Persians who were willing to bear witness to the misdeeds of Orsines, but he counselled them to refrain from*

---

[3] Probably two tiers of oars with three and four men per oar respectively.

making their accusations public until he should order it. Meanwhile in private he began to undermine Orsines' reputation with the king, so that although the satrap had not yet been charged, he was already less highly regarded. Bagoas even began to take advantage of the opportunities afforded by his sexual liaisons with Alexander, so that whenever he had aroused the king's passion for him he made accusations of acquisitiveness or even of sedition against the satrap.

12.64 Then it happened that Alexander ordered that the tomb of Cyrus should be opened, since he wished to reverence the corpse of the former monarch, which had been laid to rest within. He had supposed it to be a treasury crammed with gold and silver, for such was its widespread repute among the Persians. Yet in fact Alexander found nothing, save the king's decaying shield, two Scythian bows and a sabre. He set a golden crown upon the sarcophagus containing the body and draped it with his own cloak, musing that it was surprising that a monarch of such power and fame had been entombed with no more splendour than many an ordinary man. The eunuch, who was close beside him, gazed intently at Alexander: "What's so surprising about the tombs of kings being bare, when the mansions of satraps cannot hold all the gold gleaned from them? As for myself, I have never seen inside this vault before, but I heard from Darius that three thousand talents were buried with Cyrus. So the generous donations that Orsines has made to you were designed to purchase your favour using funds that he knew he could not anyway retain with impunity."

12.65 Thus Alexander already harboured some antipathy towards Orsines, when the witnesses to the satrap's criminality procured by Bagoas came before him. On the one hand Bagoas and on the other the testimonies of Orsines' own subjects filled the king's ears with capital charges. Before he even suspected that allegations had been made against him, the satrap found himself arraigned in fetters. Bagoas himself manhandled Orsines to his execution. At the same time Phradates was put to death, since he was suspected of having sought the throne *and Baryaxes too was executed, since he had worn the tiara upright, which is the prerogative of the Persian king.*

12.66 *The king had progressed with the army as far as the borders of Susianê, when the Indian Calanus, who was an adept philosopher and greatly respected by Alexander, decided to terminate his own life in an amazing ceremony. He had achieved the age of seventy-three without ever having suffered from sickness and considered that he had reached the limits of happiness in terms of both health and good fortune. Recently he had been ailing* from a bowel complaint *and was growing weaker day by day. He therefore petitioned the king to construct a vast pyre and to order the royal attendants to set it alight once he had clambered atop it.*

12.67 *Although Alexander sought to dissuade Calanus from this end, the philosopher proved resolute, so the king eventually agreed to arrange the* *matter. When word of the event had spread and the pyre had been erected, crowds gathered to witness the astonishing spectacle.* The *naked* philosopher rode to his death on a fine steed, but dismounted at the base of the pyre to offer prayers. After also sprinkling himself *with holy oil* and casting a lock of his hair upon the edifice, *Calanus contentedly climbed to its apex and turned to salute the Macedonian spectators, exhorting them to celebrate the day in revelry with their king. Yet he declined to bid farewell to Alexander himself, saying only that he would see him again soon in Babylon.* Then he lay down and covered his head and did not stir at all as *he was swallowed by the flames and perished. Thus he sacrificed himself in accordance with the ancient custom of the wise men of his country,* for they consider it a sacred duty when their bodies become polluted by disease to purify themselves in fire. Some of those who attended considered him insane; others again considered it an arrogant exhibition of pride in his indifference to pain; others still simply marvelled at his strength of spirit and <u>his contempt for death.</u> *Alexander duly proceeded to celebrate the funeral of Calanus with splendid festivities.*

Figure 12.2. The weddings at Susa (late 19th century, after Andreas Muller).

12.68 *The king continued onwards to Susa,* where he held magnificent wedding ceremonies. *He himself took Stateira, the elder daughter of Darius, as his wife, whilst marrying her younger sister Drypetis to Hephaistion. He also persuaded the most influential of his Friends and noblemen to take Persian brides selected from the most aristocratic* *families.* Thus he forestalled criticism of his union with the former enemy by making all the senior men complicit in his policy.

12.69 *At this juncture a band of thirty thousand Persian youths arrived at Susa,* the cream of their generation, *chosen for their comeliness and strength. They had been recruited* as boys three years beforehand *at Alexander's behest and had since completed a course of military training under expert tuition. All were elaborately outfitted with Macedonian panoplies and weaponry and they set up their camp in front of the city, where the king came to review them. They performed their military exercises and utilised their weapons with such skill, vigour, agility and discipline that Alexander was greatly pleased and issued them a commendation. However, the Macedonian troops were downcast, fearing that their king would be freed from his reliance upon them,* now that he had these young war-dancers with whom he could go on to conquer all mankind. *Indeed it was* recalled that *the Macedonians had not merely refused to march on to the Ganges in India, but were regularly insubordinate at assemblies and lampooned Alexander's adoption of Ammon as his heavenly father. Indeed it was as a counter-weight to the power of the Macedonian phalanx that Alexander had conceived and formed the new cadre from a single age-stream of Persian youths.*

12.70 **These were the concerns of Alexander** *in the twelfth year of his reign.*

6. Alexander's Route Through India

Cleitarchus probably agreed that Alexander entered India via the River Cophen (Kabul River valley) and that the bulk of the army continued down this river under the command of Hephaistion until they reached its confluence with the Indus. Alexander operated separately with a large task force in the mountain valleys north of the Cophen, receiving the surrender of Nysa and capturing Massaga/Mazaga (in the Swat valley?) and Aornus (Pir Sar). After bridging the river, he advanced to Taxila and thence to the Hydaspes. After defeating Porus on its far bank, he proceeded eastwards crossing the Acesines and the Hydraotis/Hiarotis, but the army refused to advance beyond the Hyphasis and towards the Ganges. The king returned to encamp the army near the Acesines. Cleitarchus either stated or implied that he sailed down the Acesines (although he went down the Hydaspes in Arrian) with a newly constructed fleet, the bulk of the army marching along the banks. The most important difference on Indian geography between Cleitarchus and Arrian is that the former placed the conflict with the Malli and Oxydracae south of the confluence of the Acesines with the Indus. There is some support for Cleitarchus in the geography, since Gendari Mt could be the mountain from which the alliance of the Oxydracae and the Mallians initially mounted their defence.

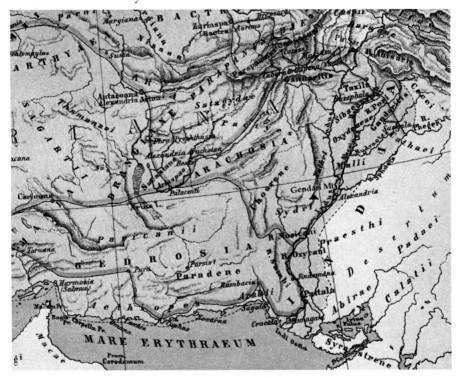

Alexander's India

Craterus and Polyperchon evidently headed back towards Persia via Arachosia with a majority of Alexander's army from the vicinity of the kingdom of Musicanus, but only a mention of Polyperchon's return in Justin would suggest that Cleitarchus noted their departure. Alexander himself sailed on to Patala and thence into the western branch of the Indus Delta and out into the Ocean, where he visited islands up to tens of kilometers offshore, then retraced his course to Patala. Arrian mentions that Alexander afterwards led an exploratory expedition down the eastern branch of the delta, but there is no sign that this appeared in Cleitarchus.

Nearchus and Onesicritus set sail for Persia via the Ocean and the Erythraean Sea from the vicinity of modern Karachi, whilst Alexander took the land route westwards, initially along the coast via Rambacia/Rhambarce (Bela). Cleitarchus was clear that Alexander's forces ran short of food on the coast of Gedrosia among the Fisheaters (Ichthyophagoi) and were reduced to a serious state of starvation after striking inland across desert wastes towards Pura. There is no sign that Cleitarchus attributed these travails to shortage of water, but rather he emphasized that Alexander had sent men ahead to dig wells. After celebrating a Dionysiac *comus* through a fertile region of Carmania, Alexander was re-united with the commanders of his fleet at Salmous, not far inland from the Gulf of Hormuz according to Cleitarchus. Thereafter he journeyed in stages to Susa via Parsagada. He was there to greet the *Epigoni*, when Cleitarchus' twelfth book ended in the early summer of 324BC.

7. Organisation And Sources

The first column outlines each successive episode in Cleitarchan terms. The second gives the extant sources for each episode. The third cites references to the Cleitarchan nature of the material and the last provides technical comments.

Book 1: Spring 336BC – Autumn 335BC; Alexander in Europe

Summary	Sources	References	Comment
Prologue: birth and ancestry of Alexander. Razing of the temple at Ephesus and descent from Aeacidae and Heraclidae.	Plutarch 2.1&3.3-5	Hammond THA 91 Sources 19-20	It has been thought that Cleitarchus opened his history with the assassination of Philip & Alexander's accession. However, a summary dealing with Alexander's birth & his youth may have been included. Hammond shows in *Sources* 19-20 that Plutarch's date for Alexander's birth comes from Timaeus, a contemporary of Cleitarchus. But Jacoby F7 of Cleitarchus from Clement of Alexandria says that both Timaeus & Cleitarchus gave 820 years for the period from the invasion of the Heraclidae to Alexander's crossing into Asia, whereas other Greek historians, such as Eratosthenes, gave wildly variant figures (cf. Jacoby F 36). This strongly indicates that Cleitarchus made use of Timaeus' work (cf. Pearson 216). If so, then Plutarch & Cicero are likely to be getting Timaeus' information on Alexander's birth via Cleitarchus. Perhaps Cleitarchus attributed the information to Timaeus. Hammond also attributes stress on Alexander's Aeacid ancestry to Cleitarchus & Jacoby F7 mentions the Heraclidae (cf. F36)
Philip sends his generals Parmenion, Amyntas & Attalus into Asia Minor	Justin 9.5.8-9	Hammond THA 93	Spring of 336BC
Philip celebrates marriage of daughter Cleopatra to Alexander of Epirus; Pausanias kills Philip in narrow passage, because he has ignored Pausanias' complaints against Attalus, who had raped him	Justin 9.6.1-8	Hammond THA 93	Summer of 336BC
Sons of Philip	Justin 9.8.1-3	Hammond THA 90-3	

Summary	Sources	References	Comment
Digression on the historical background in the Persian Empire: troubled prelude to the accession of Darius III to the throne	Justin 10 Diodorus 17.5.3-7.3		Hammond suggests this is from Diyllus in Diodorus and from Cleitarchus' father, Deinon, in Justin, but the material is similar and placed in the text in both such as to imply a common source. (cf. Jacoby F 33) Cleitarchus is the likely common source of Justin and Diodorus with a special interest in Persian events due to his father's work.
Accession & funeral of Philip; rebelliousness of Thebes; appointed general by assembly at Corinth	Justin 11.1.1-11.2.7 Diodorus 17.3-4	Hammond THA 94; Yardley & Heckel on Justin 83-5	Yardley & Heckel rightly reject Hammond's view that Diodorus used Diyllus here and prefer Cleitarchus
Balkan campaign: battle with Syrmus of the Triballi at the Danube	Plutarch 11.1-3 Justin 11.2.8 Diodorus 17.8.1	Hammond THA 94 & Sources 24; Yardley & Heckel on Justin 84-5	Spring-summer 335BC in extreme summary
Omens of the fall of Thebes	Arrian 1.9.8 Aelian VH 12.57	Hammond Sources 207	
Siege & destruction of Thebes & Council at which the destruction was proposed by the Plataeans and Phocians	Diodorus 17.8.2-14.4 Plutarch 11.4-6 Justin 11.3.1-11.4.6	Hammond THA 91-3 & Sources	
Alexander saves Pindar's house	Arrian 1.9.10 Aelian VH 13.7	Hammond Sources 207	
After razing of Thebes, its wealth (from selling Thebans into slavery…) just 440 talents & its citizens were stingy	Athenaeus 148 D-F (cf. Diodorus 17.14.4)	Jacoby, Fragment 1 of Cleitarchus	Attributed to Cleitarchus and Book 1 of Concerning Alexander – Diodorus *implies* 440 talents raised by selling the Thebans, but probably equals total proceeds
Reconciliation with Athenians upset by fate of Thebes	Plutarch 13	Hammond, Sources 27	
Visit to Delphi: Alexander declared invincible by the Pythia	Plutarch 14.4-5 Diodorus 17.93.4 [Livy 9.18] [SIG^3 251H, col. II, lines 9-10 (p.436-7)]	Hammond Sources 29 THA	Alexander is *aniketos* (invincible) & promised world-rule, cf. Siwa & Ammon. Livy too refers to the "invincible Alexander", though also the attacks on Alexander by Athenian orators, eg Hypereides, who called Alexander "king and invincible god" (ironically). Historicity of oracle visit supported by gift to shrine at this time of 150 gold coins of Philip from Alexander(?) Perhaps read of Xenophon's consultation of Delphi for *his* campaign against Persia. Pearson (Lost Histories p. 92) thinks Plutarch got Delphic visit from Onesicritus, but Cleitarchus used Onesicritus.

Book 2: Winter 335BC – June 334BC; Crosses to Asia, Battle of Granicus

Summary	Sources	References	Comment
Crossing to Asia and preparations; Alexander's gifts to his friends, Alexander took with him the most capable Thracian kings, dye on priests hands left marks foretelling victory on victims' livers	Justin 11.5.1-9 Plutarch 15.2-3 Front. Strat. 2.11.3 & 1.11.14	Hammond THA 95-6 Sources 31	
820 years from the invasion of the Heraclidae to Alexander crossing into Asia	Clement of Alexandria, Strom. I 139,4	Jacoby, Fragment 7 of Cleitarchus	Early Spring
Alexander casts a spear into the Asian shoreline	Justin 11.5.10-11 Diodorus 17.17.2		Hammond makes no suggestion for this against Justin, but this story is common to Justin and Diodorus, so Cleitarchus is overwhelmingly likely to be its source
Troops ordered not to ravage Asia, because it was their own property	Justin 11.6.1	Hammond THA 96	
Troop numbers: 32000 infantry, 4500 cavalry and 182 warships. Contrasting Alexander's world conquest with a small band of experienced troops with Darius' reliance on overwhelming strength	Justin 11.6.2-9	Hammond THA 96-7	Abbreviated(?) to 40,000 men in Frontinus, Stratagems 4.2.4 & Ampelius 16.2
Honouring the tombs of Achilles and the heroes (Patroclus) at Troy	Arrian 1.12.1 Diodorus 17.17.3 Justin 11.5.12 Plutarch 15.4 Aelian VH 9.38 & 12.7, cf. Cicero, Pro Archia poet. 24		Hammond does not explicitly identify this anecdote as Cleitarchus, but he does point out that Alexander's emulation of Achilles was probably a Cleitarchan theme (THA 64-5, 91, 109; Sources 48 n11). The story is common to Justin and Diodorus, which strongly suggests that Cleitarchus is its source
Battle of the Granicus	Diodorus 17.19.3-21.6 & 17.23.2	Hammond THA 16-17	Late spring

Book 3: July 334BC – June 333BC

Summary	Sources	References	Comment
Alexander takes the surrender of Magnesia, where lay the tomb of Themistocles (Athenian commander at Salamis) – digression on Themistocles at the court of Xerxes following his exile from Athens – he later drank bull's blood and died rather that lead Persian forces against Athens	Plutarch's Life of Themistocles 27.1-2 Cicero, Brut. 42-43	Jacoby, Fragments 33 & 34 of Cleitarchus	The surrender of Magnesia (Arrian 1.18.1) is the most likely occasion for Cleitarchus' digression on Themistocles, since the tomb of Themistocles was there. Cleitarchus' father Deinon had evidently told the story of Themistocles. It is possible that Cleitarchus drew a comparison between Themistocles' submission to Xerxes and Charidemus' allegiance to Darius, since they were both exiled Athenians serving Persian kings. Arrian (1.18.2) may implicitly be contradicting Cleitarchus when he makes a point of stating that Alexander stayed at Ephesus when Magnesia surrendered.
Miletus			Cleitarchan version lost?
Dismissed the fleet to encourage troops to fight more vigorously, when Darius reached the coast	Diodorus 23.1	Hammond THA 38	
Concentration of Persians at Halicarnassus. Memnon sends his wife (Barsine) and children to Darius for safety and trust	Diodorus 17.23.4-6	Hammond THA 39	
Halicarnassus	Diodorus 17.24.4-27.6	Hammond THA 39-40	Stalwart veterans and young shirkers – a Cleitarchan theme
Fortress of the Marmares on the border between Lycia and Pisidia	Diodorus 17.28	Hammond THA 40	Not recounted elsewhere – may be Chandir in Pamphylia
Alexander uncertain regarding future strategy	Plutarch 17.1-2	Hammond Sources 45-6	Alexander's policy is swayed by the ensuing oracles and miracles – mimics Herodotus in his account of Xerxes being swayed by dreams and oracles
Spring near Xanthus in Lydia casts forth a bronze tablet prophesying the overthrow of the Persians by the Greeks	Plutarch 17.2-3	Hammond Sources 46	
Sea gives way to Alexander on the Pamphylian coast; crowns statue of Theodectas at Phaselis during a comus	Plutarch 17.2-3 & 5	Hammond Sources 46-7, Tarn Sources 49	Cleitarchus following Callisthenes for the sea giving way? Tarn argues mentions of Alexander in a *comus* are from Cleitarchus.
Arrest of Alexander Lyncestes on charges of conspiracy due to information from a prisoner	Justin 11.7.1		Justin's timing agrees with Curtius 7.1.6, who placed the arrest in his lost second book; Hammond makes no attribution.

Summary	Sources	References	Comment
Alexander cuts the Gordian knot with his sword	Arrian 2.3.7, Justin 11.7.3-16, Curtius 3.1.14-19, Plutarch 18.1-2	Hammond Sources 47 & 217 THA 97 & 128	Knot-solver "destined to become king of the inhabited Earth" in Plutarch – chimes with World-Ruler idea from Cleitarchus (cf. Siwa oracle below)
Death of Memnon	Plutarch 18.3, Curtius 3.2.1	C3.2.1=D17.30.7 Schwartz	Completes the encouragement of Alexander to attack Darius
Parade of Darius' forces before Babylon: Charidemus of Athens is pessimistic about their chances against the Macedonians and is executed	Curtius 3.2.2-19 Diodorus 17.30.1-31.2	Hammond THA 40-1 & 116	Resembles conference of Xerxes in Herodotus 7; Curtius directly references Herodotus 7.59
Dream of Darius misinterpreted by magi	Plutarch 18.4-5, Curtius 3.3.2-7	Hammond Sources 48	Hammond does not assign this passage in THA

Book 4: July 333BC – July 332BC

Summary	Sources	References	Comment
Advance to Cilicia across Mount Taurus by a forced march on hearing of Darius' approach	Justin 11.8.1-2	Hammond THA 113	By association with Justin's version of Tarsus
Alexander tarries at Tarsus due to illness, after plunging into the Cydnus, but Darius thinks him intimidated	Plutarch 19 Curtius 3.5.1-3.6.3 Justin 11.8.3 Val. Max. 3.8 ext 6	Hammond Sources 48-9 THA 97-8 & 121	
Letter(s) from Olympias/Parmenion warning Alexander about Philip the Doctor and Alexander Lyncestes, who was arrested	Diodorus 17.32.1-2 Seneca De Ira 2.23 Val. Max. 3.8 ext 6 Curtius 3.6.4-16	Hammond THA 41	Note however that Justin 11.7.1 placed Lyncestes' arrest prior to the march to Gordium and Curtius gave it in his lost second book prior to Gordium (so too Arrian 1.25) – Diodorus may be conflating two different warning letters
Sardanapalus died of old age after he had lost the sovereignty of the Syrians	Athenaeus 530A, cf. Plutarch Moralia 326F & 336C	Jacoby, Fragment 2 of Cleitarchus	Attributed by Athenaeus to Book 4: context is Alexander's arrival before a monument and statue of Sardanapalus at Anchiale, 12 miles SW of Tarsus – here Cleitarchus is echoing his father Deinon's Persica, which may in turn have followed Ctesias' Persica. The story of Alexander's visit is also told by Athenaeus 530 A-B as a fragment of Aristobulus, so too Strabo 14.5.9 and Arrian 2.5.2-4 – this is also in Fragment 34 of Callisthenes

Summary	Sources	References	Comment
Battle of Issus: Darius defeated by Alexander	Cicero Ad f. 2.10.3 Curtius 3.8.13-3.11.27 Diodorus 17.32.3-17.38.2	Jacoby, Fragment 8 of Cleitarchus; Hammond THA 17 & 118; C3.11.7-11=D17.34.2-6 Schwartz; C3.11.20,23-6= D17.35.2,36.5,2,4 cf.J11.9.11-12 & C3.11.27=D17.36.6 Hamilton:C&D17	November 333BC
Alexander captures the chariot & bow of Darius	Plutarch 20.5-6	Hammond Sources 51	
Visit to the Persian Queens with Hephaistion, who is mistaken for Alexander	Arrian 2.12.6-7 Diodorus 17.37.5 Curtius 3.12.1-3.12.26 Justin 11.9.11-16 Plutarch 21.2-3 Val. Max. 4.7 ext 2	Hammond THA 19, 98, 118 Sources 50-52, 225; C3.12.15-17=D17.37.5-6 Hamilton:C&D17; C3.12.26=D17.38.2 Hamilton:C&D17	
Alexander seduced by Persian luxury and falls in love with Barsine and advances into Syria	Justin 11.10.1-3 Plutarch 20.6-8	Hammond THA 98 Sources 51	
Alexander sends Thessalian cavalry to capture the Persian treasure & women at Damascus	Plutarch 24.1-2	Hammond Sources 53-54	
First peace offer from Darius: Diodorus uniquely suggests that Alexander concealed the real letter and presented a forgery	Curtius 4.1.7-14 Justin 11.12.1-2 Diodorus 17.39.1-3	Hammond THA 42, 99, 122	
Siege of Tyre	Diodorus 17.40.2-17.47.6 Justin 11.10.10-14 Curtius (most of) 4.2.2-4.4.19	Hammond THA 42, 98, 121, 119; C4.2.7=D17.40.4 Schwartz; C4.2.12=D17.41.3-4 Schwartz; C4.2.18=D17.40.5 Schwartz; C4.2.20=D17.41.1 Schwartz; C4.3.6,9,11-12=D17.42.5-6,43.3 Schwartz; C4.3.22=D17.41.8 Hamilton:C&D17; C4.3.25-26=D17.44.1-3 Schwartz; C4.4.1-2=D17.45.7 Schwartz; C4.4.3-5=D17.41.5-6 Hamilton:C&D17; C4.4.10-12,17=D17.46.2-4 Schwartz	January-July 332BC

Summary	Sources	References	Comment
Phoenicians (especially Carthaginians) worship Cronos by burning a child as an offering	Schol. Plato Resp. 337A (Photius: Sardonios gelos); cf. Curtius 4.3.23	Jacoby, Fragment 9 of Cleitarchus, Hamilton Cleitarchus & Diodorus 17	Curtius relates that Tyrians proposed to resume the sacrifice of a freeborn boy to Saturn just after the arrival of Carthaginian envoys
Tyrians dreamt that Apollo wished to abandon them, so they chained his statue	Plutarch 24.4 Diodorus 17.41.7 Curtius 4.3.21	Hammond THA 42, 119 Sources 55-6	
Balonymus (Abdalonymus in J & C, Aralynomus in P Moralia) appointed king of Tyre (Sidon in J & C, Paphos in P)	Diodorus 17.47.1-6 Curtius 4.1.16-26 Justin 11.10.8-9 (cf. Plutarch Moralia 340C-E)	Hammond THA 98, 119, 121; C4.1.15-26=D17.47.1-6 Hamilton:C&D17	Diodorus incorrectly placed the story at Tyre and cited "Balonymus" – Hammond's belief that he was using Cleitarchus is probably correct, which means that Curtius and Trogus got their truer versions from elsewhere
"Now that we have described activity *concerning Alexander*, we shall turn our narrative in another direction"	Diodorus 17.47.6		Looks like a book-end from Cleitarchus, because it incorporates the title of his work: Concerning Alexander – cf. the ends of books 7 & 12

Book 5: August 332BC – June 331BC

Summary	Sources	References	Comment
Agis hires mercenaries who had escaped from Issus and invades and conquers Crete	Diodorus 17.48.1-2 Curtius 4.1.39-40	C4.1.39-40=D17.48.1-2 Schwartz	
The rebel Macedonian, Amyntas son of Antiochus led 4000 troops to Egypt and overcame the local forces in battle, but his forces were destroyed in a surprise counter-attack, when scattered for looting	Curtius 4.1.27-33 Diodorus 17.48.2-5	C4.1.27-33=D17.48.2-4 Schwartz	Hammond THA thinks this is Diyllus, but it is clear that Curtius and Diodorus used a common source and it is not tenable that they independently selected the same episodes from two separate sources as Hammond has suggested. This is therefore very likely to be Cleitarchus. Diodorus relates this episode after Tyre.
The delegates of the League of Corinth vote at the Isthmian Games to send Alexander golden crowns via 15 envoys	Curtius 4.5.11-12 Diodorus 17.48.6	C4.5.11=D17.48.6 Schwartz	Hammond THA thinks this is Diyllus, but the exact agreement of Curtius and Diodorus is suggestive of Cleitarchus
Capture of the pirate, Aristonicus of Methymne, at Chios	Curtius 4.5.19-22		This is Cleitarchus, because the delivery of Aristonicus to Alexander at Alexandria (see below) was related by Cicero, who is a source for other fragments of Cleitarchus
Second peace offer from Darius: Parmenion suggests acceptance of terms offered in a letter from Darius	Curtius 4.5.1-8 Justin 11.12.3-4 Arrian 2.25.2 (Plutarch 29.4) Val. Max. 6.4 ext 3	Hammond THA99-100, 122 Sources 62, 225	Diodorus appears to edit out this offer, but implies it was in his source by speaking of other daughter of Darius under third offer. Plutarch places his anecdote in the run-up to Gaugamela (i.e. where Cleitarchus probably recorded Darius' third offer).

Summary	Sources	References	Comment
Siege of Gaza: Alexander struck by an arrow, the city is stormed and Alexander is struck in the leg, Alexander emulates Achilles by dragging Betis behind his chariot	Curtius 4.6.1-12(?) & 4.6.17-30	Hammond Sources 57 THA 128;	Falls November 332BC – Curtius 4.6.12-16 resembles Fragment 5 of Hegesias, but this may be Cleitarchus using Hegesias as his source.
Alexander sends Amyntas son of Andromenes with 10 triremes to Macedonia Occupation of Egypt		C4.6.30=D17.49.1 Schwartz	Enthroned as Pharaoh in Memphis (Alexander Romance) December 332BC
Settles affairs in Egypt and decides to visit the Temple of Ammon (at Siwa) – meets envoys from Cyrene		C4.7.1,5,9=D17.49.2-4 Schwartz	
Enters the desert - water gives out after 4 days - a great storm provides drinking water		C4.7.12-14=D17.49.4-5 Schwartz	
Description of the oasis, its people and its situation - visit to the oracle at Siwa: Alexander, son of Ammon, would be invincible (invictus[Lat] = aniketos[Gk]) and rule all lands	Curtius 4.7.25-28 Diodorus 17.49.3-17.51.4 Justin 11.11.2-10 Plutarch 26.6-27.4 Val. Max. 9.5 ext 1	Hammond THA 43, 92, 122 Sources 58-61; C4.7.16-17,20-28=D17.50.3-51.3 Schwartz	Plutarch's version is coloured with an item from Callisthenes, a letter from Alexander to Olympias and the confusion of Paidion with Paidios, but his reference to Cambyses might be from Cleitarchus
Foundation of Alexandria	Plutarch 26.5-6 Curtius 4.8.1-6 Diodorus 17.52.1-3 Justin 11.11.11-13 Arrian 3.2.1 Val. Max. 1.4 ext 1	Hammond THA 44, 99, 128 Sources 59, 226	April 331BC Cf. Strabo 792
Pirate (captured at Chios) brought before Alexander (by Hegelochus)	St Augustine De Civ. Dei IV, 4. 25 (from a lost passage of Cicero The Republic III .24), cf. Arrian 3.2.4, Curtius 4.5.19-22		The rhetorical style of the passage, its origins via Cicero (a source of other fragments of Cleitarchus) and the location in Egypt (probably at Alexandria, which was later Cleitarchus' home) all suggest Cleitarchus as source. The pirate is Aristonicus of Methymne, whose capture is mentioned by Curtius, probably following Cleitarchus
Alexander's return march up the Levantine littoral: Story about the ultra-handsome Theias Byblios, who fell in love with his daughter Myrra	Stobaeus Flor. IV, 20, 73	Jacoby, Fragment 3 of Cleitarchus Brown, Clitarchus p.149	Attributed by Stobaeus to Book 5: presumably relates to a visit of Alexander to Byblos, an ancient Phoenician port to the north of Sidon – may reflect worship of Adonis at Byblos – must reflect Alexander's return to the vicinity after Egypt, if it is placed in Book 5
Uprising of the Spartans in Greece; heroism of King Agis of Sparta	Diodorus 17.63.4 Justin 12.1.6-11 Curtius 6.1.1-16 (& 6.3.2 in a speech) Front. Strat. 2.11.4	Hammond THA 46; Yardley & Heckel on Justin 37 & 183-8	Hammond's view (THA 113) that J's account is inconsistent with D is unconvincing

Summary	Sources	References	Comment
Fifty hostages given to Antipater by the Lacedaemonians. Antipater refers the fate of Sparta to the League of Corinth. Sparta receives permission to send envoys to Alexander.	Harpocration: homereuontas Curtius 6.1.16-20 Diodorus 17.73.5-6	Jacoby, Fragment 4 of Cleitarchus Hammond THA 133	Attributed by Harpocration to Book 5: happened after Antipater defeated Agis at Megalopolis in 331BC – it is therefore certain that Cleitarchus gave an account of the Spartan rebellion in Greece at this point, which is when it actually took place. C & J postponed mention of events in Europe until after the death of Darius (D until after Gaugamela); Curtius stated that he was deliberately doing so at 5.1.1-2. Hammond thought the matter of the League came from Diyllus, but the details are very similar in D & C, so it is likely to be from Cleitarchus
Other events in Europe, such as the death of Alexander of Epirus, given in Justin 12.2, may have been related by Cleitarchus at this point, but this is conjectural. It is however interesting that Curtius 8.1.37 mentions a complaint by Alexander of Epirus (whilst he died of a wound according to Livy) that he had encountered men in Italy, whilst his nephew was up against women in Persia (cf. Gellius, NA 17.21.33, Livy 9.19.10-11). This section of Livy has some Cleitarchan elements, such as referring to the "Invincible Alexander" (see Hammond THA 112 on Cleitarchus as Livy's likely source)			

Book 6: July 331BC – July 330BC

Summary	Sources	References	Comment
Darius hears news of Alexander's return from Egypt – his preparations for war including 200 scythed chariots		C4.9.4-5=D17.53.1-2 Hamilton:C&D17	
Run-up to Gaugamela, march into Mesopotamia	Diodorus 17.53.3-4, 17.55	Hammond THA 44-45	
Ariston, captain of the Paeonians, slays Satropates, cuts off his head and lays it at Alexander's feet	Curtius 4.9.24-25 Plutarch 39.1-2	Hamilton Plutarch Alex liii (lix in 2nd edition)	
Third peace offer from Darius: an embassy	Curtius 4.11.1-22 Diodorus17.54.1-5 Justin 11.12.7-16	Hammond THA 45, 99, 122	Diodorus has Parmenion urge acceptance on this occasion, but it is not unlikely he did so at both the second and third offers
On the death of Queen Stateira - reported to Darius by a eunuch	Plutarch 30 Curtius 4.10.18-34	Hammond Sources 63-64	Gallantry with Darius' women as with meeting in Darius' tent after Issus
Crossing of the Tigris	Diodorus 17.55	Hammond THA 45	
Size of the Persian army	Arrian 3.8.6 Diodorus 17.39.4 & 17.53.2-3	Hammond THA 42, 44 Sources 231	
Alexander and Aristander sacrifice to fear	Curtius 4.13.15 Plutarch 31.4	Hammond Sources 38, 65	(Note however that many Aristander stories seem to come from Aristobulus)
Parmenion councils a night attack	Arrian 3.10.1, Curtius 4.13.4-10 Plutarch 31.5-7	Hammond Sources 38, 232	

Organisation And Sources

Summary	Sources	References	Comment
Alexander oversleeps before Gaugamela	Justin 11.13.1-3 Diodorus 17.56 Curtius 4.13.16-24 Plutarch 32.1-2	Hammond THA 20, 100, 122-3 Sources 38	
The order of battle of Alexander's forces		C4.13.26-29=D17.57.1-4 Schwartz	
Battle of Gaugamela (Arbela in Cleitarchus)	Curtius 4.14.1-26, 4.16.8-9 Diodorus 17.57.5-17.61 & parts of Plutarch 33.1-11, Arrian 6.11.4 (for use of Arbela) Front. Strat. 2.3.19	Hammond THA 20, 123, 128 Sources 39-40 & 270	1st October 331BC (fixed by Lunar eclipse) – Cleitarchus in particular located the battle close to Arbela, though it was ~70 miles away. Hamilton, "Cleitarchus & Diodorus 17", p128 thinks Curtius used Ptolemy for parts of his account.
The attack of the scythed chariots and its defeat		C4.15.16-17=D17.58.4-5 Schwartz	
Attack on Alexanders's camp by Scythians – Sisyngambris remains aloof		C4.15.9-11=D17.59.6-7 Schwartz	
Darius' charioteer slain by spear (thrown by Alexander) – Persians suppose Darius slain – Persian flight instigated		C4.15.28-29,32=D17.60.2-4 Schwartz	
Wounds of Hephaistion, Perdiccas, Coenus & Menidas		C4.16.31-32=D17.61.3 Schwartz	
Persian casualties	Arrian 3.15.6	Hammond Sources 232	
Alexander proclaimed king of Asia, abolishes tyrannies in Greece, promises to rebuild Plataea, sends some spoils to croton in Italy	Plutarch 34.1-2 (Justin 11.14 6-7 cf. Curtius 4.10.34)	Hammond Sources 66-68	
Capture of Persian camp and treasures at Arbela	Diodorus 17.64.1-3 Curtius 5.1.10-11	Hammond THA 54; C5.1.10-11=D17.64.3 Schwartz	
Visit to Mennis in Babylonia – the cave of Naptha – anointing and igniting the boy Stephanus	Curtius 5.1.16 Plutarch 35 Strabo 16.1.15	Hammond Sources 68-69	
Babylon: description of the city – walls 365 stades in circumference and 50 cubits tall – the Hanging Gardens were built by "a later Syrian king" than Semiramis for his wife	Diodorus 2.7.3-4 & 2.10 Curtius 5.1.24-35	Jacoby, Fragment 10 of Cleitarchus, P. Schnabel, Berossus, 1923, Ch III, Pearson p.230; C5.1.25-26=D2.7.3-4 Schwartz; C5.1.34-35=D2.10.4,1 Schwartz	Cleitarchus corrects the wall height of 50 fathoms cited by Ctesias in his Persica - Nearchus fragment 3a/b notes Alexander's rivalry with Semiramis in marching across the Kedrosian desert

Summary	Sources	References	Comment
Dissolute nature of Babylonians; relaxation of army at Babylon for 34 days	Diodorus 17.64.4-17.65.1 Curtius 5.1.36-39 & 5.1.40-45, Justin 11.14.8	Hammond THA 54; C5.1.40-42=D17.65.1 Schwartz; C5.1.43-45=D17.64.5-6 Schwartz	Curtius 5.1.36-39 is attributed to Diyllus in THA 129-130, but Hammond is clearly mistaken, because the 34 days is common to Curtius and Justin and so must be Cleitarchus; the appointments of Agathon etc to commands at Babylon and the arrival of 50 sons of the Macedonian nobility are common to D & C, therefore Cleitarchus; probably all in C about Babylon is Cleitarchus
Reorganisation of the army in Sittacene	Diodorus 17.64.2 Curtius 5.2.1	C5.2.1-7=D17.65.2-4 cf.D17.27.1-2 Schwartz	Strong resemblance between C & D, though D is heavily summarised
Susa – Abulites sends forth his son – 40,000 talents found there, mother and children of Darius left there, Alexander uses a stool to rest his feet upon when sitting in Darius' throne	Plutarch 36.1-2 Diodorus 17.65.5, 17.66.3-5, 17.67.1 Curtius 5.2.13-17	Hammond THA 55 Sources 70; C5.2.8, 12-15=D17.65.5,66.2-7 Schwartz	Plutarch quotes Cleitarchus' father Deinon in 36.2 – this probably follows such a quote by Cleitarchus himself. Hammond thinks Diodorus is following Diyllus at this point in THA, but the throne story is from the same source in C & D, which is therefore Cleitarchus.
Alexander gives Sisygambis purple cloth	Curtius 5.2.18-22	Hammond THA 130-131	
Uxii and campaign against Medates – Sisygambis obtains a pardon for Medates	Curtius 5.3.1-15 Diodorus 17.67.2-5	Hammond THA 55-56, 130-131; C5.3.1,2,4-5,10=D17.67.1-2,4-5 Schwartz	
Campaign against Ariobarzanes – Susian Gates – a Lycian leads Alexander around them by a narrow path through the woods	Curtius 5.3.16-5.4.34 Diodorus 17.68.1-7 Plutarch 37.1 Front. Strat. 2.5.17	Hammond THA 56, 131 Sources 70 Hamilton Plutarch Alex liii; C5.3.17-18,23&C5.4.2-4,10,12,18=D17.68.1-6 Schwartz	
Advance to the Araxes	Curtius 5.5.1 Diodorus 17.69.1	Hammond THA 131	
Letter from Tiridates		C5.5.2-4=D17.69.1-2 Schwartz	
Alexander meets 800 mutilated Greeks who do not wish to return home	Diodorus 17.69.2-9 Curtius 5.5.5-24 Justin 11.14.11-12	Hammond THA 56, 101, 131; C5.5.5-9,12,23-24=D17.69.2-8 cf.J11.14.11-12 Schwartz	
Capture of Persepolis followed by a Winter campaign in Persis	Curtius 5.6.1-20 Diodorus 17.70.1-17.71.7 & 17.73.1	Hammond THA 132; C5.6.1-5,8,9=D17.70.1-71.2 Schwartz	The campaign is only detailed by C and mentioned after the burning of the palace in one sentence by D

Summary	Sources	References	Comment
Burning of Persepolis incited by Thais the Athenian courtesan: a *comus*	Athenaeus 576D-E Diodorus 17.72.1-6 Curtius 5.7.1-7 Plutarch 38.1-4	Jacoby, Fragment 11 of Cleitarchus Hammond THA 56, 131-132 Sources 72-73 Hamilton Plutarch Alex liii	May 330BC
Pursuit and death of Darius	Justin 11.15 Diodorus 17.73.2-3 Curtius 5.8.1-5.13.25 Plutarch 42.3-43.3	Hammond THA 57, 101, 132-133 Sources 74-76 Hamilton Plutarch Alex liii	At the death of Darius Trogus ended his Book XI and Curtius ended his Book V, further vindicating the view that this was the conclusion of Book VI of Cleitarchus

Book 7: July 330BC – June 329BC

Summary	Sources	References	Comment
Advance to Hecatompylus. Persuasion of the army to join in the pursuit of Bessus, who declares himself king and adopts royal regalia as Artaxerxes.	Curtius 6.2.15-6.4.1 Diodorus 17.74.3-17.75.1 Justin 12.3.2-3 (Plutarch 47.1-2) King Bessus: Diodorus 17.74.1 Curtius 6.6.13	(Hammond Sources 80); C6.2.15=D17.75.1 Schwartz	Hammond THA 58 & 134 argues Diyllus as the source for Curtius and Diodorus. But the details are very similar in Justin too, so the common source must be Cleitarchus. Hammond worries that Plutarch has a slightly different order of events and indeed Plutarch attributes his version to a letter from Alexander to Antipater, so it is doubtful whether Plutarch followed Cleitarchus here.
Entry into and description of Hyrcania and the Caspian Sea	Diodorus 17.75 Curtius 6.4.1-22	Hammond THA 58 & 135, C6.4.3 6=D17.75.2 Schwartz; C6.4.18,22=D17.75.3,6 Schwartz	Onesicritus may be the ultimate source of the natural history details – Aristobulus is unlikely despite noting oaks in Hyrcania
Caspian Sea equal to the Euxine (Black Sea)	Pliny NH 6.36-38 Plutarch 44.1-2	Jacoby, Fragment 12 of Cleitarchus Hammond Sources 77	This resembles a comment by Patrocles, a geographer who wrote circa 280BC and was cited by Eratosthenes, but it is possible that the comments are independent of one another or that Cleitarchus inspired Patrocles.
The isthmus between the Caspian and the Euxine is subject to inundation from either sea	Strabo 11.1.5	Jacoby, Fragment 13 of Cleitarchus, Brown, Clitarchus p.140	The "isthmus" in question is the region of the Caucasus Mountains, neither low-lying nor narrow – Brown suggests this was inspired by Polycleitus' error of confusing the Sea of Azov with the Aral Sea

Alexander the Great in India by Andrew Chugg

Summary	Sources	References	Comment
Wonders of Hyrcania: the wasp (*tenthredon*) of the hill-country	Demetrius, De Eloc. 304 Diodorus 17.75.7	Jacoby, Fragment 14 of Cleitarchus	Diodorus has *anthredon*, Tarn (vol 2, Sources, p.90 n.3) notes that Diodorus uses a peculiar phrase μεγίστην ἐπιφάνειαν and a rare verb κηροπλαστεῖν in describing this bee-like creature; the same combination occurs in one other place in Diodorus 19.2.9 in a passage Tarn attributes to Timaeus. Tarn poses the question of whether Cleitarchus is using Timaeus; our answer must be yes, given the other evidence of his doing so.
Surrender of Persian commanders (Phrataphernes, Phradates, Artabazus)	Curtius 6.4.23-24 & 6.5.1-5 Diodorus 17.76.1	Hammond THA 135	
Surrender of the Greek mercenaries	Curtius 6.5.10 Diodorus 17.76.2	Hammond THA 135	
Attack on the Mardi: theft and restitution of Bucephalus	Curtius 6.5.11-21 Diodorus 17.76.3-8	Hammond THA 135; C6.5.11-12,18-21=D17.76.3-8 Schwartz	
Surrender of Nabarzanes: entry of Bagoas into Alexander's service	Curtius 6.5.22-23 (Diodorus 17.76.1)	Hammond THA 157	
Visit of Thalestria, Queen of the Amazons, who had journeyed from the River Thermodon to conceive a child by Alexander in Hyrcania	Plutarch 46.1 Strabo 11.5.4 Curtius 6.5.24-32 Diodorus 17.77.1-3 Justin 12.3.3-7	Jacoby, Fragments 15-16 of Cleitarch. Hammond THA 59, 102 & 135 Sources 81 (Jacoby Fragment 32?); C6.5.24-26,30-32=D17.77.1-3 cf. J12.3.5-7 & Strabo11.5.4 Schwartz	The Thermodon is in northern Asia Minor, which anomaly Cleitarchus explained by making the Caucasus region very narrow. The story may have originated with Onesicritus, but could have been embellished by Cleitarchus. (Brown, Clitarchus p.149 suggests Jacoby Fragment 32 was background to the Amazon story)
Alexander's adoption of Persian dress (purple tunic with a vertical white stripe, zona belt, diadem, sceptre) and luxury: 365 concubines from Darius' harem. Macedonian resentments assuaged by gifts from Alexander.	Curtius 6.6.1-12 Diodorus 17.77.4-7 & 17.78.1 Justin 12.3.8-12 Metz 2	Hammond THA 59, 102-3, 136; Pearson 221 (Plutarch, Artaxerxes 27 for Deinon)	Here again is seen the Cleitarchan propensity for making things equal to the days in a year; probably inspired by Deinon - Pearson. The Metz Epitome opens here, replete with Cleitarchan stories
Alexander burns surplus baggage and wagons to avoid the encumbrance in crossing the mountains into India	Curtius 6.6. Plutarch 57.1-2 Polyaenus 4.3.10	Hamilton Plutarch Alex liii	Plutarch associates this with the invasion of India & Polyaenus may be following him; but Curtius is more likely correct.
Revolt of Satibarzanes, who flees to Bactra with 2000 cavalry. Alexander storms a rock occupied by rebels.	Diodorus 17.78.1 Curtius 6.6.20-34 (Justin 12.4.1) Metz 3	Hammond THA 59, 136	The Metz has Ariobazanes and states he fled to India – perhaps this is an error for Barzaentes as at Curtius 6.6.36 (which is suggested by Elizabeth Baynham in Antichthon 29, p.71)

Summary	Sources	References	Comment
Dimnus conspiracy: execution of Philotas	Curtius 6.7-6.11 Diodorus 17.79-80 Justin 12.5.2-3 Plutarch 49	Hammond Sources 87 Hamilton Plutarch Alex liii	Hammond THA 59 argues Diodorus is from Diyllus mainly because he differs from Curtius in saying Alexander "learnt everything" from Dimnus, but Cleitarchus probably said *behaviour* of Dimnus spoke eloquently of his guilt & Diodorus is summarising clumsily. There are compelling points of similarity on incidental details between Diodorus & Curtius: e.g. Cebalinus hidden in the armoury; Alexander is informed while bathing & Philotas is executed "in the manner of his country, Macedon". Hammond concedes (in Sources) that Curtius must be from Cleitarchus: it is too vividly detailed for a general history, e.g. Diyllus or Duris. Plutarch's version seems informed by details from Cleitarchus, e.g. Alexander behind curtain, but differs on material points & is probably preferring Aristobulus as Hammond suggests.
Execution of Alexander Lyncestes	Curtius 7.1.1-9 Diodorus 17.80.2	C7.1.5-9=D17.80.2 Schwartz	Hammond THA 138 suggests Diyllus, but his argument about the timing of Lyncestes' arrest being later in Diodorus than in Curtius overlooks the fact that Justin 11.7.1 suggests that the Cleitarchan tradition placed Lyncestes' arrest prior to the march to Gordium (as in Arrian). It looks as if Diodorus mentioned Lyncestes' arrest a few months late, perhaps connecting it with warnings in a letter from Olympias, which might have taken months to reach Alexander. Curtius & Diodorus follow the same source for Lyncestes' execution & the amount of detail in Curtius seems too extensive for sourcing from a general history. (Hammond's view that Curtius & Diodorus shared Diyllus as a secondary source is statistically implausible: it implies they independently made the same choice for most episodes between Cleitarchus & Diyllus: it is more likely that matches between Curtius & Diodorus means both used Cleitarchus.)

Summary	Sources	References	Comment
Assassination of Parmenion: Polydamas' camel trek	Curtius 7.2.11-34 Diodorus 17.80.3 Strabo 15.2.10	C7.2.18=D17.80.3 Schwartz	Detailed correspondence between Curtius and Diodorus implies Cleitarchus was the source for the completion of the story of the downfall of Parmenion
Alexander forms a disciplinary regiment by reading the letters which the troops sent home to Macedonia to identify malcontents	Justin 12.5.4-8 Diodorus 17.80.4 Curtius 7.2.35-38 Polyaenus 4.3.19	Hammond THA 103; C7.2.35-37=D17.80.4 cf. J12.5.4-8 Schwartz	Hammond thinks that the version in Diodorus comes from Diyllus, but its close resemblance to the version in Justin is clear evidence that this material came from Cleitarchus. Hammond THA 139 fails to attribute the corresponding passage in Curtius, but it is Cleitarchus, since it is connected with the execution of Parmenion as in the other accounts.
The march against the Euergetae: origin of the name Euergetae (Benefactors) for the Ariaspi (Arimaspi in Cleitarchus) in their succour for Cyrus' army	Diodorus 17.81.1-2 Curtius 7.3.1-4 Metz 4	Hammond THA 60; C7.3.1,3=D17.81.1-2 Schwartz	From Deinon? Strong correspondences between Diodorus and Curtius
Land of the Paropanisadae	Curtius 7.3.5-18 Diodorus 17.82 Metz 4	Hammond THA 60, 139; C7.3.5-18=D17.82 Schwartz	
Crossing the "Caucasus" (Hindu Kush) in 16 or 17 days; Rock of Prometheus; foundation of an Alexandria; advance into Bactria in pursuit of Bessus	Curtius 7.3.19-23 Diodorus 17.83.1-2 Metz 4 (for the foundation)	Hammond THA 60, 139; C7.3.22-23=D17.83.1-2 Schwartz	Diodorus 17.83.3 has a terminal one-liner, Καὶ τὰ μὲν περὶ Ἀλέξανδρον ἐν τούτοις ἦν ("These were the concerns of Alexander"), which may indicate the end of Book 7 of Cleitarchus. A similar formula ended Bk 6 at 17.73.4 and exactly the same formula ends Bk 12. Similar formulae are used in other books of Diodorus, but this one may echo Cleitarchus, because it contains the title of his history (Περὶ Ἀλεξάνδρου - Pearson p.213).

Book 8: July 329BC – Autumn 328BC

Summary	Sources	References	Comment
Bessus and Bagodaras (D) or Cobares (C) quarrel at a banquet	Curtius 7.4.1-19 Diodorus 17.83.7	Hammond THA 139	Digressions and accounts of events elsewhere often mark a book boundary in Cleitarchus.
Alexander receives news from Greece of the Spartan revolt, of Scythians coming to the aid of Bessus and of the combat between Erigyius and Satibarzanes	Curtius 7.4.32-40 Diodorus 17.83.4-6	Hammond THA 140 Heckel & Yardley on Justin 184; C7.4.33,38=D17.83.4-6 Schwartz	Spartan news is only in C: was this the arrival of the Spartan envoys/hostages in Alexander's camp? Their departure seems to have been delayed (preparing to leave in Summer 330BC - Aischines 3.133).

Organisation And Sources

Summary	Sources	References	Comment
Advance to the Oxus: march through a desert with the loss of many men – anecdote of Alexander refusing water brought in skins	Diodorus, List of Contents for 17 Curtius 7.5.9-12 Front. Strat. 1.7.7		The anecdote being in Frontinus and Curtius tends to confirm that it is Cleitarchan
Betrayal by Spitamenes, Dataphernes & Catanes and capture & chopping up (by Oxathres) of Bessus	Curtius 7.5.19-26 & 7.5.36-43 Diodorus 17.83.8-9 Justin 12.5.10-11 Metz 5-6	Hammond THA 61, 140-141	The Metz has Bessus sent to Ecbatana for punishment later, so perhaps Cleitarchus simply gave a preview of his ultimate fate at this point.
Branchidae	Curtius 7.5.28-35 (in the long lacuna in Diodorus 17, but listed in contents), Strabo 11.11.4, Plutarch Moralia 557B(?)	Hammond THA 141; C7.5.28-35 cf. DK Schwartz	Perhaps Cleitarchus gave the Branchidae story as a doublet with the destruction of Bessus: Persian and Greek traitors similarly destroyed (so Pearson).
Alexander wounded by an arrow of which the point remained fixed in the middle of his leg; the rebels sent envoys to apologise the next day; rivalry between the cavalry and the infantry over bearing Alexander's litter	Curtius 7.6.6-9	Hammond THA 142	
Advance to Maracanda – circumference of 70 stades with many rivers flowing around it	Curtius 7.6.10 Metz 7		With Diodorus missing in the great lacuna (and Justin being very thin and episodic here), the Metz Epitome (7-43) provides important confirmation that elements of Curtius are from Cleitarchus, wherever there is close correspondence between Curtius and the Metz. This is vital, because it appears that Curtius sometimes resorted to other sources. This applies until the middle of Book 10, where Diodorus resumes.
First news of the revolt of Spitamenes	Curtius 7.6.24	Hammond THA 143	
Advance to the Tanais: foundation of Alexandria on the Tanais with a circumference of 60 stades in 17 days	Curtius 7.6.25-27; Justin 12.5.12 Metz 8		Hammond THA 142 discusses Aristobulus, but the detailed correspondence of Curtius with Justin is a clear indication of Cleitarchus. Tanais is a Cleitarchan name for this river (through confusion with the Don).
Emperor of the Scythians sends his brother Carthasis to prevent Alexander crossing the Tanais. Speech of Alexander & augury of Aristander in Curtius. Plan for an attack on the Scythians.	Metz 8 Curtius 7.7.1-29	Hammond THA 143-4	Carthasis is in Curtius and the Metz has "Carcasim"

Summary	Sources	References	Comment
Insurrection of Spitamenes: routing and destruction of the Macedonian column under Menedemus. (2000 infantry and 300 cavalry are dead.)	Metz 9 Curtius 7.7.30-39	Hammond THA 143	Alexander spends the night sleepless – watches Scythian fires in Curtius, reflecting upon wrongs against him in the Metz
Alexander's attack across the Tanais via 2000 rafts (Metz) or 12000 (Curtius)	Metz 10-12 Curtius 7.8.1-9.16 (Diodorus – contents)	Hammond THA 143-4, Pearson (Lost Histories) 222	X may have been dropped from XII in the Metz. Curtius gives Scythian envoys' words verbatim from his source – arrows, shouts, markers of Dionysus are common; Pearson notes parallels with aphorisms attributed to Cleitarchus
Visit of envoys of the Sacae	Curtius 7.9.17-19	Hammond THA 143-4	
Alexander's return to Maracanda to counterattack Spitamenes who flees; burying of Greek dead and erection of a monument to Menedemus.	Metz 13 Curtius 7.9.20-22	Hammond THA 143	Reached Maracanda on the 4th day – bones covered with mound-monuments in the Metz
Pardoning of Sogdian prisoners (chieftains) who sang on their way to execution	Curtius 7.10.1-9 (Diodorus – contents)	Hammond THA 144; C7.10.4-9 cf. DκβSchwartz	
Alexander defeated the Sogdiani & slew over 120,000	(Diodorus – contents)	Hammond THA 61	Hammond notes that Theophylactus Simmocata burnt 120,000 & Goukowsky thought Cleitarchus his likely source
Return to Bactria – orders Bessus to Ecbatana for impaling – founds towns (6 or 12?) to curb the conquered nations	Metz 14 Curtius 7.10.10-16 Justin 12.5.13	Hammond THA 103 on Justin; C7.10.15-16 cf. DκδSchwartz	Crosses rivers Ochus and Oxus at Metz 14 and Curtius 7.10.15 (Hammond THA 144 thinks this is Aristobulus)
Sogdian Rock (Rock of Arimazes in C or Ariobazanen in M or Ariamazes in S or Ariomazes in Polyaenus)	Metz 15-18 Curtius 7.11.1-25 Polyaenus 4.3.29 (Diodorus – contents) Strabo 11.11.4		Both Curtius and the Metz Epitome seems to make this a climactic event of the campaigning year in 328BC – hence this should close Book 8 of Cleitarchus as well as Book 7 of Curtius. Curtius 7.11.26-29 differs from the Metz, so is probably not Cleitarchus (though Hammond THA 145 thinks it is). Hammond THA 144 thinks much of Curtius' account is Aristobulus, but commonalities with the Metz include a cavern on the ascent path, 20 (Metz) or 30 (Curtius) stadia high, 300 climbers signalling with white cloths, iron wedges, ropes.

Book 9: Autumn 328BC – May 327BC

Summary	Sources	References	Comment
Offer of daughter in marriage by the Scythian king. First campaign against Massagetae, Dahae – 3 columns through Sogdiana	Curtius 8.1.1-10	Hammond THA 145	
The hunt in Basista (Bazaira in Curtius) and the abundance of game there	Curtius 8.1.11-19 (Diodorus – contents)	Hammond THA 145; C8.1.11-19 cf. Dκσ Schwartz	Hammond thinks this is Onesicritus (but this is no bar to it being in Cleitarchus)
Killing of Cleitus at Maracanda – Alexander persuaded to forgive himself by Callisthenes	Curtius 8.1.19-8.2.12 Justin 12.6 Arrian 4.9.2-3 (Diodorus – contents)	Hammond THA 104,146 Hammond Sources 242	Arrian has legomena about Alexander's attempted suicide and concern over Lanike's reaction
Winter in Bactrian Nautacene (Metz)	Curtius 8.2.13-18 Metz 19		
Treaty with Sisimithres, who had fathered 2 sons and 3 daughters through incest with his mother, after a siege of his rock.	Curtius 8.2.19-33 Metz 19 Plutarch 58.3 Strabo 11.11.4	Hammond THA 146	Hammond Sources is silent on the mention of Sisimthres by Plutarch
Death of Philippus.	Curtius 8.2.34-39	Hammond THA 146-7	Hammond THA thinks Philippus is from Onesicritus (but this is no bar to it being in Cleitarchus too)
Beheading of Spitamenes by his wife assisted by a slave boy – delivery of head to Alexander and his gratitude and her expulsion from camp	Curtius 8.3.1-15 Metz 20-23	Hammond THA 147	
Dahae surrender Dataphernes (& Catanes?)	Metz 23 Curtius 8.3.16-17 Justin 12.6.18		Curtius 8.5.2 says that Catanes was subsequently killed in battle. Hammond is unsure of the source for this, but its presence in the Metz suggests Cleitarchus.
The proskynesis experiment	Curtius 8.5.5-24 Justin 12.7.1-3 Val. Max. 7.2 ext 11	Hammond THA 148 says speeches are Curtius' own invention, Alexander hides behind curtain like Agrippina in Tacitus Ann. 13.5.2 (but also like Alexander with Philotas [Plutarch 49], which suggests Cleitarchus) Hammond THA 103-4 for Justin: "most likely Cleitarchus"	This is postponed until the point of departure for India in Curtius. However Cleitarchus evidently placed it here, because Justin agrees with Diodorus by putting the award of silver shields to the hypaspists after Callisthenes' arrest, rather than before as in Curtius. Arrian gave the proskynesis experiment and the arrest of Callisthenes following on from the death of Cleitus, but points out (4.22.2) that the pages' conspiracy occurred at Bactra just prior to the invasion of India. It may be that Cleitarchus was correct in placing the proskynesis experiment at this point and chose to tell the whole story en bloc.

Summary	Sources	References	Comment
The conspiracy of the pages and the arrest and execution of Callisthenes	Curtius 8.6.1-8.23 Justin 12.7.2 (Diodorus – contents)		Hammond is unsure of the source for Curtius and Justin, but Diodorus' contents list confirms that this material was in Cleitarchus. It is possible that Curtius used other sources as well.
Campaign against the Nautaces and the destruction of the army in heavy snow	Metz 24-27 Curtius 8.4.1-15 (Diodorus – contents)	Hammond THA 147	
Saves a common soldier after the snow storm	Val. Max. 5.1 ext 1a Frontinus, Strat. 4.6.3 Curtius 8.4.15-17	Hammond THA 147	
Visit to (rock of) Chorienes (perhaps a re-visit to Sisimithres, but Cleitarchus now used his title rather than his name – yet it looks as though Cleitarchus believed him to be a distinct individual)	Metz 28 Curtius 8.4.21 has "cohortandus" in MSS wrongly changed to Oxyartes by Aldus		The Metz manuscript read "corianus"; Chorienes is from Arrian 4.21; Brunt & Heckel suggest that Chorienes is an official title of Sisimithres from the name of the area he ruled
Marriage to Roxane	Metz 28-31 Curtius 8.4.20-30 (Diodorus – contents)	Hammond THA 146	Metz & Diodorus mention marriages of Alexander's companions – hence probably from Cleitarchus

Book 10: June 327BC – June 326BC

Summary	Sources	References	Comment
Orders formation of 30,000 "Epigoni"	Curtius 8.5.1		This is Cleitarchan, since their arrival at Susa in 324BC is in Diodorus 17.108.1-3
Preparations for India: distribution of silver shields etc. - 120,000 men followed Alexander into India (Curtius only)	Justin 12.7.4-5 Curtius 8.5.4	Hammond THA 104, 147-8; C8.5.4 cf. DΛα, J12.7.5 Schwartz	Hammond seems inconsistent in recognising that J is using Cleitarchus, but expressing uncertainty over C – the 120,000 men may have been derived from Nearchus by Cleitarchus (see Arrian Indica 19.5 – Plutarch 66.2 gives 120,000 foot)
Digression on India: mention of processions of the kings in which trees are drawn along on four-wheeled carriages and tame birds (the Orion and the Catreus) decorate their branches and sing – "…some birds are like sirens" may reflect Cleitarchus' father Deinon's belief that there were sirens to be found in India (Pliny NH 10.136)	Strabo 15.1.69 Aelian NA 17.22-23 Curtius 8.9.23-26	Jacoby, Fragments 20-22 of Cleitarchus, Brown, Clitarchus p.148	Curtius 8.9.8 mentions the River Iomanes (Jumna), which elsewhere (e.g. Arrian Indica 8.5-6) is mentioned by Megasthenes. Hammond THA 148 also notes that Curtius 8.9 includes material that was not known until after Alexander's time (e.g. Megasthenes' info on the Ganges region), yet at least some of it is from Cleitarchus. This is *suggestive* of use of Megasthenes by Cleitarchus, but Megasthenes dates to 1st decade of 3rd century BC. Cf. digression on Pandaea below.

Organisation And Sources

Summary	Sources	References	Comment
Invasion of India: march from Bactra, Alexander greeted as third son of Zeus to enter India following Heracles and Dionysus, destruction of a city occupied by his initial opponents as an example	(Diodorus – contents) Curtius 8.10.1-6 Metz 32-35	Hammond THA 148; C8.10.5-6 cf. DΛβ Schwartz	
Alexander visits Nysa finds the ivy of Dionysus - citizens of Nysa intimidated into surrendering (probable mention of Acuphis and Alexander's request for 100 of his best men), then Alexander climbs Meron, the adjacent mountain, sacred to Dionysus with streaming waters and fruitful trees.	Schol. Apoll. Rhod. 2.904 Diodorus (in the great lacuna but listed in Contents of 17) cf. Arrian 5.1.1-6 Justin 12.7.6-7 Curtius 8.10.7-18, Metz 36-38	Jacoby, Fragment 17 of Cleitarchus Hammond THA 104 &148	See also Arrian's Indica 1.5-6, which has several mentions of Nysa and its legend of Dionysus – also Strabo 15.1.7-8 & Plutarch, Alex. 58.4-5
Dionysiac revels of companions (a comus)	Arrian 5.2.7, Justin 12.7.8	Hammond Sources 250	A legomenon
Mazaga in kingdom of Assacenus & slaughter of the Indian mercenaries – Alexander wounded in leg - Cleitarchus especially noted that the siege engines and their missiles terrified the defenders into surrendering, since they seemed supernatural – Alexander may have been seduced by Cleophis and she had a son, whom she named Alexander – Cleitarchus wrote that the mercenaries opposed the surrender, but then requested that they be allowed to leave the town – Cleitarchus did not give an excuse for Alexander's attack on them	Diodorus 84 (emerging from the great lacuna), Metz 39-45, Justin 12.7.9-11, Plutarch 59.3-4, Curtius 8.10.19-36 Polyaenus 4.3.20	Hammond Sources 106 Hammond THA 52-3, 104 & 149	Arrian blamed the slaughter of the mercenaries on their plan to slip away without Alexander's leave
Aornus – Heracles' failure to capture it due to an earthquake & Alexander's longing to outdo his ancestor – 100 stades in circumference, 16 high – poor old local man with two sons guided Alexander's assault – filled chasm in 7 days & nights	Metz 46-7, Curtius 8.11.1-25, Diodorus 17.85.1-86.1, Justin 12.7.12-13, Plutarch 58.3 on other Alexander	Hammond THA 53, 104-5 & 149; C8.11.2=D17.85.1-2, J12.7.12 Schwartz; C8.11.3-4=D17.85.4-5 Schwartz; C8.11.7-8,25=D17.85.3,8-9&D17.86.1 Schwartz	Hammond thinks Curtius supplemented his account from Chares (see Jacoby fragment 16 of Chares) especially for the heroic acts of the king, another Alexander and Charus (Strabo 15.1.8 says Alexander's flatterers reported that Heracles had thrice failed to take Aornus)
Aphrices (D) or Erices (C) blocks Alexander's advance with an army of 20,000, but his own men bring his head to Alexander	Diodorus 17.86.2-3, Curtius 8.12.1-3	Hammond THA 53, 149-150; C8.12.1-3=D17.86.2 Schwartz	Aphrices may have been the brother of Assacenus
Hephaistion's bridge of boats across the Indus	Metz 48, Curtius 8.12.4, Diodorus 17.86.3		Not explicitly attributed by Hammond but subsumed into the adjoining Cleitarchan passages

Summary	Sources	References	Comment
Mophis ruler of Taxila and son of dead Taxiles advances against Alexander seemingly in battle array, but joins forces and donates treasure and 56 or 58 elephants	Metz 49-52, Curtius 8.12.4 – 18 Diodorus 17.86.4-7 Plutarch 59.3	Hammond THA 53-4 & 149-50 Hammond Sources 106; C8.12.4-10,14=D17.86.3-7 Schwartz	Mophis is the probable Cleitarchan form, since the Metz (Motis) and Diodorus agree (the form Omphis in Curtius may be from elsewhere) – Curtius 8.12.17-18 is attributed to Onesicritus by Berve & Hammond, but Cleitarchus may well have repeated it.
The Battle Against Porus (Cleitarchus may not have named the battle after the river Hydaspes – modern Jhelum) initial diversionary tactics – precipitated by rumoured approach of Abisares (the name is probably corrupt in Diodorus, who gives both Embisarus 87.2 and Sasibisares 90.4) – Alexander's horse wounded (C, J, M), elephants arrayed like towers in a circuit wall, trampled or seized opponents with their trunks and dashed them to the ground, were attacked with missiles, axes and Kopis swords, then trampled their own men. Concentration of archers upon Porus – Porus slid off kneeling elephant, which was killed by missiles when it tried to protect its master. Porus asked how he wished to be treated – Porus replied that Alexander should consult his feelings as a king	Diodorus 17.87-88, Metz 53-61 (Justin 12.8.1-7) Curtius 8.13-14, Polyaenus 4.3.22 (cf. Strabo 15.1.42 on elephants protecting their masters in warfare) Front. Strat. 1.4.9 & 1.4.9a	Hammond THA 22-3, 54, 62, 150; C8.14.3=D17.87.5 Schwartz, Merkelbach thinks the letter from Porus in ME 56-58 is from a separate letter collection, but this is dubious	Perhaps the first half of May (Heckel & Yardley on Justin p.246), though Arrian 5.9.4 suggests late June after the solstice. Hammond's view that the version of the battle in Cleitarchus was as naïve as that in D is suspect, because of the details given by the Metz and Polyaenus. Hammond (THA 105) thinks J differs from D, but the Metz and D have common details such as concentration of bowmen on Porus and the Metz and J share the wounding/killing of Bucephalus: it seems more that D, J and the Metz are retaining different details from a lengthy original. Hammond thinks C supplemented his version from other sources. The Letter from Porus in ME 56-58 is faintly echoed in Pseudo-Callisthenes 3.2
Casualties	Metz 61, Diodorus 17.89.1-3		
Report of the revolt of Baryaxes in Media (Arrian 6.29.3) following the replacement of Oxydates as its Satrap by Arsaces (Curtius 8.3.17) or Atropates (Arrian 4.18.3) in early 327BC. Cleitarchus explained that Baryaxes had worn the tiara upright, which signified a claim to the throne of the Persians and Medes. (A location at the start of book 10 is also feasible, but Baryaxes probably waited for Alexander to be safely distant in India before he struck.)	Schol. Aristoph. Av. 487	Jacoby, Fragment 5 of Cleitarchus	The revolt of Baryaxes, though known to us solely through Arrian, is the only likely reason for Cleitarchus to have needed to explain the significance of the upright tiara at this juncture (the Fragment is specific that this was related in Book 10). A corollary is that Cleitarchus did not specifically mention that Bessus had worn the tiara upright. Also Cleitarchus may well have mentioned the arrest of Baryaxes by Atropates, who brought him to Alexander for execution at Pasargadae early in 324BC. This would place it in Book 12.

Book 11: July 326BC – Spring 325BC

Summary	Sources	References	Comment
Alexander plans to visit the ends of India and the Ocean – orders ships built with timber from neighbouring mountains – sacrificed to Helios – disbursements of gold coinage as reward to officers and proportionate rewards to troops (C only)	Metz 63, Curtius 9.1.3-4 Diodorus 17.89.4-5, 17.90.3-6	C9.1.1,3-4,6=D17.89.3-6&D17.90.1 Schwartz	This is evidence of a Cleitarchan discussion of Alexander's plans. Geographical and other digressions are characteristic of a new book in Cleitarchus. The coinage may be the famous Porus decadrachms (see Holt on the Elephant Medallions)
Foundation of a city to honour the dead Bucephalus – the naming seems to have happened later just before the voyage down to the Indus	Arrian 5.14.4, Metz 62, Curtius 9.1.6, Justin 12.8.8 Diodorus 17.90.6 & 17.95.5	Hammond Sources 257	Some details in Arrian may be from Chares. Hammond's view (THA 54 & 62) that the foundation of Bucephala in D was from a different source is contradicted by the evidence of the Metz, which concludes this episode with the foundation.
The serpents of India reach sixteen cubits in length	Aelian, NA 17.2 Diodorus 17.90.1 Curtius 9.1.4	Jacoby, Fragment 18 of Cleitarchus	This is probably lifted by Cleitarchus from the account of Nearchus (Arrian, Indica 15.19)
Indian monkeys mistaken for an army: a curious technique using mirrors for the capture of monkeys (there may be confusion between arboreal monkeys and baboons here)	Aelian, NA 17.25 Diodorus 17.90.2-3	Jacoby, Fragment 19 of Cleitarchus, Brown, Clitarchus p.144	This probably derives from Onesicritus, because there is a more intelligible version in Strabo 15.1.29 (however, Aristobulus and Nearchus cannot be ruled out as Strabo's source – see Pearson 223-4, Hamilton C&A 451 and Brown AJP 71, p144, n9)
After he recovered from his wounds, Porus invited to Macedon in Metz Epitome: re-instatement as king & Friend of Alexander	Curtius 8.14.5 Diodorus 17.89.6 Justin 12.8.7 Metz 61 & 64		Curtius and Metz preview this at the end of the battle, but Diodorus & the Metz put the actual event here in Cleitarchus
Abisares sends envoys, but Alexander replies that he will pursue him if he does not come in person	Curtius 9.1.7-8, Metz 65-6 Diodorus 17.90.4	Hammond THA 62-3, 151	
Crosses a rapid river (the Acesines?) and marches east into forests: the height, extent and trunk circumference of the banyan tree, small multicoloured snakes with deadly bites	Diodorus 17.90.5-7 Curtius 9.1.9-12 Aelian, NA 17.2	Pearson 225; C9.1.8-12=D17.90.4-7 Schwartz, Jacoby F18 (on the snakes)	Cleitarchus is plagiarising Nearchus on the banyan (Arrian, Indica 11.7) and Onesicritus (Strabo 15.1.21)
Hephaistion sent to deal with the rebel Porus, a cousin of the conquered Porus	Diodorus 17.91.1-2	Hammond THA 63, 151; C9.1.24-33=D17.91.4-D17.92.3 Schwartz	
Marches on across a desert and across the Hyraotis (Hydraotis) past a grove of wild peafowl; campaign against the Adrestians (city surrenders) & campaign against Cathaeans (sacked city & 2 surrendered cities) – custom of cremating wives on the pyres of their husbands to forestall poisoning	Diodorus 17.91.2-4 & 19.33 Curtius 9.1.13-23 Justin 12.8.9 Polyaenus 4.3.30		Cleitarchus is again following Onesicritus (see Strabo 15.1.30) on the custom of Suttee - Polyaenus names the Cathaean capital of Sangala as the sacked city – supplication with fronds at third Cathaean city

Alexander the Great in India by Andrew Chugg

Summary	Sources	References	Comment
Surrender of Sopithes with his sons: sets dogs on a lion	Curtius 9.1.24-36, Metz 66-7 Diodorus 17.91.4-92.3	Hammond THA 63, 151; C9.1.24-33=D17.91.4-D17.92.3 Schwartz	Cf. Strabo 15.1.31 & Isidore of Seville, Etymologiae 12.2.28.
Campaign of Hephaistion – his return.	Diodorus 17.93.1 Curtius 9.1.35		
Realm of Phegeus: 12 days from the Ganges which was 32 stades wide (30 in M) – warnings of an army of 200,000 infantry, 20,000 cavalry, 2000 chariots and up to 3000 elephants under Xandrames (D) or Aggrammes (C) or Sacram (M), king of the Gandaridae (D & P) or Candaras (M) or Gangaridae (C & J) or Gandridae (P Moralia 327B) and also the Prasii (C) or Praisii (P) or Praesidae (J) or Tabraesians (D) or Persidas (M) beyond the Hyphasis (7 stades wide in D) and at the Ganges. Alexander asks Porus to validate these figures. Alexander is undeterred, recalling that the Pythia had called him invincible.	Metz 68-9, Curtius 9.2.1-9 Diodorus 17.93 Justin 12.8.9 (Plutarch 62.1 has the same width for the Ganges)	Hammond THA 63, 151	Plutarch & Diodorus are probably not getting the width of the Ganges from Megasthenes (pace Bradford Welles), because Strabo 15.1.35 quotes a width of 100 stades from Megasthenes. Xandrames was king of the Nanda kingdom, probably the same as Nandrus in Justin 15.4.16.
Mutiny on the Hyphasis and retreat to the Acesines – exhaustion of the soldiers is a Cleitarchan feature – speech to soldiers - armour wearing out – Greek clothing gone and replaced by Indian stuff – dressed stone altars of extraordinary size (50 cubits tall in D) were built and the camp was enlarged to thrice its size with 5 cubit long beds/couches in huts as wonders for posterity	Metz 69, Curtius 9.2.10-9.3.19 Diodorus 17.94.1-17.95.2 Justin 12.8.10-17 (Plutarch 62.3 also mentions the upscalings, but of different things)	Hammond THA 63-4, 151-2; C9.3.10-11=D17.94.2 Schwartz; C9.3.19=D17.95.1-2, J12.8.16 Schwartz; C9.3.19=D17.95.1-2, J12.8.16 Schwartz	Speeches of Alexander (9.2.12-34) and Coenus (9.3.5-15) might be Curtius' inventions, but Diodorus 17.94.5 agrees there was a speech to the troops (speech was to the officers in A). Unclear whether Alexander's sulk in tent was mentioned by Cleitarchus (it is in C, who may have taken it from Ptolemy or elsewhere, but not in D, J, M – it is also in A & P). Whether Cleitarchus noted Coenus' role is also uncertain.
Alexander retraces his advance to the Acesines and is joined by reinforcements who bring 25,000 suits of armour inlaid with gold and silver - a fleet has been built by Porus and Taxiles at the Acesines: 800 service ships and 200 open galleys (D), 800 biremes & 300 penarias (Metz); 1000 ships in Curtius – Alexander names the cities he had earlier founded on opposite river banks: Nicaea & Bucephala [Coenus dies (C only)]	Metz 70, Curtius 9.3.20-24 Diodorus 17.95.3-5 (Justin 12.9.1 also reports a return only to the Acesines)	C9.3.20,23=D17.9 5.3,5 Schwartz	It seems to be a Cleitarchan error to state that Alexander returned only to the Acesines, when in fact he went back to the Hydaspes (according to Aristobulus and others). Hammond (THA p.62 & 152) thinks this material is from Diyllus, but ship numbers and other details match between D, C & M, so this is still Cleitarchus
Death of Alexander's infant son (or child) by Roxane	Metz 70		The Metz is the sole surviving source for this

Organisation And Sources

Summary	Sources	References	Comment
Voyage down the Acesines to its junction with the Hydaspes with Hephaistion & Craterus commanding the bulk of the army which marched down the bank	Diodorus 96.1 Justin 12.9.1 Curtius 9.3.24-9.4.1		Alexander sailed down the Hydaspes, which flowed into the Acesines, which in turn flowed into the Indus (Arrian 6.14.4-5).Cleitarchus' confusion on this point is evidence that he was not with the expedition in India, else he would not have made such an error. Hammond thinks this is Diyllus, but D, C & J essentially agree, though all are brief and omit different details.
Digression on an Indian salt-mine	Strabo 5.2.6 (& 15.1.30)	Jacoby, Fragment 28 of Cleitarchus	Likely to have been occasioned by a visit of Alexander to the ancient salt mines at Khewra in the SE foothills of the Salt Range 15km north of the Hydaspes (Jhelum) River. A fragment of Onesicritus (Strabo 15.1.30) mentions a mountain of salt in the kingdom of Sopeithes. Arrian 6.2.2 says that Hephaistion was to hurry to the capital of King Sopeithes at the start of the voyage down the Hydaspes. (It is dubious whether Sopeithes is the same as the Sophytes/Sopeithes, who ruled an Indian kingdom further east.)
At junction of the Acesines with the Hydaspes Alexander took the surrender of the Sibi (C) or Ibi (D), who were descended from followers of Heracles - Defeated Agalasseis (Agesinas etc in MSS of J?)	Diodorus 17.96.2-5 Justin 12.9.2 Curtius 9.4.1-8	C9.4.1-2,5–D17.96.1-3 Schwartz	The footsteps of Heracles is a Cleitarchan theme. Hammond THA 153 thinks this is a mixture of Diyllus and Cleitarchus, but there is a good level of agreement between D & C and foundation by Heracles is also in J. Hammond's argument (THA 64) that D gives different accounts of the failure of Heracles to take Aornus is not credible.
Sailed to confluence with the Indus – near wrecking of the flagship in rapids – Alexander says he has done battle with the river like Achilles (Iliad 21.228-382)	Diodorus 17.97.1-3 Curtius 9.4.8-14	Hammond THA 64-5, 153; C9.4.8-14=D17.97.1-3 Schwartz	Emulation of Achilles is a Cleitarchan theme – D said Alexander jumped into the river and swam to safety, but Curtius that he merely disrobed to be ready to swim
Letter from the Indian philosophers	Metz 71-4; cf. Pap. Hamb. 129	Merkelbach thinks the letter from the Indian Philosophers in ME 71-74 is from a separate letter collection, but this is dubious	Similar letter in Philo of Alexandria, Every Good Man Is Free, Section 96. Similar letter among the letters of St Ambrosius XXXVII (11), 34/35, Migne, Patrologia Latina XVI col 1139 (letter in Pseudo-Callisthenes 3.5 differs substantially)

Summary	Sources	References	Comment
Campaign against the Oxydracae & Malli - Alexander suffers an arrow wound to the chest when leading the storming of a town of the Oxydracae & Malli (Mandri/Mambros in J) – Cleitarchus said Ptolemy & Peucestas (A & C) & Limnaeus (P: wrongly Timaeus in C) & Leonnatus (A & C – Metz had Legatus) & Aristonus (C) saved Alexander (Syracousas in D; Sugambri in J; Sudracae in C; Sydracai or Oxydrakai Strabo; Oxydracae in A & Pausanias, oxudrac in Metz) - Alexander showered with missiles, jumps down inside wall, ladders collapse under weight of Macedonians, Alexander shelters next to tree, drops to knees	Curtius 9.4.15-9.5.21 Arrian 6.11.3 & 6.11.8, Metz 75-8 Plutarch Moralia 327B & 343D & 344D Diodorus 17.98.1-99.4 Justin12.9.3-12 Pausanias 1.6.2	Jacoby, Fragment 24 of Cleitarchus Hammond Sources 270 Hammond THA 65, 153-4	c. November 326BC, the Metz mentions both the Oxydracae (oxudrae) and the Malli – so probably Cleitarchan – Oxydracae is probably Cleitarchan since it is in Arrian (where he disputes the "Vulgate" version), some manuscripts of Strabo, Pausanias (where he tells Cleitarchus stories) and the Metz – Timagenes also had Ptolemy present
Risky treatment: Alexander's wound enlarged by Critobulus to remove the barbed arrow – Alexander faints, then slowly recovers	Curtius 9.5.22-30 Diodorus 17.99.4 Justin 12.9.13	Hammond THA 154 (wrongly Critodemus in Arrian 6.11.1, cf. Indica 18.7)	D & J are very brief; Pliny NH 7.37.37 notes that Critobulus was even more famous for having extracted an arrow from Philip II's eye in 354BC.
Revolt of the Greeks settled in Bactria (since they heard tell that Alexander had died from the Mallian wound)	Diodorus 17.99.5-6 Curtius 9.7.1-11	Hammond THA 66 (for 99.5 only), 154	Diodorus confuses this rebellion with another after Alexander's death (probably due to his account of a subsequent rebellion of Bactrian colonists at 18.7.1). The version in C is probably Cleitarchus. Since Cleitarchus habitually ended books with news from elsewhere, this report from his work of events in Bactria is the best indication of the boundary between his 11th and 12th books. Also chapter 17.99 in Diodorus and chapter 12.9 in Justin end here.

Book 12: Spring 325BC – June 324BC

Summary	Sources	References	Comment
Surrender of Indians - Alexander held a banquet – the contest between Coragus (D) or Coratas (C) and Dioxippus and the latter's suicide	Diodorus 17.100.1-101.6 Curtius 9.7.12-26 Aelian VH 10.22	Hammond THA 66, 154-5; C9.7.16-26=D17.100.2-D17.101.6 Schwartz	The story of Dioxippus is exclusive to D & C among the main sources, so is clearly from Cleitarchus
Submission of Sambastae(D) or Sabarcae(C), 60,000 infantry, 6000 cavalry & 500 chariots – impressed by the fleet into thinking another Dionysus was coming - Sodrae & Massani – founds an Alexandria on Indus	Diodorus 17.102.1-4 Curtius 9.8.4-8	C9.8.4-8=D17.102.1-4 Schwartz	

Organisation And Sources

Summary	Sources	References	Comment
Subjugation of the Musicani. Trial of Terioltes and Oxyartes. Conviction & execution of the former – acquittal and enlargement of realm of latter.	Diodorus 17.102.5 Curtius 9.8.9-10	Hammond THA 155	The trials were probably in Cleitarchus, though only found in C (compare and contrast with Arrian 6.15.3) D subsumes the later revolt and crucifixion of Musicanus into a single sentence entry at the arrival of Alexander in his realm (is D following Cleitarchus or does Curtius better reflect Cleitarchus?)
Dispatch of Polyperchon (& Craterus) to Babylonia with an army	Justin 12.10.1	Yardley & Heckel on Justin 260-1	This mention in J is the only indication that Cleitarchus recorded the return of a large contingent of the army with Craterus to the west – probably from the kingdom of Musicanus and before the war with Sambus. Hammond THA 106 has a curious explanation that this line is misplaced in J
Invasion of the kingdom of Porticanus – storming and burning of two cities – capture and slaying of Porticanus as he sheltered within a stronghold	Diodorus 17.102.5 Curtius 9.8.11-12	Hammond THA 155	Porticanus is Cleitarchan – he is Oxycanus in Arrian 6.16.1
The kingdom of Sambus (Ambus in Justin 12.10.2): 80,000 Indians slain by Alexander (Curtius names Cleitarchus as his source for this) – Sambus escaped to the east with thirty elephants in D but surrendered (gave up the fight?) in C	Curtius 9.8.13-15 Diodorus 17.102.6	Jacoby, Fragment 25 of Cleitarchus, Hammond THA 67, 155; C9.8.13-15=D17.102.6 Schwartz	The Sambus at the Mallian siege in Metz 75 is almost certainly a different person. The number was DCCC *milia* rather than LXXX *milia* in manuscripts of Curtius, but is emended on the basis of Diodorus
Revolt and suppression of the Brahmins and their supplication with branches	Diodorus 17.102.7		Supplication with branches is recalls the surrender of Mazaga
Revolt, capture by Pithon and crucifixion of Musicanus	Curtius 9.8.16	Hammond THA 155	It is uncertain whether this was in Cleitarchus, but it is in the same paragraph as a direct quote of Cleitarchus
The Indian town of Harmatelia, the last city of the Brahmins, refuses to submit and is attacked by 500 Agriani. Ptolemy receives a wound from a poisoned hand weapon (sword in C or arrow in J) and his life was saved by Alexander who was shown an antidote herb in a dream – followed by a eulogy of Ptolemy	Diodorus 17.103 Curtius 9.8.18-28 Justin 12.10.2-3 (cf. Strabo 15.2.7 who places this among the Oreitae) [Cic. de divinatione. 2.135 – Schwartz on Curtius]	Hamilton Cleitarchus & Diodorus 17, Hammond THA 67, 105, 155; C9.8.17-28=D17.103, J12.10.2-3 cf. Cic. de divin. 2.135 Schwartz	Definitely Cleitarchus, because the eulogy is common to Diodorus and Curtius. The mention by Curtius that Ptolemy was believed to be an illegitimate son of Philip is echoed by Pausanias 1.6.2 in a Cleitarchan context and thus probably also goes back to Cleitarchus. Dreaming cures was a standard technique in Greek medicine. Alexander had been taught herbal medicine by Aristotle according to Plutarch 8.1.

Alexander the Great in India by Andrew Chugg

Summary	Sources	References	Comment
Interview with the Indian philosophers, who were asked why they had induced King Sambus to revolt *inter alia*	Metz 78-84, Plutarch 64-5, cf. Pap. Berol. 13044	Merkelbach thinks the interview with the gymnosophists is from a separate letter collection, but this is dubious	Plutarch mentions that the 10 gymnosophists were captured after instigating the revolt of King Sabbas (probably Sambus in Curtius & Ambus in Justin). Hammond traces some of Plutarch to Onesicritus & Megasthenes, but this may nevertheless be via Cleitarchus, since it is in the Metz
Digression on the Indians (called Mandi) of Pandaea(?) – their women can bear children from the age of 7 and become old at 40 – Pandaea is the southernmost part of India extending to the sea, which Heracles gave to his daughter of that name to rule: he divided it into 365 villages, one of which would pay the royal tax each day of the year	Pliny NH 7.28-29 Polyaenus 1.3.4 Arrian Indica 9 (cf. Solinus 52.6-17)	Jacoby, Fragment 23 of Cleitarchus	Pliny co-attributes this fragment to Megasthenes & he is the source for a parallel description in Arrian's Indica, which adds the story of Pandaea. Polyaenus gives the Pandaea story in what has been thought a fragment of Megasthenes, but the usage of the number 365 in his version is highly characteristic of Cleitarchus. Solinus has a garbled version linked with Nysa. (Mandi from Pliny is similar to Mandri, which is J's name for the Malli) – Tarn, Alexander the Great II, Sources & Studies p.52 appears to confuse Pandaea with the Panchaea of Euhemerus (Brown, Onesicritus p.66 ff.)
Patala and the Patalii – pursuit of their king Soeris and a sojourn upon an island in the channel of the Indus (the island of Patala – "insulam catacam" in the Metz?), whilst seeking fresh guides	Metz 84 Curtius 9.8.28-30 (Diodorus 17.104.2 mentions Patala when Alexander returns from the Ocean)	Hammond THA 155	Reached "Patalene" about the rising of the Dog Star, i.e. mid-July 325BC (Strabo 15.1.17 from Aristobulus)
Sailing on 400 stades to visit the Ocean: during a stop Alexander's cavalry have to gallop to escape the returning tide (evidently a tidal bore) which dashed ships together – Alexander's sacrifices to Oceanus and Tethys on islands (one in the river and one out in the ocean)	Strabo 7.2.1-2, Metz 85-6, Curtius 9.9.1-27, Justin 12.10.4-5, Diodorus 17.104.1	Jacoby, Fragment 26 of Cleitarchus	Hammond THA 67 & 155 thinks D follows Diyllus & fails to attribute Curtius' account, except to note that he used a different source to Arrian and probably did not use Diyllus. But that a fragment of Cleitarchus in Strabo recorded the bore makes it likely that Curtius used Cleitarchus & the Metz agrees with C on details.
Return to Patala (mooring at a salt lake which diseased the skin of swimmers – C only) Nearchus as admiral and Onesicritus as chief pilot appointed to lead fleet along the coast keeping India on their right as far as the mouth of the Euphrates recording all they saw – burnt damaged ships	Diodorus 17.104.3 Curtius 9.10.3-4		

Organisation And Sources

Summary	Sources	References	Comment
Submission of the Abritae (D) or Arabitae (C) & the Kedrosian tribesmen	Diodorus 17.104.4 Curtius 9.10.5	C9.10.5-11,17-18,27=D17.104.4-D17.106.1 Schwartz	
Three columns under Leonnatus, Ptolemy and Alexander himself – founds an Alexandria at a sheltered harbour	Diodorus 17.104.4-8 Curtius 9.10.6-7	Hammond THA 155-6; C9.10.5-11,17-18,27=D17.104.4-D17.106.1 Schwartz	The city at Rhambakia in Arrian 6.21.5 – perhaps "Barce" (*parcem/bartem/bastemostem*) in Justin 12.10.6
The Oreitae inhabit the land separated from India by the River Arabis/Arabus and expose their dead naked to be eaten by wild animals… on the coast of Kedrosia an unfriendly and brutish people eat nothing but fish, which they tear to pieces with their nails and dry in the sun to make bread – their houses are roofed with whale ribs and scales	Pliny NH 7.30 cf. Diodorus 17.105.1-5 Curtius 9.10.6-10	Jacoby, Fragment 27 of Cleitarchus, Hammond THA 70, 156; C9.10.5-11,17-18,27=D17.104.4-D17.106.1 Schwartz	?Autumn 325BC The story of the fish eaters seems gleaned from Nearchus (cf. Strabo 15.2.2)
The march through Gedrosia (Kedrosia in Cleitarchus) - many deaths in Kedrosia – Alexander had ordered wells to be dug at regular intervals to provide water, but the army was threatened by starvation - Alexander sent to the satraps who made supplies abundantly available – Leonnatus attacked by Oreitae	Diodorus 17.105.6-8 Arrian 6.24.4 Plutarch 66.2-3 Curtius 9.10.11-21 Justin 12.10.7	Hammond Sources 124-5 & 275 Hamilton Plutarch Alex liii; C9.10.5-11,17-18,27=D17.104.4-D17.106.1 Schwartz	Arrian legomenon – Plutarch says that only a quarter of the army survived the desert, but he may have read that 30,000 infantry came through and (wrongly) compared this figure with Alexander's army of 120,000 in India – it is not clear that the Cleitarchan vulgate mentioned the men who returned with Craterus
Festivities in Carmania seven day comus	Arrian 6.28.1-2 Diodorus 17.106.1 Curtius 9.10.22-28 Plutarch 67	Hammond Sources 125 & 278 THA 156 Hamilton Plutarch Alex liii; C9.10.5-11,17-18,27=D17.104.4-D17.106.1 Schwartz	Arrian legomenon
The purging of the Satraps – first Astaspes – then Cleander & Sitalces and the rebels Ozines & Zariaspes	Curtius 9.10.19-21, 10.1.1-9, Diodorus 17.106.2-3 Justin 12.10.8		Hammond THA 70 &156 is unsure of D's & C's sources for the purging of satraps except that they were different to Arrian's
Return of Nearchus & Onesicritus – meeting with in theatre at Salmous - stories including: an island where a horse was worth a talent of gold, school of whales etc. – fleet ordered to sail to the Euphrates (kiss with Bagoas in this theatre may have been noted – Plutarch 67)	Pliny, NH 6.198 Diodorus 17.106.4-7 Curtius 10.1.10-16	Jacoby, Fragment 29 of Cleitarchus Hamilton Cleitarchus & Diodorus 17 Hammond THA 71, 156	Cf. Nearchus in Strabo 15.2.12 and Arrian, Indica 30.4-5 on whale spoutings. The use of trumpets to frighten the whales in Diodorus & Curtius matches the accounts in the fragments of Nearchus.

Summary	Sources	References	Comment
Alexander orders ship construction at Babylon using Lebanese timber to support a campaign around the eastern sea coast (Arabia?) & across N Africa to the Pillars of Heracles then back through Spain and Italy – letters from Porus & Taxiles	Curtius 10.1.17-21	Hammond THA 156-7	Was this from Cleitarchus?
Bagoas prosecuted & hanged Orsines at Parsagada (perhaps included mention of the execution of Baryaxes, who had worn the tiara upright and was brought to Parsagada by Atropates – Arrian 6.29.3)	Curtius 10.1.22-38	Hammond THA 157, Brown, Clitarchus p.153-4	Brown concludes that Cleitarchus was not unfavourable to Alexander, so C's emotive treatment of this story probably reflects his own spin on the matter. A large lacuna begins at Curtius 10.1.45 after an account of the defeat of Zopyrion by the Getae
Alexander and the army progress to Susianê. Self-immolation of Calanus (Caranus in Diodorus) on becoming ill: the disdain of the Indian gymnosophists for death	Diogenes Laertius 16 Aelian VH 5.6 Diodorus 17.107.1-5	Jacoby, Fragment 6 of Cleitarchus Hammond THA 71	Diogenes Laertius attributes this to the 12th book of Cleitarchus
Calanus would greet Alexander at Babylon	Arrian 7.18.6 Plutarch 69.3-4	Hammond Sources 132-3 & 301	
The marriages at Susa	Diodorus 17.107.6 Justin 12.10.9-10		Hammond THA 72 thinks D is Diyllus
The 30,000 Epigoni arrive	Diodorus 17.108.1-2 (Plutarch 71.1)	Hammond Sources 134-5	Hammond THA 72 thinks D is Diyllus - Curtius had mentioned the instigation of their formation and training at 8.5.1
Καὶ τὰ μὲν περὶ Ἀλέξανδρον ἐν τούτοις ἦν ("These were the concerns of Alexander")	End of Diodorus 17.108.3		This seems to indicate the end of Book 12 of Cleitarchus: the same formula is found at Diodorus 17.83.3, where Cleitarchus' Book 7 closed. This is also the boundary between chapters 12.10 and 12.11 in Justin.

Book 13: July 324BC – June 323BC

Summary	Sources	References	Comment
Death of Zopyrion in Europe	Curtius 10.1.43-45		Cf. Justin 12.1.16-17
The extravagance of Harpalus towards his courtesans – his flight to Athens	Athenaeus 586C-D Diodorus 17.108.4-8 Curtius 10.2.1-3	Jacoby, Fragment 30 of Cleitarchus	Cleitarchus commonly began (or ended) his books with news from elsewhere. Curtius emerges from a major lacuna in the midst of the Harpalus story. Hammond THA 72 & 157 thinks this is Diyllus, but this is confuted by a close match between the Cleitarchus fragment in Athenaeus and D's version

Organisation And Sources

Summary	Sources	References	Comment
The Exiles Decree	Diodorus 17.109.1 Curtius 10.2.4-7	C10.2.4,8-12,30=D17.190.1-2 Schwartz	Hammond THA 72-3 thinks D is Diyllus
Paying of troops' debts at 10,000 talents (20,000 in J & A) on planning to send 10,000 veterans home to Macedon	Diodorus 17.109.2 Curtius 10.2.8-11 Justin 12.11.1-3 Arrian 7.5.3	Hammond Sources 285; C10.2.4,8-12,30=D17.190.1-2 Schwartz	Hammond THA 72-3 & 157-8 thinks D & C are both from Diyllus, but I assert that all matches between versions in D & C are overwhelmingly likely to be from Cleitarchus – Hammond is probably wrong to suggest that Arrian used Cleitarchus
The Mutiny (at Opis) - troops taunt Alexander for claiming to be the son of Ammon – drowning of leaders of the mutiny in the river – Craterus to lead the veterans home – Antipater to come to Babylon with a force of fresh recruits	Plutarch 71.2-5 Justin 12.11.4-12.10 Diodorus 17.108.3 & 17.109.2-3 Curtius 10.2.12-10.4.3	Hammond Sources 134-6; C10.2.4,8-12,30=D17.190.1-2 Schwartz	There is no evidence that Cleitarchus located the mutiny at Opis – Diodorus implies that it took place at Susa - Curtius enters a further long lacuna during events at Opis - Hammond THA 72-3 & 157-8 thinks D & C are both from Diyllus, but I assert that all matches between versions in D & C are very likely to be from Cleitarchus
Arrival of Persian reinforcements; 20,000 archers and slingers arrive with Peucestas	Diodorus 17.110.1-2		This occurred nearly a year later in 323BC in Arrian - Hammond THA 73 thinks D is Diyllus
Arranges for the upbringing of 10,000 children of his veterans by captive women	Diodorus 17.110.3		Hammond THA 73 thinks D is Diyllus
March from Susa to Ecbatana via Carae, Sambana and the Celones, where he saw a settlement of Bocotian Greeks	Diodorus 17.110.4-5		Hammond THA 73 thinks D is Diyllus
Quarrel of Hephaistion with Eumenes	Arrian 7.13.1		The only hint that Cleitarchus may have mentioned the quarrel between Hephaistion and Eumenes is that Arrian mentions their reconciliation as a "story", which usually means he did not find it in Ptolemy or Aristobulus (the main source on the quarrel is Plutarch's Life of Eumenes) – there is a similar dearth of evidence for the quarrel between Hephaistion and Craterus in India, so perhaps Cleitarchus avoided this topic
Sightseeing trip to Bagistane - 60,000 horses where once there had been 160,000 - Atropates gives Alexander 100 Amazons	Arrian 7.13.2-3 Diodorus 17.110.5-6	Hammond Sources 293	Strabo 505 Hammond THA 73 thinks D is Diyllus
Arrival at Ecbatana – holds a drama festival - the Death of Hephaistion and Alexander's mourning – orders Perdiccas to conduct the corpse to Babylon for a magnificent funeral	Plutarch 72.1-3 Diodorus 17.110.7-8 Justin 12.12.11-12	Hammond Sources 136-140 & THA 107-8	Hammond THA 73 thinks D is Diyllus, but that J is drawing on Ephippus, perhaps via Cleitarchus and "P's much more sensational account" is Cleitarchus

Alexander the Great in India by Andrew Chugg

Summary	Sources	References	Comment
Unrest in Greece fuelled by dissolution of Satrapal armies of mercenaries on Alexander's orders	Diodorus 17.111.1-3		Hammond THA 73-4 thinks D is Diyllus
Against the Cossaeans	Diodorus 17.111.4-6		January-February 323BC - Hammond THA 73-4 thinks D is Diyllus
To Babylon – ill omens – warnings from the Chaldean scholars	Plutarch 73.1-4 Diodorus 17.112 Justin 12.13.3-5	Hammond Sources 141-3 Hammond THA 108	March-April 323BC - Hammond THA 74 thinks D is Diyllus
Embassies at Babylon including the embassy of the Romans	Pliny NH 3.57 Diodorus 17.113 (cf. Arrian 7.15.5, Livy 9.18.6) Justin 12.13.1-2	Jacoby, Fragment 31 of Cleitarchus Hammond THA 108	Possibly suggestive that Cleitarchus wrote after campaigns of Pyrrhus made Romans famous in the Greek world, but could simply be true. Livy attacks "frivolous Greeks" who harped on about Romans bowing to Alexander in his digression on Alexander vs. the Romans - Hammond THA 74 thinks D is Diyllus
Hephaistion's pyre at 10,000 talents - anecdotes of Hephaistion's status in Alexander's affections – response from Ammon brought by Philip that Hephaistion should be worshipped as God-Coadjutor (Paredros)	Arrian 7.14.8 Plutarch 72.3 & 75.2 Diodorus 17.114-115	Hammond Sources 139 & 296 Hamilton Plutarch Alex liii	Cf. Lucian, Slander17, Aelian, VH 7.8 - Hammond THA 74-5 thinks D is Diyllus & Ephippus (however, there are grounds to suspect that Cleitarchus used Ephippus' book on the Death of Alexander & Hephaistion)
Episode of the prisoner who sat on the throne	Diodorus 17.116.2-4	Hammond THA 76-7	
Visit to the marshes – Alexander's boat becomes lost for three days – diadem catches on a reed and is retrieved by an oarsman	Diodorus 17.116.5-7	Hammond THA 76-7	
Drinking party hosted by Medius the Thessalian following a ceremonial banquet in honour of Nearchus - Cup of Heracles – Alexander falls ill	Plutarch 75.3 Justin 12.13.6-10 Diodorus 17.117.1-3	Hammond Sources 151 & THA 77-8 & 108-9 Hamilton Plutarch Alex liii	Cf. Ephippus in Athenaeus 434A-B
Death in Babylon (After 3 days troops filed past, Where to find a worthy king? Body to Ammon, Funeral Games, On 6th day voice failed and gave ring to Perdiccas, "To whom do you leave your kingdom?" - "To the strongest", Divine honours when happy)	Arrian 7.26.3 Diodorus 17.117.4 Curtius 10.5.1-6 Justin 12.15	Hammond Sources 309& THA 77-8 & 108-9	Towards evening 10th June 323BC – Hammond THA 158-9 thinks C did not draw on Arrian's sources, but he is unsure of the identity of C's source

Summary	Sources	References	Comment
Conspiracy of Antipater and his sons, Cassander and Iollas (and Philip) – poison from the Styx brought in a mule's hoof - the rumour was suppressed, because of the subsequent power of Antipater and Cassander; restoration of Thebes and murders of Alexander's family by Cassander	Diodorus 17.118.1-2 Justin 12.14 Val. Max. 1.7 ext 2 Curtius 10.10.14-19 Pausanias 9.7.2	C10.10.14,18-19=D17.117.5& D17.118.2 cf. J12.13.10 Schwartz	Cleitarchus may have given this as an alternative as in Diodorus – cf. Ampelius 16.2, which Seel thought a fragment of Trogus: it says it was considered unclear whether Alexander died of drunkenness or poison (cf. Pliny NH 30.16.53) – Hammond THA 78 thinks D's version inspired by Hieronymus and THA 109-111 thinks J's version is from Satyrus and does not identify C's source, but it is more likely (e.g. Heckel LDT) that Cleitarchus took this rumour from the *Liber de Morte* – NB D & C 10.10.18-19 say this story was suppressed until Cassander died in 297BC; if this is Cleitarchus, then it is further evidence for an early 3rd century BC date for him
Death of Sisyngambris	Diodorus 17.118.3 Curtius 10.5.18-25 Justin 13.1.5-6	C10.5.21-25=D17.118.3, J13.1.5-6 Schwartz	Hammond THA 78 & 159 thinks D & C are both from Diyllus, but all matches between versions in D & C are overwhelmingly likely to be from Cleitarchus
Aftermath and entombment in Memphis? Last Plans?	Curtius 10.10.20 Pausanias 1.6.2-3 Diodorus 18.2 – 18.4		There is reason to suppose Cleitarchus extended so far as to mention the entombment in Memphis and possibly the relocation to Alexandria (how could he ignore it, if it had just happened when he wrote in Alexandria circa 280BC?). The clues are the fact that Curtius ended his history with this information and the fact that Pausanias mentions the Memphite entombment and the transfer to Alexandria in the context of his having mentioned some Cleitarchan stories (e.g. Ptolemy's birth and Alexander's wound among the Malli/Oxydracae). Pausanias uses Cleitarchan phraseology in speaking of "burial with Macedonian rites" (cf. Curtius 7.9.21). This also implies that most of the information in Curtius on the aftermath of Alexander's demise was taken from Cleitarchus. The Last Plans in Diodorus 18.4 may similarly be taken from Cleitarchus.

8. Bibliography

1)   Atkinson, JE, "A Commentary on Quintus Curtius Rufus' Historiae
       Alexandri Magni, Books 3 & 4", Amsterdam 1980.

2)   Atkinson, JE, "A Commentary on Quintus Curtius Rufus' Historiae
       Alexandri Magni, Books 5 to 7.2", Amsterdam 1994.

3)   Atkinson, JE, "Quintus Curtius Rufus' *Historiae Alexandri Magni*",
       ANRW II (H. temporini ed., Aufsteig und Niedergang der römischen
       Welt, Berlin), 34.4: 3447-83, 1998.

4)   Atkinson, John E, "Curzio Rufo: Storie di Alessandro Magno. Volume
       I (Libri III-V) & Volume II (Libri VI-X)", tr. Virginio Antelami and
       Maurizio Giangiulio, Milan: Fondazione Lorenzo Valla/Arnoldo
       Mondadori Editore, 1998 & 2000.

5)   Atkinson, JE, "Originality and its Limits in the Alexander Sources of
       the Early Empire" in *Alexander the Great in Fact and Fiction* (editors: AB
       Bosworth & EJ Baynham), Oxford 2000, pp. 307-25.

6)   Badian, E, "The Date of Clitarchus" Proceedings African Classical
       Associations 8 (1965): 5-11.

7)   Baynham, Elizabeth, "Alexander the Great: The Unique History of
       Quintus Curtius", Ann Arbor 1998.

8)   Baynham, Elizabeth, "An Introduction to the *Metz Epitome*: its
       traditions and value", Antichthon 29 (1995) 60-77.

9)   Berve, H, Gnomon 5, 1929.

10)   Billows, Richard, "Polybius and Alexander Historiography" in
       Alexander the Great in Fact and Fiction, ed. A.B. Bosworth and E.J.
       Baynham, Oxford 2000.

11)   Borza, EN, 1968, "Cleitarchus & Diodorus' Account of Alexander"
       Proceedings African Classical Associations 11:25-45.

12)   Bosworth, AB, "From Arrian to Alexander", Oxford, 1988.

13)   Bosworth, AB, "Commentary on Arrian's History of Alexander II"
       Oxford 1995.

14)   Bosworth, AB, "The Historical Setting of Megasthenes' Indica,"
       Classical Philology 91, 1996.

15)   Bosworth, AB, "In Search of Cleitarchus: Review-Discussion of Luisa
       Prandi: Fortuna è Realtà dell'Opera di Clitarco" in Histos (University of
       Durham, electronic journal of historiography), Vol. 1, Aug. 1997.

Bibliography

16) Bradford Welles, C, "Diodorus Siculus: Library of History," Vol. 8, Loeb, Harvard, 1963.

17) Brown, TS, 1949, "Onesicritus", Berkeley.

18) Brown, TS, 1950, "Clitarchus" American Journal Philology 71: 134-55.

19) Brown, TS, "The Merits and Weaknesses of Megasthenes," Phoenix 11, 1957.

20) Brunt, PA, "Arrian: History of Alexander and Indica", Loeb, Harvard, 1976 & 1983.

21) Chugg, AM, "The Journal of Alexander the Great", Ancient History Bulletin 19.3-4 (2005) 155-175.

22) Chugg, AM, "The Sarcophagus of Aleander the Great?" Greece & Rome, Vol. 49.1, April 2002.

23) Engels, Donald W, "Alexander the Great and the Logistics of the Macedonian Army", University of California, 1978.

24) Errington, RM, "Bias in Ptolemy's History of Alexander", *Classical Quarterly* 19, 1969, 233-242.

25) Errington, RM, "From Babylon to Triparadeisos, 323-320BC," *JHS* 90 (1970) 72-75.

26) Fontana, M, "Il problema delle fonti per il XVII Libro di Diodoro Siculo," *Kokalos* I (1955), 155-190.

27) Goukowsky, P, 1969, "Clitarque seul? Remarques sur les sources du livre xvii de Diodore de Sicile" Revue des Etudes Anciennes 71: 320-6.

28) Gunderson, Lloyd L, "Quintus Curtius Rufus: On His Historical Methods in the *Historiae Alexandri*" in Philip II, Alexander the Great and the Macedonian Heritage, eds. WL Adams & E N Borza, Lanham, 1982, pp.177-196.

29) Hamilton, JR, 1961, "Cleitarchus & Aristobulus" Historia 10: 448-59.

30) Hamilton, JR, "Plutarch, Alexander: A Commentary", Oxford 1969.

31) Hamilton, JR, 1977, "Cleitarchus and Diodorus 17" in Greece & the Ancient Mediterranean in History and Prehistory, ed KH Kinzl, Berlin, 126-46.

32) Hammond, NGL, "Three Historians of Alexander the Great", Cambridge 1983.

33) Hammond, NGL, "The Regnal Years of Philip and Alexander," Greek, Roman and Byzantine Studies, Vol. 33, 1992, 355-373.

34) Hammond, NGL, "Sources for Alexander the Great", Cambridge 1993.

35)   Heckel, W, "The Last Days & Testament of Alexander the Great", Historia Einzelschriften, Heft 56, Stuttgart 1988.

36)   Heckel, W, "The Earliest Evidence for the Plot to Poison Alexander" in *Alexander's Empire: Formulation to Decay*, California 2007.

37)   Heckel, W, "Who's Who in the Age of Alexander the Great", Blackwell 2006.

38)   Holt, Frank, "Alexander the Great and the Mystery of the Elephant Medallions", California, 2003.

39)   Hornblower, Jane, "Hieronymus of Cardia", OUP, 1981.

40)   Howard, CL, Review of the Teubner Edition of the *Metz Epitome*, Classical Philology 58, pp. 129-131.

41)   Hunt, JM, "An Emendation in the *Epitoma Metensis*", Classical Philology 67, pp. 287-288.

42)   Hunt, JM, "More Emendations in the *Epitoma Metensis*", Classical Philology 80, pp. 335-337.

43)   Jacoby, F, FGrH 137, "Kleitarchos".

44)   Merkelbach, Reinhold, "Die Quellen des Griechischen Alexanderromans," *Zetema Monographien zur Klassischen Altertumswissenschaft*, Heft 9, Munich 1954.

45)   Pearson, Lionel, 1960, "Cleitarchus" in The Lost Histories of Alexander the Great, American Philological Association, London and New York.

46)   Prandi, Luisa, "Callistene. Uno storico tra Aristotele e i re macedoni", Milan, 1985.

47)   Prandi, Luisa, "Fortuna è Realtà dell'Opera di Clitarco" in Historia Einzelschriften 104, Steiner, Stuttgart 1996.

48)   Schachermeyr, F, "Alexander der Grosse: Das Problem seiner Persönlichkeit und seines Wirkens", Vienna, 1973.

49)   Schachermeyr, F, "Alexander in Babylon und die Reichsordnung nach seiner Tod", Vienna, 1970.

50)   Schwartz, E, Paulys Real-Encyclopädie, Vol. 4, 1901, s.v. Q. Curtius Rufus, cols. 1871-1891, & Vol 5, 1905, s.v. Diodoros, cols. 682-684.

51)   Tarn, WW, "Alexander the Great, Vol II, Sources and Studies", Part One, The So-Called 'Vulgate' and its Sources, pp. 1-133, Cambridge 1948.

52)   Thomas, PH, Editor, "Incerti Auctoris Epitoma Rerum Gestarum Alexandri Magni cum Libro de Morte Testamentoque Alexandri" (The *Metz Epitome*), Teubner, Leipzig 1966.

53) Yardley, JC & Heckel, W, "Justin: Epitome of the Philippic History of Pompeius Trogus, Vol I, Books 11-12, Alexander the Great", Oxford 1997.

54) Zeller, Eduard, "Die Philosophie der Griechen", 4th ed., Part II, Leipzig, 1889.

Selected Ancient Sources

Aelian, Varia Historia, N.G. Wilson, Loeb, Harvard, 1997

Aelian, On The Characteristics of Animals, trans. A.F. Scholfield in 3 volumes, Loeb, Harvard, 1958

Arrian, Anabasis Alexandri and Indica, P.A. Brunt, Loeb, Harvard, 1976 and 1983

Arrian, Epitome of the History of Events After Alexander, *Photius* 92, Photius Bibliothèque, vol. II, René Henry, Paris, 1960

Athenaeus, Deipnosophistae, Charles Burton Gulick, Loeb, Harvard, 1927-41

Curtius, The History of Alexander, John C. Rolfe, Loeb, Harvard, 1946; The History of Alexander, trans. John Yardley, Penguin Classics, 1984; Historiae Alexandri Magni, ed. E. Hedicke, Teubner, 1908; De Rebus Gestis Alexandri Magni, Freinshem et al., Petrus vander Aa, Lugduni Batavorum, 1696

Diodorus Siculus, Library of History, vol. VII, Charles L. Sherman, Loeb, Harvard, 1952; vol. VIII, C. Bradford Welles, Loeb, Harvard, 1963, vol. IX, Russel M. Geer, Loeb, Harvard, 1947

Diogenes Laertius, Lives of Eminent Philosophers

Ephemerides, FrGrHist 2.117

Hegesias, FrGrHist 2.142

Homer, Iliad, trans. A.T. Murray, revised William F. Wyatt, Loeb, Harvard, 1999

Justin, Epitome of the Philippic History of Pompeius Trogus, Books 11-12, J.C. Yardley and W. Heckel, Oxford, 1997; Justin, Cornelius Nepos and Eutropius, Rev. John Selby Watson, London, 1853

Lucian, Dialogues of the Dead, XIII, vol. 7, M.D. MacLeod, Loeb, Harvard, 1961

Lucian, Essay on How to Write History, vol. 6, K. Kilburn, Loeb, 1959

Metz Epitome & Liber de Morte, P.H. Thomas, Ed., Incerti Auctoris Epitoma Rerum Gestarum Alexandri Magni cum Libro de Morte Testamentoque Alexandri, Teubner, Leipzig 1966

Nepos, Eumenes in Justin; Cornelius Nepos and Eutropius, Rev. John Selby Watson, London, 1853

Pausanias, Description of Greece, vol. 1, W.H.S. Jones, Loeb, Harvard, 1918

Pliny the Elder, Natural History, H. Rackham, W.H.S. Jones, D.E. Eichholz, Loeb, Harvard, 1938-62

Plutarch, Agesilaus, Lives vol. 5, B. Perrin, Loeb, Harvard, 1917

Plutarch, Alexander & Caesar, Lives vol. 7, B. Perrin, Loeb, Harvard, 1919

Plutarch, Eumenes, Lives vol. 8, B. Perrin, Loeb, Harvard, 1919

Plutarch, Demetrius, Antony & Pyrrhus, Lives vol. 9, B. Perrin, Loeb, Harvard, 1920

Plutarch, Moralia, vols. 3 and 4, Frank Cole Babbitt, Loeb, Harvard, 1931 and 1936

Polyaenus, Stratagems of War, trans. Peter Krentz & Everett L. Wheeler, Ares, Chicago, 1994

Polybius, The Histories, W.R. Paton, Loeb, Harvard, 1922-7

Pseudo-Callisthenes, Alexander Romance, e.g. Guilelmus Kroll, Historia Alexandri Magni, vol, 1, Weidmann, 1926

Stephanus Byzantinus, Augustus Meineke, Stephani Byzantii, Ethnicorum, Berlin, 1849

Strabo, Geography, H.L. Jones, Loeb, Harvard, 1917-32

Suidae Lexicon (a.k.a. The Suda), A. Adler (ed.), Leipzig, 1928-35

9. Acknowledgements

I would like to express my particular gratitude to the following for their assistance in the research reported in this book:-

The staff of Bristol University Arts and Social Sciences Library

Matthew Wofinden and Centonex for website support

Visitors to the Cleitarchus Reconstruction pages at www.alexanderstomb.com

C. Bradford Welles for recognizing the usefulness of a reconstruction

A. B. Bosworth for endorsing the feasibility of reconstruction

Index

A

Abdalonymus 12, 18, 20, 150
Abisares 80, 81, 82, 84, 85, 95, 138, 164, 165
Acadira 71
Acesines18, 65, 95, 106, 107, 108, 142, 165, 166, 167
Achilles 7, 11, 43, 44, 108, 118, 119, 146, 151, 167
Acuphis 51, 70, 163
Adler, Ada 180
Adonis 8, 151
Aelian 3, 15, 21, 24, 27, 43, 53, 145, 146, 162, 165, 168, 172, 174, 179
Africa 66, 117, 138, 172
Agalasseis 107, 167
Agathocles 35
Agathon 136, 154
Agesilaus 180
Agis 5, 8, 13, 58, 150, 151, 152
Agrianians 76, 87, 125
Aldus 49, 162
Aleppo 8
Alexander IV 37
Alexander Lyncestes 46, 147, 148, 157
Alexander of Epirus .. 13, 144, 152
Alexander Romance 63, 180
Alexander son of Cleophis 75
Alexandria1, 3, 11, 12, 13, 17, 24, 26, 27, 31, 32, 34, 39, 48, 53, 57, 59, 60, 124, 133, 144, 146, 150, 151, 158, 159, 167, 168, 171, 175
Alps 138
Altusacra 100
Amazons 14, 19, 25, 48, 58, 60, 156, 173

Amminais 72, 73
Ammon .. 100, 141, 145, 151, 173, 174
Ampelius 50, 53, 146, 175
Amuq Plain 8
Amyntas... 7, 25, 37, 60, 144, 150, 151
Anaximenes 11, 53
Anchiale. 7, 21, 22, 26, 44, 58, 60, 148
aniketos 11, 44, 145, 151
anthredon 22, 60, 156
Antigenes 86
Antioch 8
Antiochus 25, 29, 150
Antipater 8, 13, 17, 23, 30, 36, 37, 57, 58, 60, 152, 155, 173, 175
Antonio Tempesta 71, 77, 102
Aornus .. iv, 30, 43, 60, 64, 75, 76, 77, 107, 142, 163, 167
apes 27, 60, 94
Aphrices 78, 163
Apollonius Rhodius 4, 15
Arabus river 132, 171
Arachosia 24, 32, 133, 143
Arachosii 121
Aral Sea 25, 60, 155
Arbela 13, 102, 103, 153
Ares 119, 122, 180
Argyraspides 64
Aria 134
Ariamazes. 14, 27, 49, 52, 60, 160
Arines 68
Aristander 28, 60, 152, 159
Aristobulus .. 7, 18, 20, 21, 22, 25, 26, 27, 35, 36, 38, 50, 51, 52, 53, 60, 148, 152, 155, 157, 159, 160, 165, 166, 170, 173, 177
Aristonicus of Methymne 53, 150, 151

Index

Aristonous 115

Aristophanes 9

Aristotle 34, 169

Arrian. 3, 5, 7, 8, 9, 12, 15, 16, 18, 19, 20, 21, 22, 23, 24, 25, 26, 27, 28, 29, 30, 31, 32, 33, 35, 36, 43, 44, 45, 46, 48, 49, 50, 51, 52, 53, 54, 55, 59, 65, 66, 68, 71, 74, 78, 81, 84, 85, 86, 92, 96, 117, 142, 143, 145, 146, 147, 148, 149, 150, 151, 152, 153, 157, 161, 162, 163, 164, 165, 167, 168, 169, 170, 171, 172, 173, 174, 176, 177, 179

Asia.... 13, 18, 20, 22, 58, 93, 101, 103, 118, 119, 136, 144, 146, 153, 156

Asianic rhythms...... 11, 24, 45, 60

Assacena 71

Assacenus 72, 78, 163

Assembly 93, 101, 104, 110

Assyria 7, 29, 46

Astaspes 135, 136, 171

Athena 78

Athenaeus 4, 6, 7, 9, 13, 16, 24, 26, 28, 29, 30, 43, 44, 46, 53, 145, 148, 155, 172, 174, 179

Athenodorus 120

Athens.... 16, 25, 44, 59, 121, 147, 148, 172

Atlantic 93, 128

Atropates 9, 92, 164, 172, 173

Attalus 58, 83, 144

Augustine, St 53, 151

Augustus 47, 180

Aulus Gellius 13, 30

Azov, Sea of 25, 60, 155

B

Babylon ... 3, 6, 12, 13, 16, 17, 18, 25, 29, 31, 38, 44, 58, 59, 60, 137, 138, 140, 148, 153, 154, 172, 173, 174, 177, 178

Babyloniaca 29

Bactra 119, 120, 156, 161, 163

Bactria .. 15, 59, 68, 103, 120, 158, 160, 161, 168

Bactrians 104, 124

Bagasdaram 75

Bagoas 54, 137, 138, 139, 156, 171, 172

Balacrus 78

Banyan tree 21, 60

Barsine 37, 54, 147, 149

Baryaxes 9, 15, 54, 57, 59, 92, 139, 164, 172

Barzaentes 82, 156

Baynham ..30, 45, 48, 52, 54, 156, 176

Beira 71

Bel 29

Berossus 29, 38, 60, 153

Bessus 9, 14, 18, 59, 155, 158, 159, 160, 164

Betis 11, 43, 151

Bibliotheke 39, 47

Bigandar 129

Billows, Richard 29, 30, 45, 54, 176

biremes 106

Biton 120

Black Sea 28, 155

Bodyguards 116, 126, 135

Bosworth 3, 5, 7, 30, 32, 33, 35, 36, 42, 45, 46, 54, 60, 176

Boxus 120

Brahmins 44, 125, 126, 169

Branchidae 44, 54, 159

Brown, T. S.. 8, 19, 25, 27, 28, 33, 45

Bubacenê 64

Bucephala....30, 59, 106, 165, 166

Bucephalus ..... iii, 30, 60, 89, 156, 164, 165

Byblos 8, 13, 58, 151

C

cadet bursary 101

Caelius Rufus 42, 43

Caesar 180

Calanus 5, 10, 16, 30, 80, 139, 172

Callisthenes .. 7, 21, 22, 26, 30, 42, 48, 54, 57, 60, 147, 148, 151, 161, 162, 164, 167

Cardia 6, 17, 28, 30, 31, 39, 40, 47, 54, 178

Carmania 134, 135, 136, 137, 143, 171

Carthaginians 138, 150

Caspian Sea 14, 18, 25, 28, 58, 60, 155

Cassander 6, 17, 23, 30, 36, 37, 57, 60, 175

Cassandrea 26

Castaigne, André 88, 113, 117

Catanes 64, 159, 161

catapults 73, 78, 89, 110

Cathaea 19, 165

Cathaeans 96, 97, 165

Catreus 67, 162

Caucasus 58, 65, 155, 156, 158

Ceylon 25

Chaldean 29, 174

Chandragupta 24, 32, 33

Chares 30, 52, 53, 60, 163, 165

Charidemus 12, 25, 44, 60, 147, 148

chariots 82, 85, 100, 109, 121, 123, 124, 138, 152, 153, 166, 168

Charus 30, 76, 77, 163

Choaspes 71

Chorienes 14, 49, 162

Christian 17, 45

Cicero 10, 12, 22, 42, 53, 144, 146, 147, 149, 150, 151

Cilicia 12, 58, 101, 103, 148

Claudius 47

Cleander 136, 171

Cleitus 81, 161

Clement of Alexandria 11, 12, 24, 32, 144, 146

Cleochares 81

Cleophis 45, 72, 73, 74, 163

Coenus . 72, 78, 86, 104, 105, 106, 153, 166

Colophon 20, 34

comus 70, 136, 143, 147, 155, 163, 171

Cophen 68, 142

Coragus 16, 59, 168

Corianus 49

Corinth 34, 145, 150, 152

Corragus 121, 122

cotton 66

Crassus 8

Craterus ... 64, 69, 84, 85, 87, 107, 116, 123, 124, 135, 136, 143, 167, 169, 171, 173

Crete 13, 21, 58, 150

Critobulus 15, 59, 115, 168

Cronus 34

Ctesias 7, 26, 29, 148, 153

Curtius ... 1, 2, 3, 5, 6, 8, 9, 10, 11, 12, 13, 14, 15, 16, 18, 19, 20, 21, 23, 24, 25, 27, 28, 29, 30, 31, 34, 35, 36, 37, 40, 41, 42, 43, 44, 45, 46, 47, 48, 49, 50, 51, 52, 54, 55, 61, 66, 68, 72, 82, 99, 117, 119, 147, 148, 149, 150, 151, 152, 153, 154, 155, 156, 157, 158, 159, 160, 161, 162, 163, 164, 165, 166, 167, 168, 169, 170, 171, 172, 173, 174, 175, 176, 177, 178, 179

Cyprus 138

Cyrene 34, 151

Cyropaidia 52

Cyrus 8, 18, 44, 138, 139, 158

Cyrus the Younger 8

Index

D

Daedalian Mountains 71
Dahae 14, 85, 89, 103, 161
Damascus 8, 149
Darius 6, 9, 12, 13, 20, 25, 29, 44,
    45, 46, 48, 58, 60, 81, 117, 139,
    140, 145, 146, 147, 148, 149,
    150, 152, 153, 154, 155, 156
Deinon 6, 7, 12, 20, 26, 44, 60, 67,
    145, 147, 148, 154, 156, 158,
    162
Deipnosophistae 179
Delphi 11, 20, 44, 58, 145
Demaratus 25, 60
Demetrius .. 13, 29, 34, 37, 43, 45,
    54, 60, 156, 180
Demophon 111
Dialogues of the Dead 179
Diardines 65
Diodorus .. 1, 2, 3, 5, 6, 7, 8, 9, 10,
    11, 12, 13, 14, 15, 16, 18, 19,
    20, 21, 22, 23, 24, 25, 26, 28,
    29, 30, 31, 34, 35, 36, 37, 39,
    40, 41, 42, 43, 44, 45, 46, 47,
    48, 49, 50, 51, 52, 55, 57, 58,
    59, 61, 82, 119, 145, 146, 147,
    148, 149, 150, 151, 152, 153,
    154, 155, 156, 157, 158, 159,
    160, 161, 162, 163, 164, 165,
    166, 167, 168, 169, 170, 171,
    172, 173, 174, 175, 176, 177,
    179
Diogenes 179
Diogenes Laertius 4, 5, 10, 20, 34,
    45, 172
Diogenes of Sinope 20, 45
Dionysus 15, 44, 59, 69, 70, 71,
    103, 110, 124, 135, 160, 163,
    168
Dioxippus 16, 44, 59, 121, 122,
    123, 168

Diyllus 6, 41, 46, 145, 150, 152,
    154, 155, 157, 158, 166, 167,
    170, 172, 173, 174, 175
dogs 69, 98, 99, 166
dolphins 65
Drangianê 134
Drapis 68
Drypetis 140
Duris 42, 46, 53, 157

E

Egypt 13, 25, 26, 31, 34, 54, 58,
    150, 151, 152
Einquellenprinzip ... 37, 39, 40, 41,
    46, 47, 52, 55, 61
elephants 25, 33, 66, 67, 78, 79,
    80, 82, 85, 86, 87, 89, 90, 100,
    102, 105, 106, 117, 125, 164,
    166, 169
Eleumezen 107
Engels 8, 12, 177
Ephemerides 31, 179
Ephesus ... 11, 12, 22, 65, 144, 147
Ephippus 9, 28, 29, 31, 60, 173,
    174
Epigoni .. 15, 16, 59, 143, 162, 172
Epirus 13, 138, 152
Erymanthian boar 43
Erythraean Sea .. 65, 129, 137, 143
Erythrus 66, 137
Ethymanthus 65
Etymologiae 99, 166
Eudaemon 138
Eudamas 32, 33
Euergetae 21, 60, 158
Eumenes 31, 97, 173, 179, 180
Euphrates 8, 58, 101, 132, 137,
    138, 170, 171
Europe 9, 13, 36, 119, 144, 152,
    172
Euxine 28, 58, 60, 155

F

Florilegium............................4, 8
Fortune......84, 112, 118, 123, 135
Freinshem.........................49, 179
Frontinus 12, 14, 53, 83, 146, 159, 162

G

Gades..138
Gandara....................................96
Gangaridae..............100, 101, 166
Ganges..23, 24, 25, 32, 33, 60, 65, 100, 108, 109, 110, 141, 142, 162, 166
Gaugamela 9, 13, 150, 152, 153
Gaza 11, 13, 24, 58, 60, 151
Gedrosia..............16, 21, 143, 171
Gendari Mt......................110, 142
Gordian knot 12, 148
Gordion 12
Granicus..............12, 58, 103, 146
Greece 8, 10, 14, 17, 36, 40, 41, 58, 93, 106, 118, 120, 151, 152, 153, 158, 174, 177, 180
gymnosophist.4, 5, 20, 23, 51, 60, 170, 172

H

Hages..85
Hamah...8
Hamilton 18, 20, 26, 27, 35, 36, 40, 41, 53, 61, 149, 150, 152, 153, 154, 155, 156, 157, 165, 169, 171, 174, 177
Hammond.3, 6, 10, 13, 20, 21, 22, 23, 24, 25, 27, 28, 29, 30, 35, 37, 41, 46, 52, 144, 145, 146, 147, 148, 149, 150, 151, 152, 153, 154, 155, 156, 157, 158, 159, 160, 161, 162, 163, 164, 165, 166, 167, 168, 169, 170, 171, 172, 173, 174, 175, 177

Hanging Gardens........29, 60, 153
harem 6, 45, 156
Harmatelia 125, 127, 169
Harpalus... 16, 26, 59, 60, 76, 106, 172
Harpocration 5, 8, 152
Haustanes................................ 64
Hecatombaeon 10
Hecatompylus............. 13, 58, 155
Heckel.... 5, 18, 23, 25, 31, 34, 35, 37, 41, 47, 48, 49, 50, 52, 54, 60, 145, 151, 158, 162, 164, 169, 175, 178, 179
Hegesias... 11, 24, 42, 53, 60, 151, 179
Hegesimachus........................... 83
Hellespont...................... 103, 118
Hephaistion 15, 28, 29, 60, 69, 79, 80, 86, 96, 99, 107, 132, 140, 142, 149, 153, 163, 165, 166, 167, 173, 174
Heracleidae............. 11, 12, 22, 58
Heracles . 7, 11, 29, 37, 43, 44, 69, 75, 76, 86, 101, 103, 107, 110, 122, 128, 138, 163, 167, 170, 172, 174
Heracon 136
Herodotus 25, 60, 147, 148
Herons 67
Hiarotis 96, 142
Hieronymus . 6, 17, 28, 30, 31, 37, 39, 40, 47, 54, 55, 60, 175, 178
Hindu Kush......... 14, 58, 119, 158
hippotoxotae 85, 89
Holcias......................... 23, 48, 60
Homer....................... 43, 72, 179
Homs 8
Hormuz, Gulf of 143
Hornblower.. 6, 17, 31, 39, 40, 47, 54, 178
Hydaspes ... 15, 18, 30, 59, 80, 82, 85, 88, 94, 95, 101, 107, 108, 142, 164, 166, 167
Hydraotis ....See Hiarotis

hypaspists 114, 161
Hypereides.................. 11, 44, 145
Hyphasis . iv, 26, 93, 99, 102, 142, 166
hypomnemata 17
Hyrcania .. 14, 18, 19, 58, 60, 155, 156

I

Iberia................................ 138
Ichor................................. 72
Ichthyophagoi....... 16, 21, 59, 143
Iliad............. 43, 72, 118, 167, 179
Illyrians.............................. 118
Indica ... 18, 19, 20, 21, 23, 24, 28, 31, 32, 33, 49, 50, 65, 66, 81, 162, 163, 165, 168, 170, 171, 176, 177, 179
Indus 14, 16, 32, 43, 44, 59, 65, 68, 69, 75, 79, 108, 109, 110, 128, 132, 142, 143, 163, 165, 167, 168, 170
Indus Delta ... 14, 16, 59, 129, 143
invictus 11, 151
Iollas 23, 30, 36, 60, 175
Iomanes 23, 60, 65, 162
Ionia................................. 12
Ipsus, Battle of...................... 33
Isidore of Seville 99, 166
Issus 12, 25, 58, 149, 150, 152
Isthmian Games................ 34, 150
Italy..... 13, 46, 138, 152, 153, 172
Itinerarium Alexandri 54

J

Jacoby .. 3, 4, 5, 6, 7, 9, 11, 12, 13, 14, 15, 16, 19, 20, 21, 22, 23, 24, 25, 26, 28, 30, 34, 35, 39, 40, 42, 43, 51, 61, 62, 81, 123, 144, 145, 146, 147, 148, 149, 150, 151, 152, 153, 155, 156, 162, 163, 164, 165, 167, 168, 169, 170, 171, 172, 174, 178

Julian 8
Jumna 23, 65, 162
Justin ..2, 3, 5, 6, 9, 10, 11, 12, 13, 15, 18, 21, 23, 27, 28, 29, 30, 32, 33, 40, 41, 43, 44, 45, 46, 47, 48, 50, 52, 54, 55, 61, 143, 144, 145, 146, 147, 148, 149, 150, 151, 152, 153, 154, 155, 156, 157, 158, 159, 160, 161, 162, 163, 164, 165, 166, 167, 168, 169, 170, 171, 172, 173, 174, 175, 179

K

Kabul River 142
Karachi................................. 143
Kedrosia 133, 134, 135
Kedrosii................................ 132
Khewra 15, 107, 167
kopis sword 89, 102
Kroll 180

L

Lagus................................. 17, 36
Last Plans 17, 175
Laurel 70
Le Brun, Charles 91
Lebanon................. 8, 13, 138, 172
Leonnatus . 86, 115, 132, 135, 168, 171
Leontiscus 36
Liber de Morte 23, 31, 48, 60, 175, 179
Library.......................... 179, 181
Limnaeus........................ 115, 168
lions.................. 99, 107, 123, 166
Livy . 11, 13, 44, 48, 145, 152, 174
London 179
Lucian 179
Lysimachus 20, 60

M

Macedon..... 11, 36, 108, 117, 157, 165, 173
Maedi 118
Magnesia 12, 24, 58, 147
Malli ... 15, 16, 35, 41, 53, 59, 109, 121, 124, 142, 168, 169, 170, 175
Mamalces 129
Mandi 16, 23, 59, 60, 128, 170
Mark Antony 180
Massagetae 14, 161
Massani 124, 168
Matris 42
Mazaga iv, 52, 64, 72, 74, 78, 142, 163, 169
Media 9, 59, 92, 164
Megara 34
Megasthenes..... 16, 23, 24, 31, 32, 33, 38, 39, 50, 57, 60, 66, 162, 166, 170, 176, 177
Meleager 81
Memnon 12, 25, 58, 106, 147, 148
Memphis 16, 37, 57, 151, 175
Menon 135
Mentor 44
mercenaries .. 72, 73, 74, 150, 156, 163, 174
Merkelbach 51, 164, 167, 170, 178
Meros 70
Mesopotamia 101, 138, 152
Metz Epitome 1, 2, 3, 9, 14, 15, 18, 20, 23, 26, 27, 29, 30, 40, 43, 44, 46, 47, 48, 49, 50, 51, 52, 55, 57, 68, 72, 73, 78, 82, 84, 90, 156, 158, 159, 160, 161, 162, 163, 164, 165, 166, 167, 168, 169, 170, 176, 178, 179
Minythyia 48
Moeris 129
monkeys 15, 20, 21, 27, 59, 60, 94, 165
Mophis 79, 80, 164

Moralia .. 7, 18, 20, 26, 29, 44, 50, 53, 148, 150, 159, 166, 168, 180
Müller 3, 54
Musicani 124, 125, 169
Musicanus 124, 125, 143, 169
Myllinas................................... 76
Myrra 8, 151
Myrtle 70
Mytilene.................................. 30

N

Nature 65, 67, 72, 99, 105, 109, 110, 118, 119, 129
Nearchus 16, 18, 19, 21, 27, 28, 36, 57, 59, 60, 66, 117, 132, 136, 143, 153, 162, 165, 170, 171, 174
Nebuchadnezzar 29
Nicaea 106, 166
Nicanor 83
Nicocles 81
Nile 65
Numidia 138
Nysa iv, 15, 48, 51, 59, 64, 69, 70, 71, 142, 163, 170
Nysaeans.......................... 69, 70

O

occhus tree 19
Ocean .... iv, 15, 16, 59, 64, 71, 93, 103, 105, 106, 109, 110, 121, 124, 128, 129, 130, 131, 132, 137, 143, 165, 170
Oceanus 132, 170
Olympian gods...................... 105
Olympias 36, 37, 46, 119, 148, 151, 157
Olympic Games 122
Olynthus 21, 28
Onesicritus. 15, 16, 18, 19, 20, 21, 22, 24, 25, 26, 36, 45, 51, 52, 53, 57, 59, 60, 66, 80, 96, 99,

132, 136, 143, 145, 155, 156, 161, 164, 165, 167, 170, 171, 177
oracle 60, 121, 145, 148, 151
Oreitae ... 16, 21, 59, 60, 132, 133, 135, 169, 171
Orion 67, 162
Orsines 138, 139, 172
Orxines 54
Oxus river 14, 68, 159, 160
Oxyartes 49, 124, 162, 169
Oxydracae... iv, 16, 26, 37, 50, 53, 54, 59, 93, 109, 110, 121, 142, 168, 175
Ozines 135, 136, 171

P

Palimbothra 32
Pamphylia 21, 60, 147
Pandaea 23, 60, 128, 162, 170
papyrus 66
Parapanisadae 124
Parmenion.. 46, 58, 136, 144, 148, 150, 152, 158
Paropamisus 58
Paropanisum 124
parrot 66, 75
Parsagada 138, 143, 172
Parthyaea 134
Pasitigris 55
Patala 129, 132, 143, 170
Patrocles 28, 38, 60, 155
Patron 44
Pausanias . 16, 37, 50, 53, 54, 144, 168, 169, 175, 180
peacock 67
Pearls 98
Pearson 5, 6, 7, 11, 20, 22, 23, 24, 27, 28, 29, 30, 34, 35, 38, 45, 46, 144, 145, 153, 156, 158, 159, 160, 165, 178
Perdiccas 69, 85, 86, 97, 153, 173, 174

Persepolis 13, 36, 58, 154, 155
Persia .... iv, 9, 13, 20, 46, 92, 93, 117, 121, 135, 137, 143, 145, 152
Persian Empire 12, 20, 145
Persica 7, 20, 26, 148, 153
Peucestes 114
phalanx 69, 86, 87, 88, 97, 141
Phegeus 99, 100, 166
Philadelphus 39
Philip 6, 11, 13, 37, 46, 58, 105, 119, 126, 138, 144, 145, 148, 168, 169, 174, 175, 177
Philippic History 5, 41, 47, 48, 50, 52, 54, 55, 179
Philippus 20, 34, 161
Philodemus 11, 34, 43
Philotas 44, 157, 161
Phoenicia 8, 151
Phraates 47
Phradates 139, 156
Phrataphernes 134, 156
Pillars of Heracles 43
Pir Sar .... See Aornus
Pithon 125, 169
Pliny .3, 13, 16, 20, 25, 26, 28, 34, 35, 38, 39, 42, 50, 53, 65, 67, 155, 162, 168, 170, 171, 174, 175, 180
Plutarch ..2, 3, 5, 6, 7, 8, 9, 10, 11, 12, 14, 18, 20, 21, 22, 23, 24, 25, 26, 29, 30, 33, 34, 40, 43, 44, 46, 50, 51, 52, 53, 55, 65, 72, 76, 144, 145, 146, 147, 148, 149, 150, 151, 152, 153, 154, 155, 156, 157, 159, 161, 162, 163, 164, 166, 168, 169, 170, 171, 172, 173, 174, 177, 180
Polyaenus 3, 14, 23, 43, 44, 53, 74, 85, 156, 158, 160, 163, 164, 165, 170, 180
Polybius 29, 30, 45, 54, 65, 176, 180
Polycleitus 24, 25, 60, 155

Polyperchon 64, 75, 124, 143, 169
Porticanus.................124, 169
Porusiv, 15, 32, 33, 46, 51, 59, 64, 80, 81, 82, 83, 84, 85, 86, 87, 89, 90, 91, 92, 93, 94, 95, 96, 99, 100, 102, 106, 138, 142, 164, 165, 166, 172
pothos.................28
Prandi, Luisa ..5, 7, 26, 35, 36, 42, 46, 176, 178
Prasii 100, 166
proskynesis.................30, 44, 161
Providence.................126
Pseudo-Callisthenes 180
Ptolemy 1, 2, 9, 15, 16, 18, 25, 26, 31, 34, 35, 36, 37, 39, 40, 47, 50, 51, 53, 54, 59, 65, 71, 83, 84, 86, 115, 118, 126, 127, 132, 153, 166, 168, 169, 171, 173, 175, 177
Punjab 33
Pura 143
Pyrrhus................30, 38, 174, 180
Pythia 100, 145, 166

Q

Quintillian 34, 42

R

Radulfus de Diceto.................47
Rambacia.............See Rhambarce
Red Sea 93, 118, 137
Rhambarce 133, 143
rhinoceroses 66, 94
Rome................17, 34, 41, 48, 177
Roxane14, 37, 48, 49, 55, 59, 106, 162, 166

S

Salmous.................136, 143, 171
Samaxus 82
Sambastae 124, 168

Sambus 16, 59, 110, 125, 127, 169, 170
Sandrocottus 32, 33
Sangala 97, 165
Sardanapalus 7, 21, 22, 26, 44, 58, 60, 148
sarissas................74, 86, 87
Schachermeyr . 17, 20, 37, 39, 178
Schnabel, P. 29, 153
Schwartz .. 3, 39, 40, 61, 148, 149, 150, 151, 153, 154, 155, 156, 157, 158, 159, 160, 161, 162, 163, 164, 165, 166, 167, 168, 169, 171, 173, 175, 178
scindapsos.................70
scorpion engines 73
Scythia14, 59, 103, 120, 139, 160, 161
Scythians ... 85, 89, 104, 153, 158, 159
Seleucia 8
Seleucus............24, 29, 32, 33, 86
Semiramis.....29, 44, 60, 119, 153
septiremes 138
Sibi.................43, 107, 167
Sibyrtius...............24, 32, 33, 135
Sidon.................12, 18, 150, 151
siege-towers................73, 78
Silex.................69
Simmias 34
Sirens 20, 67
Sisenna.................42
Sisimithres 49, 50, 161, 162
Sisygambis.................16, 59, 154
Sitalces.................136, 171
Siwa . 13, 22, 31, 44, 60, 145, 148, 151
snakes .. 15, 21, 25, 59, 60, 94, 96, 104, 126, 165
Sodrae.................124, 168
Sogdian Rock.............14, 59, 160
Sogdiana 14, 48, 59, 79, 119, 160, 161
Sogdians 103, 160

Sopeithes 15, 19, 98, 99, 107, 167
Sophocles................................... 42
Sparta... 5, 8, 13, 25, 58, 129, 151, 152, 158
Stateira............................ 140, 152
Stephanus Byzantinus............. 180
Stilpo 34, 45
Stobaeus.................. 4, 8, 13, 151
Strabo 7, 13, 14, 15, 16, 18, 19, 20, 21, 22, 23, 24, 25, 26, 27, 28, 30, 32, 33, 43, 44, 45, 50, 51, 52, 65, 66, 80, 96, 99, 148, 151, 153, 155, 156, 158, 159, 160, 161, 162, 163, 164, 165, 166, 167, 168, 169, 170, 171, 173, 180
Suda........................ 8, 17, 34, 180
Sudracae 26, 50, 168
Susa 10, 55, 59, 140, 141, 143, 154, 162, 172, 173
Susianê........................ 5, 139, 172
suttee.................................. 19, 60
Swat River Valley....... 71, 72, 142
Syria........ 8, 29, 46, 138, 149, 153

T

Tanais 27, 60, 159, 160
Tarn . 3, 19, 22, 24, 25, 26, 27, 28, 35, 39, 44, 147, 156, 170, 178
Tarsus 7, 26, 58, 148
Tauron 76, 86
Taurus mountains 12
Taxila................. 79, 80, 142, 164
Taxiles . 46, 68, 79, 80, 82, 90, 92, 94, 106, 138, 164, 166, 172
Terioltes....................... 124, 169
Tethys 132, 170
Thais 36, 155
Thalestris 14, 45, 48, 58, 156
Thapsacus 8, 138
thaumasia................................ 45
Thebes 6, 7, 11, 36, 37, 39, 55, 58, 145, 175

Theis Byblios 8
Themistocles 12, 21, 44, 53, 58, 60, 147
Theophrastus 35
Theopompus.......................26, 60
Thimodes................................44
Thrace 106, 118
Thracians..................87, 138, 146
tigers................................99, 123
Tigris.........................99, 101, 152
Timaeus...... 10, 17, 22, 24, 35, 60, 144, 156, 168
Timagenes..... 1, 2, 34, 41, 48, 168
Tiridates 46, 154
tortoises.....................24, 25, 123
Trajan 8
triacontors 79
Triballi............................118, 145
Trogus .. 1, 2, 5, 12, 13, 18, 28, 40, 41, 45, 47, 48, 50, 52, 55, 150, 155, 175, 179
Troy....................................43, 146
Tyche...............................29, 45
Tyre   8, 12, 13, 18, 58, 138, 149, 150

V

Valerius Maximus......................53
Vulgate.....2, 9, 17, 29, 44, 47, 50, 53, 54, 55, 57, 83, 85, 168, 178

W

Wagner, Otto.......................48, 49
Welles 3, 5, 23, 166, 177, 179
whales 21, 60, 133, 137, 171

X

Xandrames 100, 166
Xanthus 44, 147
Xenophon.................6, 9, 52, 145
Xerxes 12, 25, 58, 60, 147, 148

Y

Yardley...5, 18, 34, 36, 41, 47, 48, 50, 52, 54, 66, 145, 151, 158, 164, 169, 179

Z

Zariaspes................. 135, 136, 171
Zeller 34, 179
Zeus 69, 70, 72, 81, 119, 163

Lightning Source UK Ltd.
Milton Keynes UK
04 May 2010

153670UK00002B/179/P